mastering
the opening
BYRON JACOBS

GLENVIEW PUBLIC LIBRARY

3 1170 00584 0933

W9-BLF-110

JUN 1 1 2003

794.122
JAC

GLENVIEW PUBLIC LIBRARY
1930 GLENVIEW ROAD
GLENVIEW, ILLINOIS 60025
847-729-7500

EVERYMAN CHESS

Everyman Publishers plc   www.everyman.uk.com

First published 2001 by Everyman Publishers plc, formerly Cadogan Books plc, Gloucester Mansions, 140A Shaftesbury Avenue, London WC2H 8HD

Copyright © 2001 Byron Jacobs

The right of Byron Jacobs to be identified as the author of this work has been asserted in accordance with the Copyrights, Designs and Patents Act 1988.

All rights reserved. No part of this publication may be reproduced, stored in a retrieval system or transmitted in any form or by any means, electronic, electrostatic, magnetic tape, photocopying, recording or otherwise, without prior permission of the publisher.

British Library Cataloguing-in-Publication Data
A catalogue record for this book is available from the British Library.

ISBN 1 85744 223 7

Distributed in North America by The Globe Pequot Press, P.O Box 480, 246 Goose Lane, Guilford, CT 06437-0480.

All other sales enquiries should be directed to Everyman Chess, Gloucester Mansions, 140A Shaftesbury Avenue, London WC2H 8HD
tel: 020 7539 7600 fax: 020 7379 4060
email: dan@everyman.uk.com
website: www.everyman.uk.com

EVERYMAN CHESS SERIES (formerly Cadogan Chess)
Chief Advisor: Garry Kasparov
Commissioning editor: Byron Jacobs

Typeset and edited by First Rank Publishing, Brighton
Production by Book Production Services
Printed and bound in Great Britain by The Cromwell Press Ltd., Trowbridge, Wiltshire

SEP 4 2002

Contents

Introduction

After the Brain Games World Championship in London last year, Garry Kasparov (who had just lost the match) said that his main failing in this battle was that he 'did not have any good openings.' This might sound like a rather surprising statement from a man who had just completed a 15-year reign as world champion, still held – in rating terms – the number one spot, and who is regarded by most serious commentators as the greatest player ever. However, the new world champion, Vladimir Kramnik, immediately replied that he thought this was a rather subjective statement as, for most of the match, he had also felt that he didn't have any good openings either!

Well, that's a fine state of affairs. The two best players in the world have several months to prepare for their match against each other. Not only do they have a great deal of time, but they are assisted in their researches by some of the world's leading grandmasters and also have substantial technical back-up in terms of chess software, databases and analytical engines. And, at the end of all that, they both volunteer the information that they felt they hadn't worked out anything worthwhile for the opening stage of the game.

Of course, there is undoubtedly an element of dissembling going on in these statements, but any player who has played at any sort of level can recognise the complaint of 'having no good openings'. Kasparov and Kramnik are extremely hard-working grandmasters with decades of chess understanding and experience between them. If they can get into a situation where they don't feel that they are finding good moves early on in the game, what chance is there for the rest of us?

How Important is the Opening?

Beyond the level of complete beginner, the opening is perhaps the most important phase of the game to get right. If you choose to play systems that you don't understand or which don't suit your style, you will find yourself starting each game with a handicap. Of course, we are not all serious professional players who can happily spend great swathes of our time studying the latest refinements in opening theory, but having a decent set of tools to aid navigation from the opening position to the middlegame struggle, is basic to survival on the chessboard.

Many players struggle long and hard to absorb huge amounts of theory in their favourite openings. For professional players this is something of an unavoidable necessity. At the rarefied level at which top grandmaster games are played, subtle errors early on can condemn a player to a long and possibly unsuccessful defence. To compete at this level, it is essential to have a highly developed understanding of numerous opening systems. However, for the vast majority of players who like to enjoy their chess lower down the evolutionary ladder, this is less of a priority. Tiny errors are not going to be ruthlessly exploited (although your opponent may indeed make you suffer if you drop a couple of pawns or a piece early on). A more important consideration is that you choose to play systems which suit your style and which lead to positions where you feel you know what you are doing.

Choosing the Right Openings

This is only a short book and it will be impossible for me to detail, even broadly, all opening systems. The canon of chess opening literature is immense and a quick survey of one of my databases revealed that the Poisoned Pawn variation of the Sicilian Najdorf (1 e4 c5 2 Nf3 d6 3 d4 cxd4 4 Nxd4 Nf6 5 Nc3 a6 is the Najdorf, and now 6 Bg5 e6 7 f4 Qb6 leads to the Poisoned Pawn), occurs in approximately 0.1% of international games. Nevertheless, whole books – much longer than the one you are currently reading – have been written on this single variation.

What I will do in this book is to look at all the major openings and the most important and popular variations within them. This is with a view to giving a feel for what different openings are like, what the main themes of play within them are, and what sort of positions they usually lead to. Unavoidably, some areas of theory will only be skirted over or even avoided altogether. However, I hope that there will be sufficient material here for you to gain a good feel for many different opening variations and thus to decide which systems might work best for you.

Byron Jacobs,
Brighton, October 2001

Chapter One

The Sicilian with d2-d4

The Sicilian Defence is the opening of choice of many of the world's top players against 1 e4. Garry Kasparov in particular has a fantastic score with this defence. Black's structure is completely sound and, by unbalancing the position at an early stage, he creates opportunities for complex play. The Sicilian rewards players who have worked hard on the opening and developed a good understanding of their systems.

In most openings White has the opportunity to play quietly and to defuse the struggle from an early stage. An attractive feature of the Sicilian is that this is not so easy for a passively-inclined White. Many of the quiet variations that White can choose that do not really promise an advantage are dynamically equal rather than just plain equal. This means that if White is determined to sit around and do nothing then Black will naturally have chances to play for the advantage and will not have to acquiesce in a dull, level position.

The Sicilian Defence is very complex and requires a fair amount of study to become familiar with the typical themes and ideas. If White is well prepared then you had better make sure that you are well prepared too, or you can find yourself blown off the board very quickly indeed. There are also a number of offbeat White systems, which although not promising much theoretically, can be difficult to face over-the-board if you are not familiar with some of the nuances.

In this chapter we will consider some of the more popular main line (involving an early White d2-d4) Sicilian variations. The next chapter will consider ways to meet the Sicilian that do not involve d2-d4. Alert readers will note that I have chosen not to include the highly popular Najdorf variation here. The reason for this is that the themes that occur in the Najdorf are frequently seen in the Scheveningen and Sveshnikov variations. Indeed, several of the illustrative games chosen for the Scheveningen actually started out as Najdorfs.

The Sveshnikov Variation

1 e4 c5 2 Nf3 Nc6 3 d4 cxd4 4 Nxd4 Nf6 5 Nc3 e5

The Sveshnikov Sicilian is typical of modern chess. By playing ...e7-e5 Black creates a *static* weakness on the d-file, ceding the d5-square to White in front of the backward pawn at d6. In return, Black gains *active* piece play and usually the two bishops (after White plays Bg5xf6 to reinforce his control over d5). In the main line, 6 Ndb5 d6 7 Bg5 a6 8 Na3, Black also gains time pushing around the white knight, which has now spent four moves to reach an unimpressive posting at a3. Finally, after 8...b5 9 Bxf6 gxf6 Black now has *two* f-pawns with which to assault the centre.

NOTE: The Sicilian Sveshnikov is not for those who like a quiet life

This all sounds splendid for Black, but the one disadvantage – the d-file weakness – is serious. If White manages both to suppress Black's activity and to maintain control over the central light squares then he will have good prospects. However, one more advantage for Black is that an attacking position is easier to play; whereas White's task of restricting counterplay requires patience and constant vigilance.

What is White's Strategy?

White's main strategy is to reinforce his grip on the central light squares. White starts by exchanging his queen's bishop for the black knight on f6. His offside knight can be rerouted to the key square e3 via c2 or sometimes c4. If Black's counterplay can be contained then the long-term weakness on the d-file will assume ever greater importance. White can also probe the queenside with the thrusts a2-a4 or c2-c4.

What is Black's Strategy?

Although Black can no longer cover the d5 square with a pawn, he has not entirely given up control of this square. Both the queen's knight and bishop can provide cover from e7 and e6 respectively. Also, after White's usual Bg5xf6, if Black recaptures ...g7xf6 then the front f-pawn will advance to challenge the centre, while the half-open g-file may be useful for an attacking rook. If ...Be7xf6 is played, a common later ploy is ...Bf6-g5 to remove a white knight appearing on e3.

WARNING: If Black does not maintain dynamic counterplay he can find himself left with a difficult defensive task in a position with numerous pawn weaknesses.

Tactical/Strategic/Dynamic?

The Sveshnikov typifies the conflict between strategic and dynamic elements. White has a strategic advantage based on the weak d5-square and backward d6-pawn. Black counts on the dynamism of his position to create counterplay.

Theoretical?

All Sicilian main lines have been tested and investigated repeatedly at the highest level. Therefore they are generally highly theoretical – and the Sveshnikov is no exception. Nevertheless, the fixed central pawn structure defines the plans for both sides so the Sveshnikov is somewhat easier to learn than other Sicilian systems.

How Popular is it?

The statistics show Black scoring an impressive 49% in the Sveshnikov, a high proportion of which are wins. So it is not surprising that the Sveshnikov is extremely popular at all levels of chess, and is a favourite of World Champion Vladimir Kramnik.

Illustrative Games

Game 1

☐ **Short** ■ **Kramnik**

Novgorod 1994

1 e4 c5 2 Nf3 Nc6 3 d4 cxd4 4 Nxd4 Nf6 5 Nc3 e5

Although Vladimir Kramnik (currently world champion) has now adopted a more solid style of play with the black pieces, earlier in his career he played very dynamic defences such as the King's Indian and, as we see here, the Sicilian Sveshnikov.

6 Ndb5 d6 7 Bg5 a6 8 Na3 b5 9 Bxf6 gxf6 10 Nd5 Bg7 11 c3 f5 12 exf5 Bxf5 13 Nc2 Be6 14 g3 0-0 15 Bg2 a5 16 0-0 Rb8 17 Re1 Qd7 18 Qh5 f5 19 Rad1 e4 20 Nce3

White has done well so far and now prepares to take absolute control of the d-file. However, Black simply ignores it and builds his counter-play on the kingside behind his pawn duo. White would have done better to challenge the e4-pawn with 20 f3.

20...Ne5 21 Re2 Ng6 22 Red2 Be5 23 a4 bxa4 24 Nc4 Qf7 25 Qg5 Kh8 26 Kh1 Rg8 27 Qe3 Qg7 28 Bf1 Rbf8 29 Be2 Re8 30 Qb6

A definite mistake which allows Black a trick.

30...Nf4 (Diagram 1) 31 Nxf4 Bxf4 32 Rd4 d5

Despite White's consistent strategy Black has managed to gain control of d5 after all by tactical means. If now 33 Ne3 Be5 34 Rxa4 f4 and the attack is very strong.

33 Rxd5 Bxd5 34 Rxd5 Bc7 35 Qc6 f4 36 Nd6 Re6 37 Bc4 Qe7 38 Re5 Rxd6 39 Rxe7 Rxc6 40 Bxg8 Kxg8 41 Rxe4 a3 White resigns

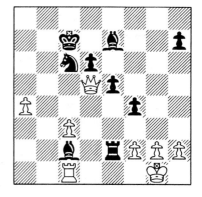

Diagram 1

Black is about to gain control of d5

Diagram 2

White's a-pawn is useful

Game 2
□ **Shirov** ■ **Topalov**
Leon 'Advanced Chess' 2001

In 'advanced chess' each player has access to a computer during the game – both to a database and playing program.

1 e4 c5 2 Nf3 Nc6 3 d4 cxd4 4 Nxd4 Nf6 5 Nc3 e5 6 Ndb5 d6 7 Bg5 a6 8 Na3 b5 9 Bxf6 gxf6 10 Nd5 f5 11 Bxb5

White wrests the initiative with a speculative sacrifice, gaining two or three pawns and transforming his passive Na3 into a dangerous attacking piece. While the sacrifice may not be the critical test theoretically speaking, it is not so easy for Black to defend at the board.

11...axb5 12 Nxb5 Ra4 13 b4 Rxb4 14 Nbc7+ Kd7 15 0-0 Qxc7

An interesting counter-sacrifice – Black obtains three pieces for the queen.

16 c3 Rxe4 17 Qh5 Kd8 18 Nxc7 Kxc7 19 Qxf7+ Be7 20 Rab1 Ba6 21 Rfd1 Rf8 22 Qb3 Rb8 23 Qe6 Rxb1 24 Rxb1 Bd3 25 Rd1 f4 26 Qd5 Bc2 27 Rc1 Re2 28 a4 (Diagram 2)

The game is still fairly balanced but now Black makes a mistake, after which his pieces are forced to take up passive positions to cope with the advancing a-pawn. 28...Be4 was better.

28...e4 29 a5 Bd3 30 Ra1 Rb2 31 c4 Rb7 32 a6 Ra7

With Black's activity reduced to nothing the white queen runs the game.

33 f3 Ne5 34 fxe4 Bxc4 35 Rc1 Rxa6 36 Rxc4+ Nxc4 37 Qxc4+ Rc6 38 Qf7 Kd8 39 Qg8+ Kd7 40 Qxh7 Rc5 41 Qf7 Rc1+ 42 Kf2 Rc8 43 Qf5+ Kc7 44 Qe6 Black resigns

Game 3
□ **Anand** ■ **Lautier**
Belgrade 1997

1 e4 c5 2 Nf3 e6 3 d4 cxd4 4 Nxd4 Nf6 5 Nc3 Nc6 6 Ndb5 d6 7 Bf4 e5 8 Bg5 a6 9 Na3 b5 10 Bxf6 gxf6 11 Nd5 Bg7 12 c4 f5

Black ignores the attack on his queenside structure and begins his own counter-attack in the centre.

13 cxb5 Nd4 14 Bd3 Be6 15 0-0 0-0 16 Nc2 Nxc2 17 Bxc2 fxe4 18 bxa6 Rxa6 19 Bxe4 f5 20 Bd3 Rc6 21 Be2 Rc5 (Diagram 3)

White has two passed queenside pawns for the endgame, but Black has a mobile central pawn mass which gives him good chances in the middlegame.

22 Nc3 e4 23 Rc1 d5 24 Na4 Rxc1 25 Qxc1 d4 26 Nc5 Bd5 27 Bc4

Kh8 28 Ne6 Bxe6 29 Bxe6 d3 30 Qc4 Qf6 31 b3 Re8 32 Bd5 Rd8
33 g3 Qe5 34 Bb7 Qe7 35 Bd5 Qe5 36 Bb7 Qe7 37 Bd5 Qd6 38
Bb7 Qb6 39 Qc6 Qd4 40 Qe6

A terrible mistake which allows Black to advance his d-pawn deci-
sively. If White replies with 41 Rd1 then 41...Qa1 42 Rxa1 Bxa1
breaks the blockade.

40...d2 41 Qxf5 Rf8 White resigns

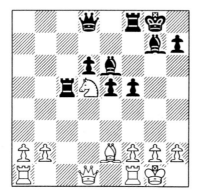

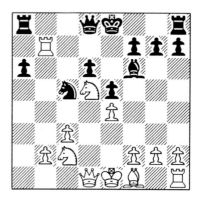

Diagram 3	**Diagram 4**
Black has a strong centre	An amazing exchange sacrifice!

Game 4
□ **Kasparov** ■ **Shirov**
Horgen 1994

**1 e4 c5 2 Nf3 e6 3 d4 cxd4 4 Nxd4 Nf6 5 Nc3 Nc6 6 Ndb5 d6 7 Bf4
e5 8 Bg5 a6 9 Na3 b5**

Reaching the usual position a move later, with both sides having
'wasted' a tempo: White with Bc1-f4-g5, Black with ...e7-e6-e5. White
now forces the bishop recapture on f6.

**10 Nd5 Be7 11 Bxf6 Bxf6 12 c3 Bb7 13 Nc2 Nb8 14 a4 bxa4 15
Rxa4 Nd7 16 Rb4 Nc5 17 Rxb7 (Diagram 4)**

A surprising positional sacrifice by which White takes total control
over d5. Further justification is that after the key move 18 b4 the
black knight will remain on the sidelines for a long time, leaving
Black without active play.

**17...Nxb7 18 b4 Bg5 19 Na3 0-0 20 Nc4 a5 21 Bd3 axb4 22 cxb4
Qb8 23 h4**

Another important move, putting the question to the bishop. If it retreats to d8 then the knight's route to e6 is blocked, while if the
bishop drops back to h6 Black loses control of the d8-h4 diagonal.

23...Bh6 24 Ncb6 Ra2 25 0-0 Rd2 26 Qf3 Qa7 27 Nd7 Nd8

Tamely returning material and leaving White with his positional superiority for nothing. Black was no doubt concerned about 28 Ne7+ Kh8 29 Qxf7, but 27...Ra8 allows him to defend by 29...Rxd3 30 Nf8 Qa2!.

28 Nxf8 Kxf8 29 b5 Qa3 30 Qf5 Ke8 31 Bc4 Rc2 32 Qxh7 Rxc4 33 Qg8+ Kd7 34 Nb6+ Ke7 35 Nxc4 Qc5 36 Ra1 Qd4 37 Ra3 Bc1 38 Ne3 Black resigns

The Scheveningen Variation

1 e4 c5 2 Nf3 d6 3 d4 cxd4 4 Nxd4 Nf6 5 Nc3 e6

With 5...e6 Black plays a more patient game. He covers the central squares in his own half of the board and intends to develop behind them. The major advantage of this for Black is that he has no weaknesses and, with his extra central pawn, has more control over the central squares, albeit only those in his own half of the board. After first organising his forces Black will then start his counterplay from a sound foundation.

By the direct Scheveningen move order (given above) White has some violent responses, notably 6 g4 (Keres Attack), which have discouraged some Black players. However, the small centre ...d6, ...e6 formation can arise via several other Sicilian defences; for instance, the Taimanov and Kan variations (if Black plays ...d6) or the Najdorf (5...a6 followed by ...e7-e6). For this reason the Classical Scheveningen is of central importance to the understanding of the Sicilian Defence in general.

TIP: The Scheveningen is a good choice for those who want a dynamic opening as Black but do not wish to weaken their position at an early stage.

White's initiative in the early stages of the game can reach tsunami proportions, and if Black is not to be swept aside, he often has to defend very carefully. However, the small centre is very resilient and should the attack founder, White is very often unable to cope with the inevitable counter-attack. It is for this that Black has waited and plotted long.

What is White's Strategy?

In the Classical Scheveningen White has a choice: either to attack on the kingside or in the centre. He may also seek to restrain Black on the queenside by playing a2-a4, or not bother and use the extra tempo for his own plans. White can conduct his kingside attack either with pieces (typically the manoeuvre Qe1-g3, followed by e4-e5 to drive away the black Nf6) or launch a pawn storm with g2-g4-g5.

What is Black's Strategy?

Black will develop Be7, Qc7, 0-0, Nc6 (or Nbd7); the queen's bishop generally ends up on the long diagonal, either directly at b7 or via d7-c6, to put pressure on the e4-pawn. If White has allowed the advance ...b7-b5 then Black may play ...b5-b4 to drive away the defending white knight.

Tactical/Strategic/Dynamic?

As the Closed Ruy Lopez is the strategic battleground in the open games (1 e4 e5), the Classical Scheveningen is the equivalent for the Sicilian Defence. However, there is one big difference: In the Closed Ruy Lopez White's attack is built up slowly and is often described as slow torture. In the Scheveningen the attack usually comes more swiftly, but if Black survives he can look forward to good chances in the long term.

Theoretical?

As with all Sicilian defences a large body of theory has built up on the Scheveningen. While a lot of this can be overlooked for general use, Black at least needs to know two things: firstly how to defend his kingside against White's inevitable attack, and then how, when and where to strike back.

How Popular is it?

The Scheveningen formation with the small centre ...d6, ...e6 is very popular. The direct move order has lessened in popularity as many players (notably Kasparov) prefer to avoid the Keres Attack. But as the Classical positions can be obtained from several other Sicilian systems, it still appears regularly at all levels of play.

Illustrative Games

Game 5
□ **Tal** ■ **Andersson**
Stockholm 1976

1 e4 c5 2 Nf3 d6 3 d4 cxd4 4 Nxd4 Nf6 5 Nc3 e6 6 Be2 Be7 7 0-0 0-0 8 f4 Nc6 9 Be3 a6 10 Qe1 Nxd4 11 Bxd4 b5 12 Rd1 Bb7 13 Bf3 Qc7 14 e5 dxe5 15 fxe5 Nd7 16 Bxb7 Qxb7 17 Ne4

White has a ready-made kingside attack but it is not all plain sailing – Black's kingside is quite secure and he can target the e5-pawn. Tal wins the game powerfully, but Black's defence has since been improved.

17...Rad8 18 Rd3 Qc6 19 Rg3 Qxc2 20 Qe3 Qc4 21 b3 Qd5 22 Nf6+

A typical attacking ploy: Black is forced to weaken his dark squares.

22...Bxf6 23 exf6 g6 24 Rg4 Kh8 25 Bb6 Rc8 26 Qh6 Rg8 27 Rd4 (Diagram 5)

The decisive move – if Black retreats the queen to b7 or c6 then 28 Qxh7+ Kxh7 29 Rh4 mates.

27...Nxb6 28 Rxd5 Nxd5 29 Rf3 Rc3 30 Rxc3 Nxc3 31 Qe3 b4 32 Qa7 Rf8 33 Qc5 Rb8 34 Qd6 Black resigns

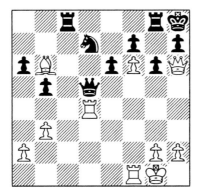

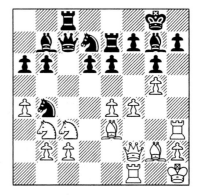

Diagram 5
White's attack wins material

Diagram 6
Kasparov's brilliant defensive play

Game 6
□ **Karpov** ■ **Kasparov**
Moscow World Championship 1985

1 e4 c5 2 Nf3 d6 3 d4 cxd4 4 Nxd4 Nf6 5 Nc3 a6 6 Be2 e6 7 0-0 Be7 8 f4 0-0 9 Kh1 Qc7 10 a4 Nc6 11 Be3 Re8 12 Bf3 Rb8 13 Qd2 Bd7 14 Nb3 b6 15 g4 Bc8 16 g5 Nd7 17 Qf2 Bf8 18 Bg2 Bb7 19 Rad1 g6

Black is patiently defending and reorganising. Karpov, who needed to win to retain the title, finds a way to rejuvenate his attack.

20 Bc1 Rbc8 21 Rd3 Nb4 22 Rh3 Bg7 23 Be3 Re7 (Diagram 6)

Kasparov's famous 'mysterious' rook move. With White having missed the optimum moment to thrust f4-f5, Black forestalls it by defending f7 and planning to use the e-file should it open up.

24 Kg1 Rce8 25 Rd1 f5 26 gxf6 Nxf6 27 Rg3 Rf7 28 Bxb6 Qb8 29 Be3 Nh5 30 Rg4 Nf6 31 Rh4 g5 32 fxg5 Ng4 33 Qd2 Nxe3 34 Qxe3 Nxc2 35 Qb6 Ba8 36 Rxd6

Having spent most of his time trying to force the required win, Karpov now blunders.

36...Rb7 37 Qxa6 Rxb3 38 Rxe6 Rxb2 39 Qc4 Kh8 40 e5 Qa7+ 41 Kh1 Bxg2+ 42 Kxg2 Nd4+ White resigns

WARNING: White often wants to advance his kingside pawns in the Scheveningen but this can leave holes which Black can later exploit.

Game 7
□ **Kasparov** ■ **Short**
Moscow Olympiad 1994

---

1 e4 c5 2 Nf3 d6 3 d4 cxd4 4 Nxd4 Nf6 5 Nc3 a6

Short, not noted as a Sicilian specialist, is being very provocative here as Kasparov is a virtuoso on the black side of these lines.

6 Be2 e6 7 f4 Be7 8 0-0 Qc7 9 Qe1 Nbd7 10 Bf3 0-0 11 Kh1 Kh8 12 a4 Rb8 13 g4

This natural attacking advance is especially strong here, since Black's queen's knight blocks the retreat of his king's knight.

13...b6 14 g5 Ne8 15 Bg2 Bb7 16 b3 Qd8 17 h4 g6 18 Bb2 Ng7 19 Rd1 Rc8 20 f5 e5 21 f6 exd4 22 fxe7 Qxe7 23 Rxd4 (Diagram 7)

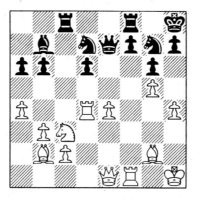
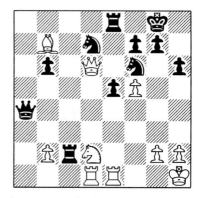

Diagram 7
The b2-bishop is very strong

Diagram 8
Black has a winning position

White already has a huge advantage with the two bishops, one of which glares ominously down the a1-h8 diagonal at the black king.

23...f6 24 Qd2 fxg5 25 Rxf8+ Rxf8 26 Rxd6 Ne5 27 Rxb6 gxh4 28 Nd5 Bxd5 29 Qxd5 Re8 30 Bh3 Qc7 31 Re6 Rxe6 32 Bxe6 Nc6 33 Qg5 Qd6 34 Bd5 Nb4 35 Qf6 Qxf6 36 Bxf6 Nxc2 37 Bc3

The queenside pawns advance for an easy win while the black knights look on helplessly.

37...h6 38 b4 Kh7 39 b5 axb5 40 axb5 Nh5 41 b6 Ng3+ 42 Kh2
Black resigns

Game 8
□ **J.Polgar** ■ **Kasparov**
Linares 1994

---

1 e4 c5 2 Nf3 d6 3 d4 cxd4 4 Nxd4 Nf6 5 Nc3 a6 6 f4 e6 7 Be2 Be7
8 0-0 Qc7 9 Qe1 Nbd7 10 a4 b6 11 Bf3 Bb7 12 Kh1 Rd8

Kasparov plays these positions with great virtuosity. Here 12...Rd8
negates White's intended thrust e4-e5, since after an exchange on e5
the Nd4 would be en prise.

13 Be3 0-0 14 Qg3 Nc5 15 f5 e5 16 Bh6 Ne8 17 Nb3 Nd7 18 Rad1
Kh8 19 Be3 Nef6 20 Qf2 Rfe8 21 Rfe1 Bf8 22 Bg5 h6 23 Bh4 Rc8

Having consolidated his kingside defences Black begins his queenside
counterplay.

24 Qf1 Be7 25 Nd2 Qc5 26 Nb3 Qb4 27 Be2 Bxe4 28 Nxe4 Nxe4
29 Bxe7 Rxe7 30 Bf3 Nef6 31 Qxa6 Ree8 32 Qe2 Kg8 33 Bb7 Rc4
34 Qd2 Qxa4 35 Qxd6 Rxc2 36 Nd2 (Diagram 8)

Black has played powerfully to reach a won position, but now an al-
tercation arose: Kasparov put his knight on c5 and then, seeing it was
a mistake, moved it to f8. Polgar claimed he had let go of the piece on
c5, Kasparov said he hadn't. The truth is now irrelevant, 36...Nf8 was
allowed by the arbiter and the game continued.

36...Nf8 37 Ne4 N8d7 38 Nxf6+ Nxf6 39 Qxb6 Ng4 40 Rf1 e4 41
Bd5 e3 42 Bb3 Qe4 43 Bxc2 Qxc2 44 Rd8 Rxd8 45 Qxd8+ Kh7 46
Qe7 Qc4 **White resigns**

The Dragon Variation

1 e4 c5 2 Nf3 d6 3 d4 cxd4 4 Nxd4 Nf6 5 Nc3 g6

The Dragon is perhaps the most logical of the various Sicilian defences. With White's d4-pawn cleared away, the fianchettoed bishop
at g7 is able to gaze – breathe fire – down the long diagonal, supporting a direct attack (should White castle long) or otherwise the natural
minority attack ...b7-b5-b4.

The critical variation is the Yugoslav Attack, in which Black and
White castle on opposite sides. The game often becomes fiercely tactical, requiring great accuracy from both players as they launch violent
attacks against each other's kings. One mistake in defence and there
can be no way back for either side. The Yugoslav Dragon almost
qualifies as an 'extreme sport', to which many Dragon players show a
loyalty bordering on addiction, remaining true to the system for decades.

What is White's Strategy?

Although White can play the Dragon quietly (Be2, 0-0), the most testing variation involves Be3, Qd2, 0-0-0 and a direct attack against the black king's position. White will advance the h-pawn to open the h-file for his major pieces, and try to exchange the dark-squared bishops with Be3-h6. The knight on f6 can be removed by Nc3-d5 or g4-g5.

What is Black's Strategy?

If allowed Black may break in the centre with ...d6-d5, unleashing his bishop after e4xd5 ...Nxd5. Otherwise the game can become a race between two attacks. While Black keeps an eye on the kingside, most of his concentration is reserved for his own queenside attack, possibly with ...b7-b5, or ...Rc8, ...Nc4, ...Qa5. Black's typical device is the exchange sacrifice, either ...Rxc3 to destroy White's defences, or sometimes ...RxBd4 so that Black's dark-squared bishop is unopposed. In both defence and attack the Dragon bishop on g7 is Black's key piece.

Tactical/Strategic/Dynamic?

The main lines of the Yugoslav Attack can be enormously tactical as both sides rush on with their attacks on opposite sides of the board. Even in the quieter variations Black is guaranteed dynamic counter-play thanks to his potent Dragon bishop at g7.

Theoretical?

The Dragon is also enormously theoretical. Often the game proper doesn't begin until move 16 and every nuance of the respective attacks has been investigated. That the Dragon has still not been fully exhausted is evidence of the infinite possibilities in chess, but entering into complications of the Yugoslav Attack with insufficient knowledge can be suicidal.

How Popular is it?

The many attractive tactics and sacrifices in the Dragon make it popular at all levels. It also received a boost in 1995 when Kasparov unexpectedly used it in his World Championship title against Anand.

Illustrative Games

Game 9
□ **Karpov** ■ **Korchnoi**
Moscow Candidates final 1974

1 e4 c5 2 Nf3 d6 3 d4 cxd4 4 Nxd4 Nf6 5 Nc3 g6 6 Be3 Bg7 7 f3

Nc6 8 Qd2 0-0 9 Bc4 Bd7 10 h4 Rc8 11 Bb3 Ne5 12 0-0-0 Nc4 13 Bxc4 Rxc4 14 h5 Nxh5 15 g4 Nf6 16 Nde2

White has sacrificed a pawn to open the h-file, but now takes time out to over-protect his queen's knight and forestall Black's typical exchange sacrifice on c3. At the time 16 Nde2 was a prepared novelty. Black's next allows the trade of dark-squared bishops. Subsequently 16...Re8 has been preferred to answer Be3-h6 with ...Bg7-h8.

16...Qa5 17 Bh6 Bxh6 18 Qxh6 Rfc8 19 Rd3

Again supporting the Nc3. In these main lines both players are on a knife edge. One mistake and the game can be irrevocably lost. Black's next is one such mistake.

19...R4c5 20 g5 Rxg5 21 Rd5 Rxd5 22 Nxd5 Re8 23 Nef4 Bc6 24 e5 (Diagram 9)

Blocking the fifth rank so that if 24...dxe5 White wins by 25 Nxf6+ exf6 26 Nh5! gxh5 27 Rg1+.

24...Bxd5 25 exf6 exf6 26 Qxh7+ Kf8 27 Qh8+ Black resigns

If 27...Ke7 28 Nxd5+ Qxd5 29 Re1+ wins the rook.

 WARNING: You should not consider playing the Dragon as Black without a great deal of preparatory work.

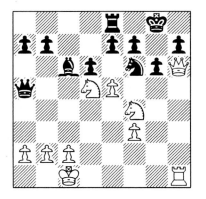

Diagram 9
Black's f6-knight is undermined

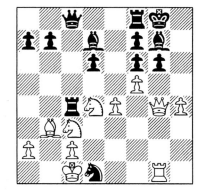

Diagram 10
Black blocks the a2-g8 diagonal

Game 10
□ **Oll** ■ **Topalov**
Moscow Olympiad 1994

1 e4 c5 2 Nf3 d6 3 d4 cxd4 4 Nxd4 Nf6 5 Nc3 g6 6 Be3 Bg7 7 f3 Nc6 8 Qd2 0-0 9 Bc4 Bd7 10 h4 Ne5 11 Bb3 h5

Black blocks the h-file and gains more time for his queenside attack.

The drawback is that ...h7-h5 weakens his kingside defences which White will assault with g2-g4.

12 0-0-0 Rc8 13 Bg5 Rc5 14 g4 hxg4 15 f4 Nc4 16 Qe2 Qc8 17 f5 Nxb2

The major threat behind ...Nc4. Here White should capture with 18 Kxb2 Rxc3 19 fxg6 Rxb3+ 20 axb3 fxg6 and Black is slightly better. Instead he stakes everything on an insufficient attack.

18 Bxf6 Nxd1 19 Qxg4 exf6 20 Rg1 Rc4 (Diagram 10)

The winning move. Black blocks the a2-g8 diagonal, preventing White's intended Qxg6, and keeps a decisive material advantage.

21 Nxd1 d5 22 h5 Rxd4 23 hxg6 fxg6 24 Qxg6 Rf7 25 Nf2 Qc3 26 Kb1 Qe3 27 Rg2 Kf8 28 exd5 Qe1+ 29 Kb2 Qe5 30 Kb1 Qxf5 White resigns

TIP: The Dragon is a good choice of opening if you want to try and beat a stronger player. In positions with wild complications, anything can happen!

Game 11
□ Adams ■ Fedorov
Wijk aan Zee 2001

1 e4 c5 2 Nf3 d6 3 d4 cxd4 4 Nxd4 Nf6 5 Nc3 g6 6 Be3 Bg7 7 f3 Nc6 8 Qd2 0-0 9 0-0-0

As White has left his king's bishop on f1 Black has to change his plans. To continue as before with ...Nc4 would donate two tempi to White, who has not used time on Bf1-c4-b3. However, the absence of the bishop from the a2-g8 diagonal allows Black to make the following pawn sacrifice. Black can also play 9...Nxd4 10 Bxd4 Be6.

9...d5 10 exd5 Nxd5 11 Nxc6 bxc6 12 Nxd5 cxd5 13 Qxd5 Qc7 (Diagram 11)

For the pawn Black has obtained open files and diagonals against the white king, and has scored well from this position. Note that if White takes the rook, 14 Qxa8, then 14...Bf5 forces him to give up his queen, when Black has a good game.

14 Qc5 Qb8 15 Qa3 Be6 16 Ba6 Qe5 17 g3 Rad8 18 Bf4 Qf6 19 Rhe1 Bf5 20 Rxd8 Rxd8 21 c3 Qb6 22 Be3 Bh6 23 f4 Qc6 24 Bd2 Qd5 25 Re2 e5 26 Qa4 exf4 27 gxf4 Bxf4

The winning move. White cannot capture the bishop: if 28 Bxf4 Qh1+ mates, or 28 Qxf4 Qxa2 creates the decisive threat of ...Qb1 mate.

28 Re8+ Kg7 29 Qxf4 Rxe8 30 Bc4 Qh1+ 31 Bf1 Kg8 White resigns

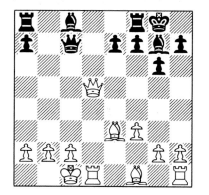

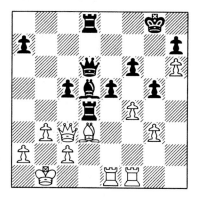

Diagram 11
Black has dangerous counterplay

Diagram 12
g7 is a vulnerable spot for Black

Game 12
□ **Morozevich** ■ **Kir.Georgiev**
Sarajevo 2000

1 e4 c5 2 Nf3 d6 3 d4 cxd4 4 Nxd4 Nf6 5 Nc3 g6 6 Be3 Bg7 7 f3 Nc6 8 Qd2 0-0 9 0-0-0 d5 10 exd5 Nxd5 11 Nxc6 bxc6 12 Bd4

A more positional approach than in the previous game. Usually Black replies 12...e5 to prevent the exchange of bishops. But Georgiev is an expert on the Dragon so his choice must also be taken seriously.

12...Bxd4 13 Qxd4 Qc7 14 Qc5 Nxc3 15 Qxc3 Be6 16 Bd3 Rad8 17 Rde1 c5 18 Kb1 Rd4 19 h4 Qd6 20 h5 g5 21 h6 (Diagram 12)

White sticks an annoying thorn in the black kingside. Although there are no immediate threats, in the long term White plans to open lines with f3-f4.

21...Rd8 22 b3 f6 23 g3 Bd5 24 Rhf1 e5 25 f4 e4 26 Be2 Rf8 27 fxg5 f5 28 Rf4 Be6 29 Ref1 Qe5 30 Qa5 Rf7 31 g4 fxg4 32 Rxf7 Bxf7 33 Qxa7

The h-pawn finally has its say. Apart from providing the possibility of Qg7 mate, if now 33...Qe8 34 g6! hxg6 35 h7+ is decisive.

33...Be8 34 Rf5 Black resigns

The Taimanov Variation

1 e4 c5 2 Nf3 e6 3 d4 cxd4 4 Nxd4 Nc6 5 Nc3 a6

The Taimanov is a very flexible system. Black begins with 'universal' Sicilian moves (...a6, ...e6), and keeps his options open as to his kingside development. Meanwhile he can mobilise his queenside and perhaps take the initiative in that sector.

One problem is that the black king remains in the centre for a long time and is sometimes caught there, facing a fierce white onslaught. But when this happens it is usually because Black has takes too many liberties in the opening. The Taimanov pawn structure (d7, e6, f7) is resilient and has resisted White's attempts to smash or to smother it.

Black also has a choice of move orders: he can play 4...a6 before ...Nc6, or perhaps 4...Qc7 first, or even delay ...e7-e6. It depends on what Black most wants to avoid – for instance, against 4...a6 White can reply 5 Bd3. The Taimanov move order prevents Bd3 but then Black has to contend with Nd4xc6.

What is White's Strategy?

As White is not under any immediate pressure he can formulate his own plans for the middlegame undisturbed – possibly to take space in the centre with c2-c4 or prepare a kingside attack with f2-f4. Against ...Nb8-c6 the capture Nd4xc6 also comes into consideration; this is not usually a good idea in the Sicilian as ...b7xc6 strengthens Black's centre, but here it enables White to accelerate his development.

What is Black's Strategy?

Primarily Black's area for action is on the queenside, but having played non-committal moves so far Black has many options: advance on the queenside with ...b7-b5; exchange pieces by ...Nxd4 and follow with ...Ne7-c6; develop the king's bishop actively to c5 or b4; or return to Scheveningen positions with ...d7-d6.

Tactical/Strategic/Dynamic?

The quiet beginning of the Taimanov would seem to indicate a strategic game, but it has supporters amongst GMs of all styles. It can in fact be strategic, tactical or dynamic according to taste.

Theoretical?

The flexible nature of the Taimanov makes it less theoretically taxing than other Sicilian main lines, which is one of its main appeals. Black can get away with a general understanding of the positions, although some grasp of transpositional possibilities is useful.

How Popular is it?

The Taimanov and its close relative, the Kan, are both popular at Grandmaster level, but not so much at club level. The reason is perhaps that amateur players, who undertake to learn a Sicilian system, want a higher reward for their work than just a flexible, sound position. Hence they opt for one of the more aggressive defences such as the Dragon or Sveshnikov.

Illustrative Games

Game 13
□ **Psakhis** ■ **Romanishin**
Irkutsk 1986

1 e4 c5 2 Nf3 e6 3 d4 cxd4 4 Nxd4 Nc6 5 Nc3 a6 6 Be2 Nge7 7 Bf4 Ng6 8 Nxc6 bxc6 9 Bd6

A drawback of Black's d7/e6 structure is the weakness at d6. Here White manages to create a blockade on d6, rendering Black's pieces completely passive.

9...Bxd6 10 Qxd6 Qe7 11 0-0-0 Qxd6 12 Rxd6 Ke7 13 Rhd1 Ra7 14 g3 f6 15 f4 Rd8 16 Na4 Nh8 17 c4 Nf7 18 c5 (Diagram 13)

A strong exchange sacrifice which can hardly be accepted – if 18...Nxd6 19 cxd6+ Kf7 20 Nc5 White's dark control is absolute and Black has virtually no moves.

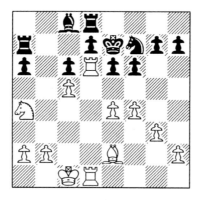

Diagram 13
Black is suffering on the dark squares

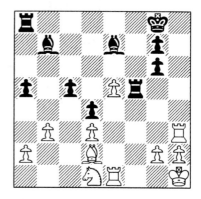

Diagram 14
Black is very active

18...a5 19 R6d4 e5 20 R4d2 Ba6 21 Bg4 d6 22 fxe5 dxe5 23 Rxd8 Nxd8 24 Nb6 Rc7 25 Kc2 g6 26 Kc3 h5 27 Rd7+ Rxd7 28 Bxd7

Black has freed his position, but the white queenside pawn majority makes the endgame very difficult.

28...Ne6 29 Bxc6 Nxc5 30 Nc4 Bb7 31 Bxb7 Nxb7 32 b4 axb4+ 33 Kxb4 Ke6 34 a4 f5 35 a5

Knights are very bad at stopping rook's pawns.

35...Nxa5 36 Kxa5 f4 37 Kb5 g5 38 Nd2 g4 39 Nf1 Kf6 40 Kc5 Kg5 41 Kd5 Kf6 42 Kd6 **Black resigns**

Game 14
□ **Gallagher** ■ **Razuvaev**
Geneva 1994

---

1 e4 c5 2 Nf3 e6 3 d4 cxd4 4 Nxd4 Nc6 5 Nc3 Qc7 6 f4 a6 7 Nxc6 bxc6 8 Bd3 d5

Black frees his position immediately. However, his centre is rigid as d5xe4 or d5-d4 would leave behind weaknesses.

9 0-0 Nf6 10 Qe2 Bb7 11 Bd2 Be7 12 Rae1 Nd7 13 Nd1 0-0 14 Bc3 Qb6+ 15 Kh1 d4 16 Bd2 Nc5 17 Rf3 Nxd3 18 cxd3 c5 19 b3 f5 20 Rh3 e5

A dual-purpose move: Black both destroys his opponent's centre and clears the third rank for his queen.

21 Qh5 Qg6 22 Qxg6 hxg6 23 exf5 Rxf5 24 fxe5 a5 (Diagram 14)

Black's pawns look a mess, but in fact it is the white pawns which are weak as Black now demonstrates.

25 Kg1 a4 26 Nf2 axb3 27 axb3 Ra2 28 Ne4 Rxe5 29 Bf4 Rf5 30 Rf3 Rb2 31 Bg3 Bd5 32 Rxf5 gxf5 33 Nxc5 Bxc5 34 Re5 Bxg2 35 Rxc5 Bh3 36 Rc7 Rg2+ 37 Kh1 f4 38 Rc4 Rd2 39 Be1 Rd1 40 Kg1 Rxe1+ 41 Kf2 **White resigns**

Game 15
□ **Timman** ■ **Ljubojevic**
Brussels World Cup 1988

---

1 e4 c5 2 Nf3 e6 3 d4 cxd4 4 Nxd4 Nc6 5 Nc3 a6 6 g3 d6 7 Bg2 Bd7 8 0-0 Rc8 9 Nxc6 Bxc6 10 a4 Be7 11 Qg4 h5

Black takes the opportunity to open the h-file for a possible later attack. Much later as it turns out – the attack doesn't come to fruition until another 30 moves have passed.

12 Qe2 h4 13 Rd1 hxg3 14 hxg3 Qc7 15 Bf4 Nf6 16 Rd2 Nd7 17 Nb5 axb5 18 axb5 Ne5 19 bxc6 Qxc6 20 b3 g5 21 Be3 g4 22 Rad1 Rg8 23 Bf4 Qc5 24 Be3 Qc6 25 c4 Rg6 26 Rd4 Kf8 27 Bc1 Qc5 28 Be3 Qa3 29 Rb1 Kg7

Having evacuated his king and cleared the back rank in a rather un-orthodox way Black is finally ready to make use of the h-file.

30 Qd1 Rh8 31 Ra1 Qc5 32 Rd5 Qc7 33 Rb5 Nc6 34 Ra2 Bf6 35 Bb6 Qb8 36 Rd2 Be5 37 c5 Na7 38 Ra5 Nc6 39 Rb5 Na7 40 Ra5 Nc6 41 Ra4 dxc5 42 Bxc5 Rh5 43 Bb6 Qh8 44 Rda2 Rh2 (Diagram 15)

White has no defence to the following attack.

45 Be3 Rxg2+ 46 Kxg2 Qh3+ 47 Kg1 Bxg3 48 fxg3 Qxg3+ 49 Kf1 Qxe3 50 Qe2 Rf6+ White resigns

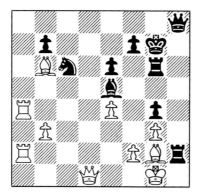

Diagram 15
The bishop on e5 controls the board?

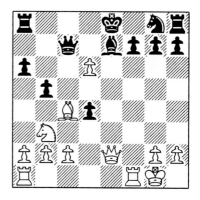

Diagram 16
Black has a bad lack of development

Game 16
□ **Hector** ■ **Mortensen**
Reykjavik 1995

---

1 e4 c5 2 Nf3 Nc6 3 d4 cxd4 4 Nxd4 Qc7 5 Nc3 e6 6 Be3 a6 7 Bd3 b5 8 0-0 Bb7 9 Nb3 Ne5

Novices are taught not to move the same piece twice in the opening. Nowadays such axioms are often disregarded as players pursue other objectives in the opening than quick development. But this entails the risk of being crushed by more swiftly mobilised opposing forces.

10 f4 Nc4 11 Bd4 d6 12 Qe2 e5 13 Nd5 Bxd5 14 exd5 Be7 15 fxe5 dxe5 16 Bxc4 exd4 17 d6 (Diagram 16)

White is already ahead in development. Now he accelerates this with a piece sacrifice, which Black must accept because of the threat to f7.

17...Qxc4 18 Qf3 Rb8 19 Rae1 Nf6 20 Rxe7+ Kf8 21 Na5 Qc5 22 Qb3

21...Qb4 would have prevented this, but White still intended to put his queen on the diagonal by 22 Qd5! Nxd5 23 Rfxf7+ winning.

22...Qh5 23 Nc6 Rc8 24 d7 Rd8 25 Re8+ Black resigns

Chapter Two

The Sicilian without d2-d4

 Closed Systems with 2 Nc3

 The c3 Sicilian

One of the problems with taking on the main lines of the Sicilian Defence is the necessity for learning substantial amounts of theory. If you commit yourself to playing 2 Nf3 and 3 d4, you must be familiar with a large number of possible variations, many of which are very sharp and require a reasonably detailed understanding of what is going on. Consequently, methods of countering the Sicilian other than the afore-mentioned 2 Nf3 and 3 d4 are very popular, particularly at club level.

In this chapter we will consider two of these possibilities and identify their strengths and weaknesses.

Closed Systems with 2 Nc3

Playing 2 Nc3 against the Sicilian is usually an indication that White is going to adopt some form of 'Closed' Sicilian. This means that White will decline to advance with d2-d4 and will instead concentrate on arranging his forces for a kingside advance. A typical set-up for White arrives with the following moves: Nc3, g2-g3, Bg2, d2-d3, 0-0 and f2-f4. This is the classical form of the Closed Sicilian. White has staked out a claim to space on the kingside and this will usually lead to a general advance in that sector, with further moves such as h2-h3, g3-g4 and f4-f5. More often than not Black castles kingside in the Closed Sicilian, thus supplying a handy target for White's expansionist ambitions.

Another way to play with 2 Nc3 is the immediate advance 3 f4, followed by 4 Nf3. The light-squared bishop is then developed either at c4 or b5 and White again aims for a kingside attack. However, in this case the attack will usually be carried out by pure piece play rather than with pawn advances. These systems are collectively known as the Grand Prix Attack and they can be quite dangerous against an unwary opponent.

From White's point of view, the Closed systems rely very much on an understanding of some fairly straightforward plans and can therefore be mastered quite easily. Despite their simplistic nature they can, nevertheless, be dangerous against ill-prepared opposition. The downside is that they are rather quiet and do not really promise any theoretical advantage. White's systems are not terribly complex – he is basically after a kingside attack and there is not a lot else in the armoury if that particular weapon is defused. Nowadays many black players are wise to the nuances of these systems and can often neutralise them with careful play.

What is White's Strategy?

As has already been made clear, White is planning a swift kingside attack, either with piece play or pawn advances. Sometimes White can also advance in the centre but there are drawbacks to this. In order to occupy the centre White has to play c2-c3 and d3-d4, but he has already developed the knight on c3 and spent a tempo advancing the d-pawn to d3.

What is Black's Strategy?

Black will generally counter White's kingside advance with an advance of his own on the opposite wing. Play can often develop into a race. Although White has the black king as a target, his advances on the kingside weaken his own king's position. If Black successfully gets 'in round the back', this can prove fatal. Black can also consider trying to blunt White's attempted initiative with a move such as ...f7-f5.

Tactical/Strategic/Dynamic?

The pure Closed Sicilian with 2 Nc3 and 3 g3 tends to be very strategic. The two armies often do not really engage each other until much later in the game and positional understanding is paramount. However, the Grand Prix Attack is a more confrontational opening and can liven up much earlier. The Grand Prix Attack is also quite dynamic, whereas the Closed is less so.

Theoretical?

The Closed systems are not particularly theoretical but there are a few important principles that need to be understood. The Grand Prix Attack is quite theoretical and there are a few specific moves and ideas which need to be understood.

How Popular is it?

Closed systems, and in particular the Grand Prix Attack, are most popular at club level but, even so, are seen reasonably frequently at international level. They are also very popular with British players. For example, Nigel Short is often seen playing lines with 2 Nc3. The more classically minded players from Russia and the Eastern European countries are not great fans, although Anatoly Karpov did use the Closed Sicilian in his youth and Boris Spassky, world champion from 1969-1972 is a major enthusiast.

Illustrative Games

Game 17
□ **Spassky** ■ **Geller**
Candidates Quarter-Final, Sukhumi 1968

1 e4 c5 2 Nc3 d6 3 g3 Nc6 4 Bg2 g6 5 d3 Bg7 6 f4 Nf6 7 Nf3 0-0 8

0-0 Rb8 9 Nh4 Nd4 10 f5 b5 11 Bg5 b4 12 Nb1 Nd7 13 Nd2 Ne5 14
Kh1 a5 15 Rb1 a4 16 Nhf3 exf3 17 Nxf3 Nb5 18 Qd2 a3 19 bxa3
Nxa3 20 Rbe1 (Diagram 1)

White has built up a promising attacking position on the kingside and
all his pieces are participating in his initiative on that side of the
board. Meanwhile Black has broken through on the queenside and
now wins rook for bishop. However, this is at the cost of his crucial
defensive dark-squared bishop and this proves to be too high a price
to pay.

20...Bc3 21 Qf2 Bxe1 22 Rxe1 f6

Having jettisoned the fianchettoed bishop, Black hurries to shore up
the dark square weaknesses around his king.

**23 Bh6 Rf7 24 g4 e6 25 Nh4 g5 26 Nf3 exf5 27 gxf5 Kh8 28 h4 g4
29 Nh2 g3 30 Qxg3 Nxc2 31 Rg1 Bb7 32 Bf3 Qd7 33 Bh5 Re7 34
Ng4 Rg8 35 Qf2 Nd4 36 Nxf6 Rxg1+ 37 Qxg1 Black resigns**

**NOTE: In Closed Sicilian positions the black dark-squared bishop is
a key piece and, in double-edged middlegames, is often more
valuable than a rook.**

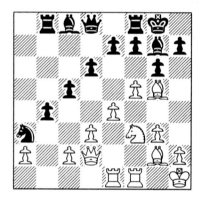

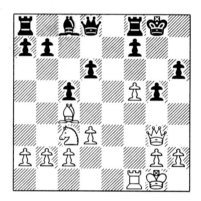

Diagram 1
White has a powerful kingside build-up

Diagram 2
White has a strong attack

Game 18
□ **Hodgson** ■ **Malisauskas**
St. Petersburg 1984

1 e4 c5 2 Nc3 Nc6 3 f4 g6 4 Nf3 Bg7 5 Bc4 d6 6 d3 e6 7 f5

This is White's typical ploy in the Grand Prix Attack. It is a purely
positional pawn sacrifice designed to open lines for his pieces.

7...exf5 8 0-0 Nge7 9 Qe1 h6

Black must already be very careful. A serious mistake here is 9...0-0 as after 10 Qh4 White already has what is close to a winning kingside attack.

10 Qg3 Ne5 11 Nxe5 Bxe5 12 Bf4 Bxf4 13 Rxf4 g5 14 Rxf5

A promising gambit.

14...Nxf5 15 exf5 0-0 16 Rf1 (Diagram 2)

A typically successful enterprise for White in the Grand Prix Attack. He has given up the exchange but has wonderful control of key central squares such as e4 and d5. Additionally, Black has weakened himself badly on the kingside and White's forces are well placed to come in.

16...Qf6 17 Ne4 Qe5 18 Qh3 Kg7 19 f6+ Kh7 20 Qh5

White is busy exploiting all the holes in the black position.

20...Be6 21 Bxe6 fxe6 22 f7 Qd4+ 23 Kh1 Kg7 24 Nf6 Qh4 25 Ne8+ Kh7 26 Qe2 e5 27 g4 d5 28 Qxe5 Raxe8 29 Qf5+ Black resigns

NOTE: The Grand Prix is a slow-burning attacking system. White often sacrifices a pawn or the exchange purely to create structural weaknesses in the black camp which are then gradually exploited.

Game 19
☐ **Fedorov** ■ **Kasparov**
Wijk aan Zee 2001

---

1 e4 c5 2 d3 Nc6 3 g3 g6 4 Bg2 Bg7 5 f4 d6 6 Nf3 Nf6 7 0-0 0-0 8 h3 b5 9 g4

This is not exactly a Closed Sicilian, as White has omitted the move Nc3. However, the principle is exactly the same – White is charging forward on the kingside and is not unduly concerned about developments on the other wing.

9...a5 10 f5 b4 11 Qe1 Ba6 12 Qh4 c4 13 Bh6 cxd3 14 cxd3 Bxd3 15 Re1 Bxh6 16 Qxh6 Qb6+ 17 Kh1 Ne5 18 Nbd2 Rac8 19 Ng5 Rc2 (Diagram 3)

Although White has set up a strong attacking position on the kingside (he need only deflect the knight from f6 to force checkmate with Qxh7), Black has invaded down the queenside and broken into the centre. He now copes easily with White's threats.

20 Rf1 Bxf1 21 Rxf1 Rfc8 22 fxg6 hxg6 23 Nb3 Rxg2 24 Kxg2 Rc2+ 25 Kg3 Qe3+ White resigns

WARNING: White's strategy in many variations of the Closed Sicilian is rather one-dimensional. If the attempted mating attack does not come off there is often not much else in White's armoury.

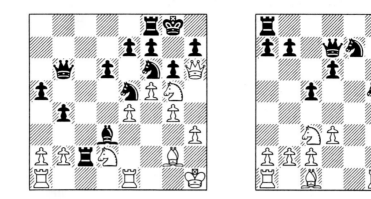

Diagram 3
Black has invaded on the queenside

Diagram 4
White's king is also exposed

Game 20
□ **Hellers** ■ **Gelfand**
Novi Sad 1990

1 e4 c5 2 Nc3 d6 3 f4 Nc6 4 Nf3 g6 5 Bc4 Bg7 6 0-0 e6 7 f5 exf5 8 d3 Nge7 9 Qe1 h6 10 exf5 Bxf5 11 g4

A violent idea from White which appears to seriously disrupt the black king.

11...Bxg4 12 Bxf7+ Kxf7 13 Ne5+ Kg8 14 Nxg4 Nd4 15 Qf2 Ndf5 16 Qg2 Qd7 (Diagram 4)

Black has beaten off the white initiative and is a good pawn up. His king is a little uncomfortable but, then again, so is his opponent's. White has very little compensation.

17 Ne4 Rf8 18 c3 b6 19 Bf4 d5 20 Nd2 d4 21 Ne4 g5 22 Be5 Bxe5 23 Nxe5 Qe6 24 Ng4 dxc3 25 Rae1 Qc6 26 bxc3 Kg7 27 d4 Ng6 28 dxc5 bxc5 29 Qf2 Nd4 30 Nef6 h5 31 cxd4 hxg4 32 Ne8+ Qxe8 White resigns

The c3 Sicilian

2 c3 is a perennially popular way to meet the Sicilian Defence. White immediately tries to set up a powerful central position with the advance d2-d4. Unlike in the open Sicilian, White will be able to meet the capture ...c5xd4 by taking back with the c-pawn rather than a piece and thus maintaining a solid central structure. The drawback of White's second move is that it takes away the natural development square for the queen's knight. It is therefore not surprising that Black's most popular counters rely on immediately attacking the

white e-pawn with either 2...d5 or 2...Nf6 as White is no longer able to defend this pawn in the most natural way (i.e. Nb1-c3).

The c3 Sicilian often leads to open, attacking positions. Even if positions arise which are not theoretically advantageous for White, they often exhibit a reasonable degree of complexity which will allow the player more familiar with the positions to create problems for their opponent. The c3 Sicilian is not overly theoretically complex, but at the same time usually manages to lead to dynamic play.

White often ends up with a slight positional inferiority (an isolated queen's pawn being the most obvious manifestation of this) and must justify this by active play. If White is unable to keep the position complex then he can find himself with a dreary defensive task.

What is White's Strategy?

White is basically hoping for easy development followed by good piece play. All his pieces should come out easily and he will then be well placed to take the initiative. In a perfect world this can lead to a powerful attack. White generally has more space in the centre and his position is usually quite easy to play.

What is Black's Strategy?

Black will usually be able to force White into a modest positional concession. This most obviously happens in the 2...d5 variation, e.g. 1 e4 c5 2 c3 d5 3 exd5 Qxd5 4 d4 Nf6 5 Nf3 e6 6 Bd3 cxd4 7 cxd4 and White has an isolated queen's pawn. Another line is 1 e4 c5 2 c3 Nf6 3 e5 Nd5 4 d4 cxd4 5 cxd4 e6. Here White has slightly weakened his centre and the black knight has taken up an attractive outpost on d5. However, note that the advanced white pawn on e5 may well be the fulcrum for an eventual kingside attack. Black usually has to limit his ambitions in the early part of the game to containing the white initiative and hoping to profit from his positional pluses at a later stage.

Tactical/Strategic/Dynamic?

The c3 Sicilian is more a strategic than a tactical opening. There are complex lines which rely on theoretical knowledge, but they tend to be byways rather than the main lines. Although it is not unheard of, the game rarely explodes into a tactical mess in the early stages. Lines with c3 are a reasonably dynamic way to meet the Sicilian. White will always get his pieces out quickly and even if Black negotiates the opening with a satisfactory position, White is likely to retain active play.

Theoretical?

The c3 Sicilian has become much more theoretical in recent years as it has become increasingly popular at a high level. However, it is the kind of opening that is well suited to players who prefer to gain an understanding of ideas, rather than learning moves by rote.

How Popular is it?

This variation has always been popular at a club level but until relatively recently it was scorned at a high level. However, over the last few years, some quite strong players have taken an interest in it. Even at international level around 10% of Sicilians feature c3 lines.

Illustrative Games

Game 21
☐ **Adams** ■ **Benjamin**
New York 1996

1 e4 c5 2 Nf3 e6 3 c3 Nf6 4 e5 Nd5 5 d4 cxd4 6 cxd4 b6 7 Bc4 Ba6 8 Bxa6 Nxa6 9 0-0 Be7 10 Nbd2 0-0 11 Ne4 Nac7 12 Bg5 (Diagram 5)

A typical position for this line. White has easy development and active play for his pieces, but Black has good control over the important d5-square. However, over the next few moves, Black's structure deteriorates while White maintains excellent piece play.

12...f6 13 exf6 Nxf6 14 Bxf6 gxf6 15 Rc1 d5 16 Ng3 Qd7 17 Nh4 Bd6 18 f4 f5 19 Nh5 Qf7 20 Rf3

Black cannot now play 20...Qxh5 on account of 21 Rg3+. Black now has weaknesses everywhere and cannot hope to survive.

20...Kh8 21 Rh3 Rg8 22 Nf3 Qe7 23 Qe2 Ne8 24 Rc6 Qd7 25 Ne5 Qe7 26 Rxd6 Nxd6 27 Nc6 Black resigns

28 Qe5+ will follow with disastrous consequences for Black.

Game 22
☐ **Egin** ■ **Bagaturov**
Elista 1998

1 e4 c5 2 Nf3 e6 3 c3 d5 4 exd5 Qxd5 5 d4 Nf6 6 Be3 cxd4 7 cxd4 Nc6 8 Nc3 Qd6 9 a3 Be7 10 Bd3 0-0 11 0-0 b6 12 Qe2 Bb7 13 Rad1 Rac8 14 Rfe1 Rfd8 15 Bb1 Qb8 16 Bg5 g6 17 h4 Re8 18 Ba2 Nh5 19 Qd2 Rcd8 (Diagram 6)

White has a wonderful IQP (isolated queen pawn) attacking position. Black has failed either to control the d5-square or to strengthen his kingside defences. White now powers through.

20 d5 e5 21 Bxe7 Nxe7 22 Rxe5 Nf6 23 Qd4 Nd7 24 Rxe7 Rxe7 25 d6

White's pieces are all cooperating beautifully.

25...Nf8 26 Qf6 Re6 27 Bxe6 Nxe6 28 Ne5 Rf8 29 Ng4 h5 30 Nh6+ Kh7 31 Nxf7 Bxg2 32 Qxe6 Black resigns

WARNING: Black must keep the d5-square under control in IQP positions.

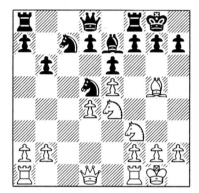

Diagram 5
White has active piece play

Diagram 6
Black's position is uncoordinated

Game 23
□ **Donguines** ■ **Kouatly**
Manila 1992

1 e4 c5 2 c3 Nf6 3 e5 Nd5 4 d4 cxd4 5 Nf3 e6 6 cxd4 b6 7 Nc3 Nxc3 8 bxc3 Qc7 9 Bd2 d6 10 Bd3 Nd7 11 0-0 Bb7 12 Re1 dxe5 13 Nxe5 Nxe5 14 Rxe5 Bd6 15 Rh5 g6 16 Rh3 0-0 17 Qg4 f5 18 Qh4 Rf7 19 Rc1 Qc6 20 f3 b5 (Diagram 7)

White has tried to get going on the kingside but Black has stayed calm. White' pawn duo on c3 and d4 constitute a long term weakness and Black's last move pins these pawns down.

21 Bg5 Re8 22 Bf6 Be7 23 Bxe7 Rfxe7 24 Qg5 Qd5 25 Rh4 Rc7 26 Qg3 Rec8 27 Qg5 a6 28 a4

This does not work out well, but White's backward c-pawn would prove indefensible in the long run.

28...bxa4 29 c4 Qd8 30 Qh6 Qf6 31 Re1 a3

White has freed up his central pawns but at the cost of providing Black with a big passed a-pawn.

32 Ra1 Rd8 33 Qf4 Rcd7 34 Qh6 Qe7 35 d5 exd5 36 Kf1 d4 37 Re1 Qf6 38 Rf4 Re7 39 Ra1 Qe5 40 h4 a2 41 h5 Qe3 42 hxg6 Qxd3+ 43 Kf2 Qe3+ 44 Kg3 hxg6 45 Rh1 Qe5 46 Qg5 d3 White resigns

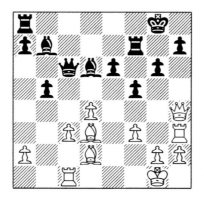

Diagram 7

Black has good central control

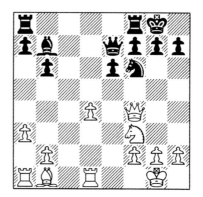

Diagram 8

White's initiative has burnt out

Game 24
□ **Sanz** ■ **Stean**
Amsterdam 1978

1 e4 c5 2 c3 d5 3 exd5 Qxd5 4 d4 e6 5 Nf3 Nc6 6 Bd3 cxd4 7 cxd4 Nf6 8 Nc3 Qd6 9 0-0 Be7 10 Qe2 0-0 11 Rd1 Nb4 12 Bb1 b6 13 Bg5 Bb7 14 a3 Nbd5 15 Ne4 Nf4 16 Qe3 Nxe4 17 Bxe7 Qxe7 18 Qxf4 Nf6 (Diagram 8)

Black has forced simplifications which have robbed the White position of its dynamism. Consequently he merely has a weak d-pawn and no compensating active play.

19 Ne5 Rfd8 20 a4 Rac8 21 Ra3 Nd5

The d5-square is a wonderful square for the black pieces in positions such as this.

22 Qg4 f5

This blunts the strength of White's bishop. Meanwhile Black's bears down powerfully against White's king.

23 Qg3 Qb4 24 Qg5 Qe7 25 Qd2 Qb4 26 Qg5 Qe7 27 Qd2 Qh4 28 Ba2 Nf4 29 Re3 Bxg2 30 f3 Bh3 31 Rc3 Qg5+ 32 Kf2 Qh4+ 33 Kg1 Rc5 34 Rxc5 bxc5 35 d5 exd5 36 Qe3 Qg5+ 37 Kf2 Qh4+ 38 Kg1 Qg5+ 39 Kf2 Qg2+ 40 Ke1 Qxb2 White resigns

Chapter Three

1...e5: The Spanish and Others

- The Spanish: The Classical Main Lines

- The Spanish: Other Variations

- Others after 1 e4 e5

The Sicilian Defence is a perfectly good opening for Black but can be a little too combative for those who prefer a quiet life. Such players are well served by the solid 1...e5, when the opening often becomes the Spanish (1 e4 e5 2 Nf3 Nc6 3 Bb5) – one of the oldest openings known.

The Spanish Opening (also known as the Ruy Lopez) is generally regarded as White's best try for the advantage after 1 e4 e5 and, until about the last ten years or so, was the almost automatic choice of strong grandmasters. Great players such as Bobby Fischer, Anatoly Karpov and Garry Kasparov excelled at playing on the white side of this opening and scored many fine victories with it. White seems to have a 'natural' advantage in the Spanish and players of such a high class were able to nurture and increase this advantage remorselessly. Such games, where Black is remorselessly worn down without ever making any obviously terrible mistakes, have led to the White strategy being described as the 'Spanish Torture'.

However, the Spanish is not all doom and gloom for Black. After all, anyone playing with the black pieces against players such as Fischer, Karpov and Kasparov is likely to be in for a hard time whatever defensive system they choose. The main lines are solid and reliable and there are also a number of counterattacking schemes which, although more risky, can be powerful weapons.

If White wants to avoid the Spanish, then there are many options for obscure gambit play. Lines such as the King's Gambit (1 e4 e5 2 f4) and the Two Knights Defence (1 e4 e5 2 Nf3 Nc6 3 Bc4 Nf6) are full of wild and woolly lines and anyone wishing to play 1 e4 e5 as Black needs to be well prepared against these various tries. However, at a high level, they are generally regarded as innocuous. An alternative to the Spanish which has gained acceptance over the past decade or so is the Scotch Game which opens 1 e4 e5 2 Nf3 Nc6 3 d4 exd4 4 Nxd4. Play now often continues 4 ... Nf6 5 Nxc6 bxc6 6 e5 when White, at the cost of some time, obtains the superior pawn structure. Many players, including Kasparov, have demonstrated that life is not so easy for Black in these lines.

The Spanish: The Classical Main Lines

1 e4 e5 2 Nf3 Nc6 3 Bb5 a6 4 Ba4 Nf6 5 0-0 Be7 6 Re1 b5 7 Bb3 d6 8 c3 0-0

In this variation White slowly builds up his position with a view to advancing reasonably soon with d2-d4 and claiming a stake in the centre. He has wasted a little time with the bishop manoeuvres but, by provoking the advance of the b-pawn, has created a slight weakness in the black queenside. However, Black is very solid and can complete development quite easily whilst maintain a firm foothold in the centre by protecting the e5-pawn.

What is White's Strategy?

White is looking for a patient build-up with a view to expanding on his small space advantage as the middlegame progresses. White's position is highly flexible and, depending upon which scheme of development Black adopts, he has various opportunities. Typical manoeuvres are Nb1-d2-f1-e3 (which targets a potential weakness on d5 as Black often plays ...c7-c5) or d2-d4-d5 and then a general pawn advance on the queenside. White's initiative can also convert into a kingside attack with moves such as Nb1-d2-f1, h2-h3 and g2-g4, Nf1-g3-f5 and Qd1-f3.

What is Black's Strategy?

Black has two main ways to handle these positions. The classical way to play is to remain as solid as possible, defending the e5-point and concentrating, in the short term at least, on nullifying White's manoeuvres. Black wants to equalise the position and will then consider if there are ways to try for the advantage. This especially becomes possible if White has been a little over-exuberant and created weaknesses in his own position.

A more modern way for Black to play is to look for counterplay by giving up the centre and then undermining it. A typical sequence in this respect is for Black to play ...e5xd4 and meet c3xd4 with ...c7-c5. This is a risky strategy as White may power through in the centre and on the kingside but it does create pressure for Black and gives him a useful queenside pawn majority.

Tactical/Strategic/Dynamic?

The main lines of the Spanish are generally strategic. If the centre is opened up then hand-to-hand fighting can break out but it is more usual that a period of trench warfare ensues before contact is made. Black can handle the position dynamically but can also adopt a more restrained approach.

Theoretical?

The Spanish is such an old opening and has been played so much that a huge body of theory has developed around it. However, although this vast canon of literature exists, actual move orders are not as important as getting a good feel for what happens in different positions. Playing through a number of well annotated grandmaster games will be at least as useful as trying to remember specific variations.

How Popular is it?

These lines are very popular at all levels. Almost all strong grandmasters have been seen on one side of these variations and often on both. The kind of positions that develop favour the player with the greater general chess understanding.

Illustrative Games

Game 25
□ **Kasparov** ■ **Karpov**
World Championship, Lyon/New York 1990

1 e4 e5 2 Nf3 Nc6 3 Bb5 a6 4 Ba4 Nf6 5 0-0 Be7 6 Re1 b5 7 Bb3 d6 8 c3 0-0 9 h3 Bb7 10 d4 Re8 11 Nbd2 Bf8 12 a4 h6 13 Bc2 exd4

A double-edged decision. Black gives up any ideas of strong-pointing e5 and clears the centre in order to create counterplay.

14 cxd4 Nb4 15 Bb1 c5 16 d5 Nd7 17 Ra3 f5

Continuing his strategy of undermining the white centre, but now the black king will come under a ferocious attack.

18 Rae3 Nf6 19 Nh2 Kh8 20 b3 bxa4 21 bxa4 c4 22 Bb2 fxe4 23 Nxe4 Nfxd5 24 Rg3 Re6 25 Ng4 Qe8 26 Nxh6

The game has reached a crisis; mind-boggling complications ensue.

26...c3 27 Nf5 cxb2 28 Qg4 Bc8 29 Qh4+ Rh6 30 Nxh6 gxh6 31 Kh2 Qe5 32 Ng5 Qf6 33 Re8 Bf5 (Diagram 1)

White's next is that most rare of events in a World Championship match – a queen sacrifice. However, the more mundane 34 Nf7+ would actually have forced mate in six moves.

34 Qxh6+ Qxh6 35 Nf7+ Kh7 36 Bxf5+ Qg6 37 Bxg6+ Kg7 38 Rxa8 Be7 39 Rb8 a5 40 Be4+ Kxf7 41 Bxd5+ Black resigns

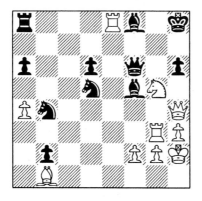

Diagram 1
White to play and win

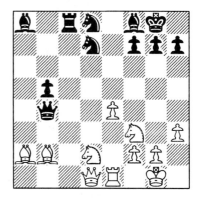

Diagram 2
White's centre has been swept away

Game 26
☐ **Kasparov** ■ **Karpov**
World Championship, Moscow 1985

1 e4 e5 2 Nf3 Nc6 3 Bb5 a6 4 Ba4 Nf6 5 0-0 Be7 6 Re1 b5 7 Bb3
d6 8 c3 0-0 9 h3 Bb7 10 d4 Re8 11 Nbd2 Bf8 12 a4 Qd7 13 axb5
axb5 14 Rxa8 Bxa8 15 d5 Na5 16 Ba2 c6 17 b4 Nb7

Black's pieces are slightly tangled, but he has begun a promising undermining of the white centre.

18 c4 Rc8 19 dxc6 Qxc6 20 c5 Nd8 21 Bb2 dxc5 22 bxc5 Qxc5 23
Bxe5 Nd7 24 Bb2 Qb4 (Diagram 2)

This is a model performance by Black in the Spanish. The white centre has been swept away, the Black pieces are active and he has a
good passed pawn on the queenside.

25 Nb3 Nc5 26 Ba1 Bxe4 27 Nfd4 Ndb7 28 Qe2 Nd6 29 Nxc5
Qxc5 30 Qg4 Re8 31 Rd1 Bg6 32 Qf4 Qb4 33 Qc1 Be4 34 Re1 Qa5
35 Bb3 Qa8 36 Qb2 b4 37 Re3 Bg6 38 Rxe8 Qxe8 39 Qc1 Ne4 40
Bd5 Nc5 41 Nb3 Nd3 White resigns

Game 27
☐ **Fischer** ■ **Bisguier**
New York 1963

1 e4 e5 2 Nf3 Nc6 3 Bb5 a6 4 Ba4 Nf6 5 0-0 Be7 6 Re1 b5 7 Bb3 0-0
8 c3 d6 9 h3 Na5 10 Bc2 c5 11 d4 Qc7 12 Nbd2 Nc6 13 dxc5 dxc5

Black has adopted a classic system of development.

14 Nf1 Rd8 15 Qe2 Nh5 16 g3 g6 17 h4 Be6 18 Ne3 f6 19 Nd5
(Diagram 3)

The drawback to Black's system is this hole on d5 which White now
jumps in to exploit. If Black takes the bait then 19...Bxd5 20 exd5
Rxd5 21 c4 grants White a strong initiative.

19...Qb7 20 Nxe7+ Qxe7 21 Nh2 Ng7 22 Ng4 c4 23 Qf3 Bxg4 24
Qxg4 Ne6 25 h5 Kh8 26 Kg2 g5 27 Be3

White is slowly but surely gaining a grip on the position.

27...Nf4+ 28 Kh2 Nd3 29 Bxd3 cxd3 30 Red1 Rd7 31 Rd2 Na5 32
b3 Qd6 33 Rad1 Re8 34 Rxd3 Qxd3 35 Qxd7 Black resigns

Game 28
☐ **Timman** ■ **Portisch**
Brussels 1988

1 e4 e5 2 Nf3 Nc6 3 Bb5 a6 4 Ba4 Nf6 5 0-0 Be7 6 Re1 b5 7 Bb3
d6 8 c3 0-0 9 h3 Nb8 10 d4 Nbd7

Black has adopted the Breyer system of defence. This is a line where Black adopts a very solid set-up and which often leads to prolonged manoeuvring.

11 Nbd2 Bb7 12 Bc2 Re8 13 Nf1 Bf8 14 Ng3 g6 15 a4 c5 16 d5 c4 17 Bg5 h6 18 Be3 Nc5 19 Qd2 h5 20 Bg5 Be7 21 Bh6 Nh7 22 Ra3 Rb8 23 Rea1 Bc8 24 axb5 axb5 25 Be3 Bf6 26 Ne2 Bd7 27 Ra7 Qc8 (Diagram 4)

White has a modest initiative but Black is rock solid. White's next is overambitious and he soon regrets granting Black the bishop pair.

28 Bxc5 dxc5 29 Qe3 Bd8 30 R7a6 Qc7 31 Nc1 Bc8 32 Rc6 Qe7 33 d6 Qd7 34 Qxc5 Bb7 35 Rca6 Bxa6 36 Rxa6 Qb7 37 Ra7 Bb6 38 Rxb7 Bxc5 39 d7 Red8 40 Rxb8 Rxb8 41 Nxe5 Rd8 42 b3 f6 43 Nf3 Rxd7 44 b4 Bb6 45 Ne2 Ra7 46 Nfd4 Ra2 47 g3 Ng5 48 h4 Nh3+ 49 Kg2 Nxf2 50 Bb1 Rb2 51 Kxf2 Bxd4+ 52 cxd4 Rxb1 White resigns

WARNING: Early violence is rarely successful against the solid black defences in the Spanish. A patient build-up is usually needed.

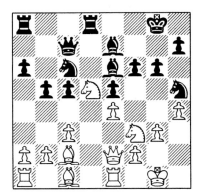

Diagram 3
White uses the d5-hole

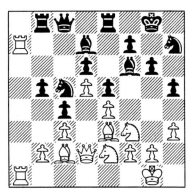

Diagram 4
Black is passive but solid

The Spanish: Other Variations

Many players like to defend with 1...e5 but feel uncomfortable with the rock solid defences in the main line Spanish and prefer something a little more dynamic. Fortunately, they have plenty of variations to choose from. Most of these attempt to give Black a bit more space and better piece development than he can expect in the main lines, but usually at the expense of some positional concessions. For example, schemes based on ...Bf8-c5, instead of ...Bf8-e7, have become popular recently. On the g1-a7 diagonal the black bishop is more actively placed, pressurising the white centre and also possibly eyeing the f2-

square. However, the drawback is that White's natural advance of d2-d4 is lent impetus by the presence of the bishop on c5 and also Bc1-g5 can become an irksome move for Black as his king's knight can be awkwardly pinned.

Another popular system is the Open Variation (1 e4 e5 2 Nf3 Nc6 3 Bb5 a6 4 Ba4 Nf6 5 0-0 Nxe4) where Black gets good play for his pieces but at the cost of slight structural weaknesses.

What is White's Strategy?

White must keep a good eye out for tactical threats. Many of the counterattacking systems for Black in the Spanish can be quite dangerous for those unfamiliar with the theory. A degree of knowledge is required from White as quiet responses are generally not too testing for Black. For example, in the Schliemann (1 e4 e5 2 Nf3 Nc6 3 Bb5 f5) White can certainly hope for an advantage with the main lines after 4 Nc3, whilst the quiet 4 d3 generally gives Black an easy game. However, in order to play 4 Nc3, White needs to know a few things.

What is Black's Strategy?

Black is trying to destabilise White's smooth plan of development. When adopting one of these dynamic counterattacking systems, there is usually no turning back for Black. He must pursue the initiative even if it means loosening his own position or costing material.

Tactical/Strategic/Dynamic

These lines tend to be very dynamic and tactical. Early tactical eruptions are quite common.

Theoretical?

If you want to take on all these unusual systems as White you will need to know a moderate amount of theory. Most of the time there is a simple straightforward response for White but a degree of knowledge will be required.

How Popular is it?

These systems tend to wander in and out of fashion. In the 1970s and 1980s the Open Spanish was popular (mainly because Korchnoi was always playing it against Karpov in their World Championship matches), whereas more recently the Archangel systems based on an early ...Bf8-c5 are what the fashion conscious grandmasters are playing. Most of these systems are popular at club level.

Illustrative Games

Game 29
□ **Timman** ■ **Speelman**
Candidates Semi-Final, London 1989

1 e4 e5 2 Nf3 Nc6 3 Bb5 f5

This is the Schliemann Defence – a risky and highly tactical line which leads to great complications.

4 Nc3 fxe4 5 Nxe4 d5 6 Nxe5 dxe4 7 Nxc6 Qg5 8 Qe2 Nf6 9 f4 Qxf4 10 Ne5+ c6 11 d4 Qh4+ 12 g3 Qh3 13 Bc4 Be6 14 Bg5 0-0-0 15 0-0-0 Bd6 16 Nf7 Bxf7 17 Bxf7 Rhf8 18 Bc4 Rde8 (Diagram 5)

Such positions are well known to theory. With the bishop pair White should have a slight edge but his next move, blocking the position, is a mistake.

19 d5 c5 20 Rhf1 Kb8 21 Bf4 Rd8 22 Bg5 a6 23 Bxf6 gxf6 24 Qxe4 Qxh2 25 Rh1 Qxg3 26 Rxh7 Rfe8 27 Qf5 b5 28 Bf1 Re1 29 Qh5 Qf4+ 30 Kb1 Qxf1 White resigns

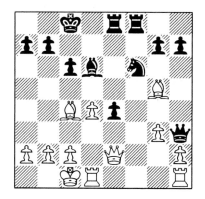

Diagram 5
Black has active play

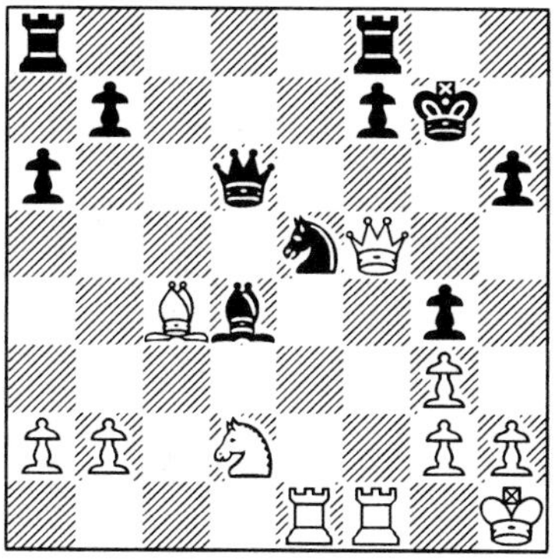

Diagram 6
Black's king is wide open

Game 30
□ **Svidler** ■ **Leko**
Linares 1999

1 e4 e5 2 Nf3 Nc6 3 Bb5 Nf6 4 0-0 Bc5 5 c3 0-0 6 d4 Bb6

In this variation Black pressurises the white centre with piece play.

7 Qd3 d6 8 Bg5 h6 9 Bh4 Bd7 10 Nbd2 a6 11 Bc4 exd4 12 cxd4 g5

A risky strategy from Black, who accepts serious kingside weaknesses in order to undermine White's centre.

13 Bg3 Nh5 14 e5 Kg7 15 exd6 Nxg3 16 dxc7 Qxc7 17 fxg3 g4 18 Nh4 Ne5 19 Nf5+ Bxf5 20 Qxf5 Bxd4+ 21 Kh1 Qd6 22 Rae1 (Diagram 6)

Black's plan has backfired. He no longer has pressure in the centre and must now face prolonged pressure due to his weak kingside.

22...Rad8 23 Bb3 Bxb2 24 Nc4 Nxc4 25 Qxg4+ Qg6 26 Qxc4 b5 27 Qb4 Rc8 28 Re3 Qg5 29 Qd2 Bf6 30 h4 Qc5 31 Re4 h5 32 Ref4 Rc6 33 Rf5 Qc3 34 Qf4 Rd8 35 Rxh5 Qd2 36 Qg4+ Kf8 37 Rh8+ Ke7 38 Rh7 Rf8 39 Qe4+ Kd7 40 Bxf7 Black resigns

---

Game 31
□ **Short** ■ **Timman**
Candidates Final, El Escorial 1993

---

1 e4 e5 2 Nf3 Nc6 3 Bb5 a6 4 Ba4 Nf6 5 0-0 Nxe4 6 d4 b5 7 Bb3 d5 8 dxe5 Be6 9 c3 Bc5 10 Nbd2 0-0 11 Bc2 f5 12 Nb3 Bb6

This is a balanced position. White has the better structure but Black has active play.

13 Nfd4 Nxd4 14 Nxd4 Bxd4 15 Qxd4 c5 16 Qd1 h6 17 f3 Ng5 18 Be3 Rc8 19 Qd2 a5 20 Rad1 Qe7 21 Bb1 Kh8 22 Rfe1 Rc7 23 Bf2 b4 24 h4 Nh7 25 Qd3 (Diagram 7)

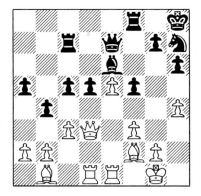
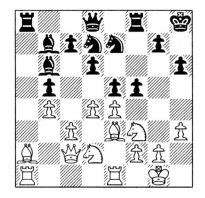

Diagram 7	**Diagram 8**
White plans a queenside invasion	The white centre is under fire

White is now threatening a queenside probe on the light squares and so Black initiated kingside play.

25...g5 26 Qa6 Rfc8 27 Re2 Rc6 28 Qd3 gxh4 29 f4 Rg8 30 Qf3 bxc3 31 bxc3 Rb6 32 Bc2 Rg4 33 Kh2 Rb8 34 Rxd5 Bxd5 35 Qxd5 Rxf4 36 Bxc5 Qg7 37 Bd4 Re8 38 Qd6 Qg3+ 39 Kg1 h3 40 Rf2 h2+

Play has become very complex and now, on the last move of the time control, Timman blunders. After 40...Rxd4 the position is unclear.

41 Kh1 Rxd4 42 Qxd4 Nf6 43 Re2 Nh5 44 e6+ Qg7 45 Kxh2 f4 46 Bg6 Black resigns

---

Game 32
□ **Short** ■ **Kamsky**
Linares 1994

---

1 e4 e5 2 Nf3 Nc6 3 Bb5 a6 4 Ba4 Nf6 5 0-0 b5 6 Bb3 Bb7 7 Re1 Bc5 8 c3 d6 9 d4 Bb6 10 Be3 0-0

Black has adopted the Archangel Variation. This is another system which pressurises the white centre with piece play.

11 Nbd2 h6 12 h3 Nd7 13 a3 Ne7 14 Ba2 Kh8 15 b4 a5 16 Qc2 axb4 17 axb4 f5 (Diagram 8)

Black, at a small risk to his kingside, tears open lines for his bishops to operate on.

18 dxe5 Bxe3 19 Rxe3 Nxe5 20 Nxe5 dxe5 21 Rae1 Ra6 22 exf5 Nxf5 23 Rxe5 Nh4

Black's pieces are converging powerfully against the white king.

24 Ne4 Rg6 25 Ng3 Bxg2 26 R1e3 Rd6 27 Bb1 g6 28 Rh5 Bf3 29 Rxh6+ Kg7 30 Rxh4 Qxh4 31 Kh2 Bg4 32 Ne4 Bf5 33 Kg2 Re6 34 Qe2 Rfe8 35 f3 Qxh3+ 36 Kg1 Rh8 37 Qg2 Qxg2+ 38 Kxg2 Rd8 39 Kf2 Rd1 40 Bd3 c6 41 Ke2 Ra1 42 Kd2 Ra2+ 43 Kc1 Rh2 44 Re1 Re8 45 Bc2 Reh8 White resigns

Other Openings after 1 e4 e5

There are quiet ways to play after 1 e4 e5 that do not involve the Spanish Opening. One example is the Bishop's Opening (1 e4 e5 2 Bc4), which can be similar to the quiet lines of the Spanish where White contents himself with an early d2-d3 instead of d2-d4. However, if white players want to try something other than the Spanish the usual reason is that they are looking for a tactical hack and have some sort of gambit in mind. Lovers of obscure sacrificial play are spoilt for choice after 1 e4 e5, as there are many weird and wonderful variations where rooks drop off in the corner, kings frequently wander around in the middle of the board and material equality is unheard of. Many of these lines have an ancient pedigree and consequently have wonderful names such as the Gullam-Khasim Gambit, the Fried Liver Attack and the Quaade-Rosentreter Gambit. However, all of this stuff should not really pose a problem for Black, as long as he has a reasonable grasp of the theory.

The major non-Spanish approach after 1 e4 e5 that does not involve extreme violence is the Scotch Game (1 e4 e5 2 Nf3 Nc6 3 d4 exd4 4 Nxd4). This is a serious attempt to gain a small positional advantage and 1...e5 players need to know a sound line here.

What is White's Strategy?

In many of these lines White's only idea is to know more tricks than his opponent and to win the game on theoretical knowledge. This rarely works at a high level but at club level many of these lines are devastating against an unprepared opponent.

What is Black's Strategy?

When facing a violent gambit line, Black should always be on the lookout for a good opportunity to return any excess material in order to defuse White's initiative. There are often opportunities to do this early on and if you are not inclined to learn large amounts of theory to take on the main lines, then this is the way to go. For example, the Belgrade Gambit which starts 1 e4 e5 2 Nf3 Nc6 3 Nc3 Nf6 4 d4 exd4 5 Nd5 can be quite dangerous after 5...Nxe4 6 Bc4 or 5...Nb4 (often recommended in theoretical works) 6 Nxd4. However, Black can simply play 5...Be7, which will almost certainly equalise the game.

Tactical/Strategic/Dynamic?

Obviously these lines are highly tactical and even the more positional openings, such as the Scotch Game, often erupt into tactics as Black tries to get active to overcome a small structural inferiority.

Theoretical?

The main lines are hugely theoretical but there are usually opportunities early on to steer the game into safe territory with a minimum of theoretical knowledge.

How Popular is it?

The only really popular alternative to the Spanish at a high level is the Scotch Game. The obscure gambits find their adherents at club level but rarely much higher.

Illustrative Games

Game 33
☐ **Kasparov** ■ **Anand**
Riga 1995

1 e4 e5 2 Nf3 Nc6 3 Bc4 Bc5 4 b4

This move caused a minor sensation when it was played. This variation, the Evans Gambit, was all the rage in the 19th century but, until this game, had hardly been seen at all in top class chess for about 100 years. Such crude gambits rarely make headway against the refined defensive technique which all top players have.

4...Bxb4 5 c3 Be7 6 d4 Na5 7 Be2 exd4 8 Qxd4 Nf6 9 e5 Nc6 10 Qh4 Nd5 11 Qg3 g6 12 0-0 Nb6 13 c4 d6

White's opening has been successful. There are weaknesses in the black camp and it is not easy for him to complete development.

14 Rd1 Nd7 15 Bh6 Ncxe5 16 Nxe5 Nxe5 17 Nc3 f6 (Diagram 9)

Tearing open more lines.

18 c5 Nf7 19 cxd6 cxd6 20 Qe3 Nxh6 21 Qxh6 Bf8 22 Qe3+ Kf7 23 Nd5 Be6 24 Nf4 Qe7 25 Re1 Black resigns

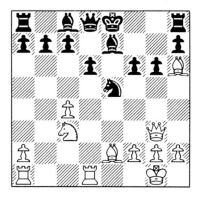

Diagram 9
Black is struggling to develop

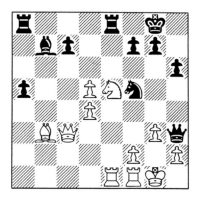

Diagram 10
Black finds a clever win

Game 34
□ **Morozevich** ■ **Adams**
Wijk aan Zee 2001

1 e4 e5 2 Nf3 Nc6 3 Bc4 Bc5 4 b4 Bxb4 5 c3 Ba5 6 d4 exd4 7 0-0 Nge7 8 Ng5 d5

This is a very modern approach to defending against gambit play. Black returns the material and achieves a comfortable position.

9 exd5 Ne5 10 Bb3 0-0 11 cxd4 Ng4 12 Qf3 Nf6 13 Ba3 h6 14 Ne4 Nxe4 15 Qxe4 Re8 16 Bb2 Nf5 17 Qf4 Bb4 18 Na3 Bd6 19 Qd2 Qh4

White's bishops are stuck behind the doubled d-pawns and, although material is equal, Black has a very pleasant position.

20 g3 Qh3 21 Nc4 b5 22 Ne5 Bb7 23 Rae1 a5 24 a3 b4 25 axb4 Bxb4 26 Bc3 Bxc3 27 Qxc3 (Diagram 10)

A neat finish. The mate threat wins the white queen.

27...Nh4 White resigns

TIP: A useful rule of thumb is that the break ...d7-d5, if timed correctly, is nearly always a good antidote to White's random gambit lines after 1 e4 e5.

Game 35
□ **Kasparov** ■ **Sokolov**
Yerevan Olympiad 1996

1 e4 e5 2 Nf3 Nc6 3 d4 exd4 4 Nxd4 Nf6 5 Nxc6 bxc6 6 e5 Qe7 7 Qe2 Nd5 8 c4 Ba6 9 g3 g6

In the Scotch Game White gives up time early on to create a weakness in the black queenside. If he can keep the game under control then this can give him a useful positional advantage.

10 b3 Bg7 11 Bb2 0-0 12 Bg2 Rfe8 13 0-0 Nb6 14 Re1 d5 15 Qc2 Qc5 16 Nd2 Rad8 17 Rac1 d4 18 Nf3 d3

Black is hoping that this pawn will generate counterplay, but his queenside minor pieces are locked out of the game.

19 Qd2 Bc8 20 h3 h5 21 Rcd1 Bf5 22 e6 Rxe6 23 Rxe6 Bxe6 24 Bxg7 Kxg7 25 Qc3+ Kg8 26 Rxd3 Rxd3 27 Qxd3 Nd7

The position has simplified and Black is left with chronic queenside weaknesses for which he has no compensation.

28 Qc3 Bf5 29 Nd4 Qe5 30 Qd2 c5 31 Nxf5 Qxf5 32 Qa5 Ne5 33 Qxa7 h4 34 Qa8+ Kg7 35 Qe4 Qf6 36 Qxh4 Black resigns

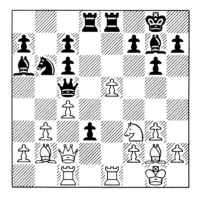

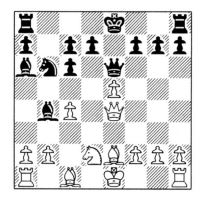

Diagram 11
Black's queenside pieces are smothered

Diagram 12
The white centre is under attack

Game 36
□ **Timman** ■ **Adams**
Sarajevo 1999

1 e4 e5 2 Nf3 Nc6 3 d4 exd4 4 Nxd4 Nf6 5 Nxc6 bxc6 6 e5 Qe7 7 Qe2 Nd5 8 c4 Nb6 9 Nd2 Qe6 10 Qe4 Bb4 11 Be2 Ba6

White has played inaccurately in the opening and now his centre is under great pressure.

12 b3 Bc3 13 Rb1 Qxe5 14 0-0 Qxe4 15 Nxe4 Bb4 16 Bg5 d5 17 a3 Be7 18 Bxe7 Kxe7 19 Nc5 Bc8

Although Black is a pawn ahead his queenside weaknesses are apparent. However, Adams skilfully untangles and is soon a pawn ahead for nothing.

20 Rbd1 Rd8 21 f4 a5 22 Rfe1 Kf8 23 cxd5 cxd5 24 Bb5 g6 25 Rd4 Ra7 26 Rc1 Rd6 27 Kf2 Bf5 28 Be2 h5 29 h3 h4 30 Bd3 Bxd3 31 Nxd3 Nd7 32 Ne5 Nf6 33 Nf3 c5 34 Rd3 a4 35 Nd2 axb3 36 Rxc5 Rxa3 37 Rb5 Ra2 38 Rbxb3 Re6 39 Kg1 Re2 40 Nf3 Rxg2+ 41 Kh1 Ne4 White resigns

Chapter Four

The French Defence

For many years 1...e5 and the Sicilian Defence have been the favoured replies to 1 e4 for the world's best players. Aggressive tactical players have favoured the Sicilian, whilst those more peaceably inclined have generally opted for 1...e5. Recently, however, many world class players have begun to look again at the French Defence and it is gradually increasing in popularity. This is not to suggest that the French has ever been regarded as unsound – it has always been seen as a dependable opening. Now, however, the possibilities that the French offers for Black to create a dynamic struggle from a sound position are becoming more appreciated.

Black invariably suffers from a slight space disadvantage in the French (White generally plays with pawns on d4 and e5 versus black pawns on e6 and d5). However, the modern view is that, within reason, this is no bad thing and allows plenty of opportunities for counterplay at a later stage. There are many examples of a proud White centre being dismantled by some well-timed undermining blows. When this happens Black can obtain excellent central control and White can be left without a worthwhile plan.

The Winawer Variation

1 e4 e6 2 d4 d5 3 Nc3 Bb4

This is a dynamic, and hence also double-edged, way for White to take on the French. As well as 3...Bb4, Black can also try 3...Nf6, also a very popular move. However, I will not examine that move here as the positions that arise are similar to those reached in the Tarrasch with 3...Nf6 and also, to a certain extent, the Advance.

The Winawer is a good example of an unbalanced opening as both sides can boast of their pluses. The move ...Bb4xc3+ usually occurs at some stage, meaning that White will have the advantage of the bishop pair and can point to possible dark square weaknesses in the black camp, while Black can take comfort from the weaknesses he has inflicted on the white pawn structure.

Play often sees 4 e5 c5 5 a3 Bxc3+ 6 bxc3 Ne7 and now 7 Qg4. This is a blunt attempt to take advantage of the absence of the black bishop from the kingside by threatening the g7-pawn. There is no simple solution for Black and all moves involve some sort of concession: 7...Kf8 is an uncomfortably early move for the king, 7...0-0 sets up the black king as an easy target for White, while 7...Qc7 (the most popular response) involves a sacrifice of a pawn. Nevertheless, all these moves are playable and lead to complex play.

It is also possible for White to turn down the opportunity for 7 Qg4 (normally because he does not fancy accepting the gambit pawn after 7...Qc7) and to instead take the struggle into complex strategic channels with a move such as 7 a4, planning Bc1-a3.

What is White's Strategy?

White invariably gains the bishop pair and eliminates Black's important dark-squared bishop in the process. If he can get going with a good kingside attack it will be granted greater strength by the absence of this piece. Therefore White is usually looking to take the initiative quickly, and the move Qd1-g4 is a key method of doing this.

What is Black's Strategy?

White's queenside is seriously compromised and thus Black's counterplay bites very quickly. In the main lines with Qd1-g4 Black must decide whether to go for the initiative with the gambit lines or to play more circumspectly, hoping to beat off White's attack. In the positional lines plans with ...b7-b6 and ...Bc8-a6 are important. If Black can exchange off White's light-squared bishop without seriously compromising his position elsewhere, this will be quite a boon for him.

Tactical/Strategic/Dynamic?

The French Winawer is a very dynamic, complex opening. If you want to play it you will have to know a decent amount of theory but will also need a good strategic understanding of the various plans available to both sides.

Theoretical?

The gambit lines where White captures on g7 are very theoretical and cannot be played unless you have had a good long look at the theory. However, lines where White adopts a more restrained strategic approach with a line such as 7 a4 are also quite theoretically complex.

How Popular is it?

The Winawer has always been popular as it unbalances the position and leads to lively play. The player with the better knowledge and feel will usually emerge on top and it is attractive from Black's point of view as it is hard for White to play this opening 'safely'.

Illustrative Games

Game 37
□ **Morozevich** ■ **Dolmatov**
Moscow 1996

1 e4 e6 2 d4 d5 3 Nc3 Bb4 4 e5 c5 5 a3 Bxc3+ 6 bxc3 Ne7 7 Qg4 0-0 8 Bd3 Nbc6 9 Qh5 Ng6 10 Nf3 Qc7 11 h4 c4

Black hopes to deflect the white bishop from its direct line to the black king, but White ploughs on...

12 Ng5! h6 13 Bxg6 fxg6 14 Qxg6 hxg5 15 hxg5 (Diagram 1) 15...Nxe5

Black feels obliged to return the piece to blunt the power of White's attack along the h-file. Nevertheless, White's initiative is so strong that he is not obliged to accept the piece at once.

16 Qh5 Bd7 17 f4! Ng4 18 Qxg4 Be8 19 Qxe6+ Bf7 20 Qf5 Qe7+ 21 Kf2 Rfe8

Roles have reversed and now Black has invested some material hoping to profit from the uncomfortable position of White's king. However, despite this, he still has problems with the safety of his own monarch.

22 g6 Qe2+ 23 Kg3 Be6 24 Qg5 Qxc2 25 Rh5 Qxc3+ 26 Kh2 Qxa1 27 Qh4

Another role reversal! White gambits a rook to get at Black's king.

27...Kf8 28 f5 Bg8 29 Rh8 Qxc1 30 f6!! Qh6

Unfortunately for Black this is the only defence against White's threatened 31 Rxg8+.

31 Rxh6 Re4 32 Qh5 gxf6 33 g7+ Ke7 34 Qf5 Re6 35 Qxd5 Rd8 36 Qxc4 Rc6 37 Qb4+ Rcd6 38 Qxb7+ R6d7 39 Qe4+ Be6 40 Rh8 Rxd4 41 Qh7 Black resigns

WARNING: The perennial difficulty for Black in the Winawer is the weakness on the dark squares and he must be careful that this does not become a chronic problem.

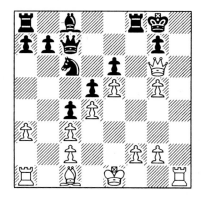

Diagram 1
A powerful gambit from White

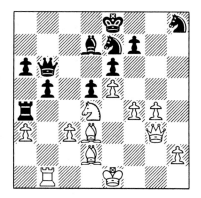

Diagram 2
White's h-pawn is ready to roll

Game 38
□ **Short** ■ **Kosten**
Hastings 1988/89

1 e4 e6 2 d4 d5 3 Nc3 Bb4 4 e5 c5 5 a3 Bxc3+ 6 bxc3 Ne7 7 Qg4 Qc7 8 Qxg7 Rg8 9 Qxh7 cxd4 10 Ne2 Nbc6 11 f4 Bd7 12 Qd3 dxc3 13 Qxc3

A standard position for this line. Black is a pawn down but White is badly underdeveloped and has many weaknesses in his camp.

13...Rc8 14 Rb1 Nf5 15 Bd2 a6 16 Rg1

Black's play has been a little slow and now White prepares to advance his pawn mass on the kingside.

16...b5 17 g4 Nh4 18 Rg3

White often has to resort to artificial looking moves in order to coordinate his pieces in this variation.

18...Qb6 19 Qd3 Rh8 20 Rh3 Ne7 21 Nd4 Rc4 22 c3 Ra4 23 Qg3 Nhg6 24 Rxh8+ Nxh8 25 Bd3 (Diagram 2)

White has driven back the black forces and is now a good pawn up. He has the plan of advancing his h-pawn and Black has no real counter.

25...Nhg6 26 h4 Rxa3 27 h5 Nf8 28 h6 Neg6 29 f5 Ne7 30 Qh2 exf5 31 h7 Neg6 32 gxf5 Nh8 33 Qh5 Qc7 34 Kf1 Rxc3 35 e6 Rxd3 36 exf7+ Kd8 37 Qg5+ Kc8 38 Rc1 Rxd4 39 Rxc7+ Kxc7 40 Ba5+ Kb7 41 Qd8 Rf4+ 42 Kg1 Rg4+ 43 Kh2 Black resigns

---

Game 39
□ **Svidler** ■ **Ivanchuk**
Linares 1999

1 e4 e6 2 d4 d5 3 Nc3 Bb4 4 e5 c5 5 a3 Bxc3+ 6 bxc3 Ne7 7 Qg4 Qc7 8 Qxg7 Rg8 9 Qxh7 cxd4 10 Ne2 Nbc6 11 f4 Bd7 12 Qd3 dxc3 13 Rb1 0-0-0 14 Nxc3 Na5 15 g3 Kb8

Black makes his king secure and creates the possibility of bringing his rook to the c8-square to press against the weak white pawn on c2.

16 Ne2 Ba4 17 c3 Nf5 18 Bh3 (Diagram 3)

White has not managed to develop happily, nor has he activated his kingside pawns. As the centre now opens White finds himself struggling to cope with Black's active pieces.

18...d4 19 Bd2 Nb3 20 Bxf5 dxc3 21 Qxc3 Nxd2 22 Qxc7+ Kxc7 23 Rc1+ Bc6 24 Bh3 Kb6 25 Rxc6+

White has no good way to hold the material balance.

25...bxc6 26 Kf2 c5 27 Bg2 c4 28 h4 Nb3 29 h5 Rd2 30 Ke3 Ra2 31 h6 Rxa3 32 h7 Rh8 33 Nc3 Ka5 34 Ne4 Nc5+ 35 Ke2 Nxe4 36 Bxe4 Rxg3 37 Rb1 Rh3 38 Kd2 Rd8+ 39 Kc2 Rd4 White resigns

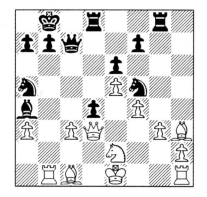

Diagram 3
White is badly under-developed

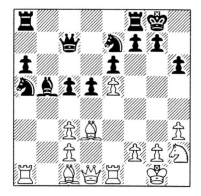

Diagram 4
Black eliminates the dangerous bishop

Game 40
□ **Cabrilo** ■ **Drasko**
Vrnjacka Banja 1999

1 e4 e6 2 d4 d5 3 Nc3 Bb4 4 e5 Ne7 5 a3 Bxc3+ 6 bxc3 c5 7 a4 Qc7 8 Nf3 b6 9 Bb5+ Bd7 10 Bd3 Nbc6 11 0-0 h6 12 Re1 0-0 13 Ba3 Na5

A typical position for the 'quiet' white treatment of the Winawer. Black is hoping to exploit White's queenside weaknesses, whilst White has in mind an initiative on the other wing.

14 h3 Bxa4 15 Nh2

This manoeuvre is a little too slow to generate much for White.

15...a6 16 dxc5 bxc5 17 Bc1 Bb5 (Diagram 4)

Black eliminates a dangerous attacking white piece. White does not have much to show for his pawn and now feels obliged to launch a rather desperate attack involving a highly speculative piece sacrifice. Black brushes this aside without too much trouble.

18 Bxh6 Bxd3 19 Qxd3 gxh6 20 Ng4 Kg7 21 Qf3 Ng8 22 Nf6 Nc4 23 Ra4 Nxe5 24 Nh5+ Kh8 25 Qg3 f6 26 Nf4 Qf7 27 Rea1 Ne7 28 Rxa6 Rxa6 29 Rxa6 Nf5 White resigns

NOTE: In dynamic positions White's queenside weaknesses can appear to be almost irrelevant. However, as the position simplifies and pieces are exchanged, they assume a greater importance.

The Tarrasch Variation

1 e4 e6 2 d4 d5 3 Nd2

The Tarrasch is often regarded as the 'safe' way to play against the French. White avoids the structural complexity that arises in the Winawer after 3 Nc3 Bb4 in favour of smooth piece development. Black has two main tries against 3 Nd2. The first of these, 3...Nf6 usually elicits the response 4 e5 from White and thus leads to standard French Defence positions with a blocked centre. Alternatively Black can opt for the simpler 3...c5. With this move Black achieves easy development for his pieces but usually at the cost of an isolated queen's pawn as White will typically play 4 exd5 exd5 and then the c5-pawn will sooner or later be exchanged for White's d-pawn. There is one further way for Black to handle this position – he can play 3...c5 with the intention of meeting 4 exd5 with 4...Qxd5. This avoids the difficulties associated with the isolated queen's pawn, but the black queen will provide a target for the White minor pieces. White can then develop a little more swiftly than would otherwise have been possible and this can lead to a useful initiative.

What is White's Strategy?

White keeps a completely sound position and maintains the option of meeting Black's ...c7-c5 thrust with ...c2-c3, maintaining a solid central structure. If Black plays a system with ...Nf6, he will advance with e4-e5 and then play to restrict Black as much as possible. If Black plays a system based on a quick ...c7-c5 then White will either try to exploit his lead in development or develop solidly and look for a long term advantage based on his superior pawn structure.

What is Black's Strategy?

Black can take heart from the fact that the white knight is not ideally placed on d2, as it blocks in the dark-squared bishop. It thus slows down the development of White's queenside and it is often difficult to relocate the knight. It does not want to move to b3 which is an even worse square than d2, while if it moves to f3, it interferes with the natural development of its colleague.

If Black plays with an early ...Ng8-f6, meeting e4-e5 with ...Nf6-d7, then he can often mount a quick attack on the d-pawn with ...c7-c5, ...Nb8-c6 and ...Qd8-b6. He will then usually either look for queenside play or a break in the centre with ...f7-f6.

If Black plays with 3...c5, meeting 4 exd5 with 4...exd5, then he is just playing quietly hoping that the d-pawn does not prove to be too much of a problem. He might also try to generate play on the open e- and c-files and the squares e4 and c4 can provide useful outposts for his pieces. If he meets 4 exd5 with 4...Qxd5, he will hope to nullify White's early initiative and reach a position where he has a slightly superior pawn structure (extra centre pawn after the white d-pawn is exchanged for the black c-pawn).

Tactical/Strategic/Dynamic?

As is usual in the French, the play is generally of a strategic nature. 3 Nd2 is not the most dynamic response to the French but it is probably the most solid and one which offers good chances for a small plus.

Theoretical?

The lines with 3...Nf6 are quite theoretical as play revolves around Black's attempts to swiftly undermine the white centre with ...c7-c5 and ...f7-f6. When this happens play can become quite sharp. 3...c5, on the other hand, is a more sedate line.

How Popular is it?

Not as popular as it used to be. When Karpov was world champion and played 1 e4, he used to beat the French time and again by gaining a small edge with the Tarrasch. Now, however, technique at a high level has improved and players hope for more than just a tiny edge from the openings and thus many strong players now prefer 3 Nc3. At lower levels, however, it remains very popular, especially as it is quite easy to play for White.

Illustrative Games

Game 41
□ **Anand** ■ **Shirov**
Frankfurt 2000

1 e4 e6 2 d4 d5 3 Nc3

Although this game actually starts with 3 Nc3 it soon transposes into a line of the Tarrasch, as we will see.

3...Nf6 4 e5 Nfd7 5 Nce2 c5 6 c3 Nc6 7 f4 Qb6 8 Nf3

This position is more normally reached by a sequence such as 3 Nd2 Nf6 4 e5 Nfd7 5 f4 c5 6 c3 Nc6 7 Ndf3 Qb6 8 Ne2.

8...Be7 9 a3 0-0 10 h4

White is taking a slight risk making so many pawn moves. If Black succeeds in blowing open the centre he can regret this. However, if Black fails to generate counterplay quickly, the pawn mass can quickly squash him. 10 h4 is a useful move for preventing a potential Black ...g7-g5. If this seems an unlikely move to you, see the game

Emms-Kosten given later in this section.

10...f6 11 Rh3 Na5 12 b4 cxb4 13 axb4 Nc4 14 Ng3 a5 15 Bd3 f5 16 Ng5 Rd8 17 Qh5 Bxg5 18 Qxg5 Rf8 19 Nh5 Rf7 20 Rg3 g6 21 Bxc4 dxc4 22 b5 (Diagram 5)

It has all gone horribly wrong for Black. White has a huge attack on the kingside and the light-squared bishop is a sorry piece.

22...Qxb5 23 Ba3 b6 24 Qh6 Bb7 25 Rxg6+ hxg6 26 Qxg6+ Kh8 27 Qxf7 Rg8 28 Bf8 Black resigns

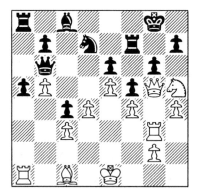

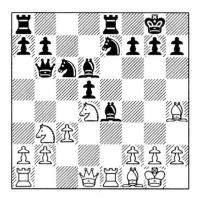

Diagram 5

White is piling in on the kingside

Diagram 6

White has complete control of d4

Game 42
□ **Karpov** ■ **Uhlmann**
Madrid 1973

1 e4 e6 2 d4 d5 3 Nd2 c5 4 exd5 exd5 5 Ngf3 Nc6 6 Bb5 Bd6 7 dxc5 Bxc5 8 0-0 Nge7 9 Nb3 Bd6 10 Bg5 0-0 11 Bh4 Bg4 12 Be2 Bh5 13 Re1 Qb6 14 Nfd4 Bg6 15 c3 Rfe8 16 Bf1 Be4 (Diagram 6)

A typical position for the Tarrasch with 3...c5. Black has had no problem developing his pieces but is hampered by the constant need to defend his vulnerable isolated d-pawn. As the game progresses this become more problematic.

17 Bg3 Bxg3 18 hxg3 a5 19 a4 Nxd4 20 Nxd4 Nc6 21 Bb5 Red8 22 g4 Nxd4 23 Qxd4 Qxd4 24 cxd4

White has systematically simplified the position with exchanges. Although structurally the situation has improved for Black (White now also has an isolated d-pawn), he is now in trouble because White has much more active pieces. This is a classic example of the transfer of an advantage from a structural to a dynamic form.

24...Rac8 25 f3 Bg6 26 Re7 b6 27 Rae1 h6 28 Rb7 Rd6 29 Ree7 h5 30 gxh5 Bxh5 31 g4 Bg6 32 f4

This is very simple and elegant play from White. The pawn advances on the kingside will drive the black forces back and enable the white rooks to run riot on the seventh rank.

32...Rc1+ 33 Kf2 Rc2+ 34 Ke3 Be4 35 Rxf7 Rg6 36 g5 Kh7 37 Rfe7 Rxb2 38 Be8 Rb3+ 39 Ke2 Rb2+ 40 Ke1 Rd6 41 Rxg7+ Kh8 42 Rge7 Black resigns

---

Game 43
☐ **Emms** ■ **Kosten**
British Championship, Edinburgh 1985

---

1 e4 e6 2 d4 d5 3 Nd2 Nf6 4 e5 Nfd7 5 f4 c5 6 c3 Nc6 7 Ndf3 cxd4 8 cxd4 Qb6 9 g3 Bb4+ 10 Kf2

White has constructed a huge centre but at the cost of falling behind in development and having to wander around with his king. Black now acts very swiftly.

10...g5! 11 Be3 f6 12 Bh3 0-0 13 Bg4 fxe5 14 fxe5

White seems to have everything just about defended, but now there follows an extraordinary move.

14...Bc5!! (Diagram 7)

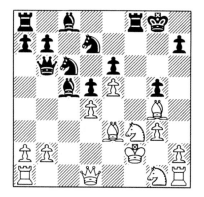

Diagram 7
A fantastic sacrifice from Black

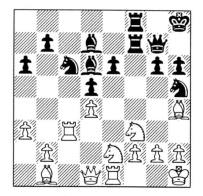

Diagram 8
Black prepares a kingside advance

A fantastic idea to undermine the white centre. After White captures this sacrifice the Black pieces spring to life and the position of the white king becomes very problematic.

15 Bxe6+ Kh8 16 dxc5 Qxb2+ 17 Bd2 g4! 18 Bxd5

The problem with 18 Bxg4 is 18...Qd4+ forking king and bishop.

18...Ndxe5 19 Bxc6 bxc6 20 Rb1 Qd4+ 21 Be3 Nd3+ 22 Ke2 gxf3+ 23 Nxf3 Qe4 24 Qxd3 Ba6 25 Qxa6 Qxf3+ 26 Kd2 Rfd8+ 27 Kc2 Qe4+ 28 Kb2 Rab8+ 29 Ka3 Qxe3+ 30 Rb3 Qxc5+ 31 Kb2 Rd2+ 32 Kb1 Rxb3+ 33 axb3 Qc2+ 34 Ka1 Qb2 checkmate

TIP: When the white king is not secure and his development lags, Black can take huge liberties (often involving substantial sacrifices) to open the position.

Game 44
□ **Marjanovic** ■ **Timman**
Sarajevo 1984

1 e4 e6 2 d4 d5 3 Nd2 Nf6 4 e5 Nfd7 5 c3 c5 6 Bd3 Nc6 7 Ne2 cxd4 8 cxd4 f6 9 exf6 Nxf6 10 0-0 Bd6 11 Nf3 Qc7 12 Nc3 a6 13 Bg5 0-0

This is another typical structure for the Tarrasch variation. Black must be careful as if White manages to exchanges dark-squared bishops and clamp down on the e5-square, he will have a very good position. However, Timman now handles the black forces very dynamically and creates good counterplay whilst preventing White from achieving this aim.

14 Bh4 Nh5 15 Rc1 g6 16 Bb1 Qg7 17 Kh1 Bd7 18 Re1 Rf7 19 Ne2 Kh8 20 a3 Raf8 21 Rc3 h6 (Diagram 8)

Black has developed smoothly and is now well placed to advance on the kingside.

22 Bg3 Nxg3+ 23 Nxg3 Rf4 24 Ne2 R4f6 25 Ng3 Be8 26 Rce3 Bf7 27 Kg1 Bg8 28 Qd3 Bf4 29 R3e2 Qf7 30 b4 g5 31 h3 Bc7 32 Nf1 Bb6

Black has cleverly relocated his bishops in order to both protect his own weakness on e6 whilst simultaneously pressing against White's vulnerable d-pawn. When White is preoccupied defending this pawn, Black's kingside advance will gain strength.

33 N1d2 Qg7 34 Nb3 Rf4 35 Rd1 g4 36 Nh4 Ne7 37 g3 gxh3 38 Kh1 Rxh4 39 f4 Rg4 40 Kh2 Nf5 White resigns

The Advance Variation

1 e4 e6 2 d4 d5 3 e5

The move 3 e5 was one of the earliest attempts to combat the French Defence and is, in many ways, the most logical. White immediately claims a space advantage and prevents the black king's knight from developing on its natural square of f6. The black queen's bishop (a perennial problem piece in the French Defence) is now hemmed in behind the black pawn chain and this can create long term difficulties for Black.

Black has the usual French counters of ...f7-f6 and ...c7-c5 to try to undermine the white centre and these usually form the basis of his counterplay. A slight difficulty for White is that 3 e5 is his third pawn move and thus he is often finds himself slightly behind in development in the early stages. Black can exploit this slight lead by a quick counter against d4 with ...c7-c5, ...Nb8-c6 and ...Qd8-b6. This pressure can be a little awkward for White and he sometimes responds by gambiting this pawn.

Another typical theme, perhaps more prevalent in the Advance than in other variations of the French, is the idea for Black to exchange the problem light-squared bishop with ...b7-b6 and ...Bc8-a6. This loses a little time and Black can end up with a misplaced knight on a6 (if White captures with Bxa6), but at least he has eliminated his worst piece.

What is White's Strategy?

White is trying to cramp Black and to use his space advantage to create long term pressure on the kingside. If Black does not organise himself well, White will have a position that is easy to play with a natural attacking plan. If Black changes the nature of the position by castling queenside then White will have to try to force open lines there instead. White can sometimes consider a plan based on c2-c4. This is most usually appropriate when Black adopts a plan involving the light-squared bishop exchange with ...b7-b6 and ...Bc8-a6.

What is Black's Strategy?

Black can either cooperate in the blocking up of the position and rely on his own advances (usually on the queenside) to compensate for White's kingside initiative, or he can try to sweep away the white centre with the standard undermining moves ...c7-c5 and ...f7-f6. He can also consider a very quick attack against the white d-pawn with ...c7-c5, ...Nb8-c6 and ...Qd8-b6. If White is not then willing to gambit this pawn, he can often be forced into an ugly mode of development such as Nb1-a3-c2.

Tactical/Strategic/Dynamic?

The Advance French tends to be a rather strategic opening. Black often joins White in closing the position up by advancing with ...c7-c5 and then ...c5-c4. This creates a completely blocked structure in the centre and then play revolves around advances on opposing wings.

Theoretical?

The Advance French is not particularly theoretical. There are lines where White gambits the d-pawn where some theoretical knowledge is necessary but on the whole White can get by with a good feel for the ideas rather than knowledge of specific moves.

How Popular is it?

Very popular at club level, slightly less so at international level. Most Grandmasters tend to prefer the greater complexity which is generated by the moves 3 Nd2 or 3 Nc3.

Illustrative Games

Game 45
□ **Illescas** ■ **Short**
Linares 1995

1 e4 e6 2 d4 d5 3 e5 c5 4 c3 Nc6 5 Nf3 Bd7 6 Be2 f5

This is probably a little too committal. After this White knows he need never worry about the undermining ...f7-f6 and can develop in comfort.

7 0-0 cxd4 8 cxd4 Nge7 9 b3 Nc8 10 Ba3

White exchanges his worst piece – the dark-squared bishop which is hemmed in by the central pawns.

10...Bxa3 11 Nxa3 0-0 12 Qd2 Qe7 13 Nc2 Be8 14 b4 a5 15 b5 Nd8 16 Rfc1 Bh5 17 Nce1 (Diagram 9)

White has a pleasant position with a useful space advantage. Black now tries to generate counterplay but only succeeds in creating weaknesses.

17...g5 18 h3 Qg7 19 Rc3 Bxf3 20 Nxf3 h6 21 Rac1 Nb6 22 Nh2 Kh8 23 Nf1 a4 24 a3 Rf7 25 Ng3 Qf8 26 Nh5 Re7 27 Nf6 Nd7 28 Nh5 Nb6 29 Rc7 Nc4 30 Rxe7

This is a key breakthrough as now 30...Nxd2 is met by 31 Rcc7 Ne4 32 f3 and White wins.

30...Qxe7 31 Bxc4 dxc4 32 Rxc4 Qxa3 33 Rc7 Qf8 34 Qa2 a3 35 Nf6 Nf7 36 Qxe6 a2 37 Qxf7 a1Q+ 38 Kh2 Qxf7 39 Rxf7 b6 40 Rh7 checkmate

NOTE: One of Black's key undermining moves is ...f7-f6, so he should be careful about advancing ...f7-f5, which eliminates this option altogether.

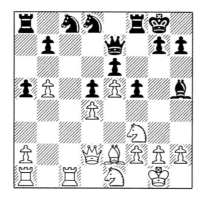

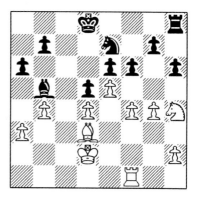

Diagram 9

White has a useful space advantage

Diagram 10

White has an endgame initiative

Game 46
□ **Anand** ■ **Gurevich**
Manila 1990

---

1 e4 e6 2 d4 d5 3 e5 c5 4 c3 Nc6 5 Nf3 Bd7 6 Be2 Nge7 7 Na3 cxd4 8 cxd4 Nf5 9 Nc2 Nb4 10 Nxb4 Bxb4+ 11 Bd2 Qa5 12 a3 Bxd2+ 13 Qxd2 Qxd2+ 14 Kxd2

Although Black has simplified the position with exchanges, White can still hope to create trouble by a gradual advance on the kingside.

14...f6 15 Rac1 Ne7 16 b4 Kd8 17 Bd3 Rc8 18 Rxc8+ Nxc8 19 g4 h6 20 Nh4 Ne7 21 f4 a6 22 Rf1 Bb5 (Diagram 10) 23 f5

White plays to force open lines on the kingside.

23...h5 24 Ng6 Nxg6 25 exf6

White can even play tactically in the endgame. If now 25...Bxd3 26 fxg6! Bxf1 27 gxh5! gxf6 28 g7 Rg8 29 h6 and White will promote a pawn by force and will have good winning chances.

25...gxf6 26 fxg6 Ke7 27 g5 f5 28 Bxb5 axb5 29 Rc1 Kd6 30 Ke3 Rg8 31 Kf4 b6 32 Rc3 Rxg6 33 Rh3 Rg8 34 Rxh5 Rc8 35 g6 Rc4 36 Rg5 Rxd4+ 37 Ke3 Re4+ 38 Kf2 Black resigns

---

Game 47
□ **Adams** ■ **Epishin**
Ter Apel 1992

---

1 e4 e6 2 d4 d5 3 e5 c5 4 c3 Nc6 5 Nf3 Bd7 6 a3 f6

In contrast to the Short-Illescas game, Black uses the f-pawn to nibble away at the white centre.

7 Bd3 Qc7 8 0-0 0-0-0 9 Bf4 c4 10 Bc2 h6 11 h4 Be8 12 b3 cxb3 13 Bxb3 Bh5 14 Nbd2 fxe5 15 dxe5 Bc5 (Diagram 11)

Black has successfully undermined the white centre and has good play thanks to his active bishops.

16 Qb1 Nge7 17 c4 Rhf8 18 Bh2 Bxf3 19 Nxf3 Rxf3!

This exchange sacrifice shreds the white kingside.

20 gxf3 Nd4 21 Kg2 Nef5 22 Bg3 Qf7 23 f4 g5! 24 cxd5 gxf4 25 dxe6 Qh5 26 e7 Nxh4+ White resigns

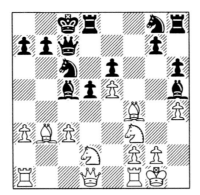

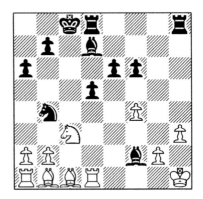

Diagram 11
White's centre has been undermined

Diagram 12
White's centre has been dismantled

Game 48
□ **Apicella** ■ **Bellet**
French Team Championship 1995

1 e4 e6 2 d4 d5 3 e5 c5 4 c3 Nc6 5 Nf3 Qb6 6 Bd3 cxd4 7 cxd4 Bd7 8 Nc3 Nxd4 9 Nxd4 Qxd4 10 Qe2 a6

This is a dangerous gambit line. Black's last move is an important one, preventing an annoying incursion by a white piece on b5.

11 0-0 Ne7 12 Kh1 Nc6 13 f4 Nb4 14 Rd1 Bc5

This is good play by Black. Rather than trying to hang on to the gambit pawn, he returns it to emphasise his own positional trumps.

15 Bxh7 Qf2 16 Qxf2 Bxf2 17 Bb1 0-0-0 18 h3 f6 19 exf6 gxf6 (Diagram 12)

The white centre has been swept away and Black has all the chances.

20 Rf1 Ba7 21 Bd2 Bc6 22 a3 d4 23 Ne4 d3 24 Bxb4 Bxe4 25 Kh2 f5 26 Ba2 Kd7 27 Rae1 Rh6 28 Bc3 Ke7 29 g4 d2 30 Bb4+ Ke8 31 Rxe4 fxe4 32 g5 Rh5 33 Bb3 Rd3 White resigns

Chapter Five

The Caro-Kann Defence

▨ **The Caro-Kann Main Lines**

▨ **The Advance Variation**

The Caro-Kann adopts a similar philosophy to the French Defence in that Black decides to fight for a share of the centre by supporting a pawn on d5. The Caro-Kann has an advantage over the French in that the light-squared bishop is not blocked in and can easily be developed to squares such as f5 or g4. The Caro-Kann is perhaps a modest opening, but has the reputation of being very difficult to crack. While it is too non-confrontational for many tactical players, it has been favoured by some of the great strategic masters such as Jose Raul Capablanca, Tigran Petrosian and Anatoly Karpov.

The Caro-Kann can often be a good choice against hyper-aggressive white players. Playing an opening like as the Sicilian gives such players ample opportunity to create dynamic, unbalanced positions. However, in the Caro-Kann achieving this is a little more problematic, as many of the more belligerent lines carry a substantial degree of risk.

In this chapter we shall look at typical developments in the main lines of the Caro, as well as what can happen if White takes the bull by the horns with the Advance Variation (1 e4 c6 2 d4 d5 3 e5) – the most direct attempt to bludgeon the Caro intro submission.

The Caro-Kann Main Lines

1 e4 c6 2 d4 d5 3 Nc3 dxe4 4 Nxe4

In the main lines of the Caro-Kann, Black meets 3 Nc3 (or 3 Nd2) by 3...dxe4. Giving up the centre by exchanging the well-supported d-pawn may seem a little odd, but Black has no better move – none of his minor pieces can yet develop to a reasonable square. After 4 Nxe4 then 4...Bf5 seems the most consistent, developing the bishop before closing the diagonal by ...e7-e6. Nevertheless, Black often plays instead 4...Nd7, preparing to challenge the white knight by ...Ngf6 (or occasionally ...Ndf6) and then reverts to French-type positions with ...e7-e6 blocking the queen's bishop in after all.

The pawn formation d4 vs. e6 guarantees White a space advantage and a knight outpost on e5. Consequently White will generally have the initiative for a long time. However, Black's position is both solid and sound, and with patient defence Black has good prospects for a draw – or sometimes more.

What is White's Strategy?

White's strategy first of all is one of containment and the d4-pawn is crucial. White will therefore try to keep a pawn on this square – unless something tangible is to be gained by its removal, such as open lines for an attack or a useful posting for the pawn on e5. White may play c2-c3 to defend the d-pawn against Black's ...c6-c5, or c2-c4 to control d5 and support a possible further advance of the d-pawn.

What is Black's Strategy?

Despite having exchanged the opposing e-pawn Black remains slightly cramped. Partly because the preliminary ...c7-c6 now obstructs the development of his queen's knight. Black will therefore aim for ...c6-c5 to free his position and undermine the potential enemy outpost at e5. This is virtually obligatory in the 4...Nd7 lines. With 4...Bf5 Black may manage without ...c6-c5, first developing ...Nb8-d7, ...Ngf6 and ...Bf8-d6, ...Qd8-c7, ...0-0-0 or ...Bf8-e7, ...0-0.

Tactical/Strategic/Dynamic?

The prime feature of these positions is strategic as White tries to maintain his positional advantages and Black tries to neutralise them. However, as these tasks are largely undertaken by pieces, the Caro-Kann main lines can also be regarded as dynamic – for White at least.

Theoretical?

Since the Caro-Kann is so solid, White has put in a lot of work trying to find an advantage and theory has expanded accordingly. However, there are few traps to worry either player in the opening, so both sides may survive without having to learn too much.

How Popular is it?

The Caro-Kann is not particularly popular at the moment, occurring about half as often as the French Defence. The 12th World Champion, Anatoly Karpov, still uses 1...c6 as his main defence to 1 e4, but as Karpov has dropped out of the limelight in recent years so his opening preferences are less influential on general praxis.

Illustrative Games

Game 49
□ **Adams** ■ **Leko**
Linares 1999

1 e4 c6 2 d4 d5 3 Nd2 dxe4 4 Nxe4 Bf5 5 Ng3 Bg6 6 h4 h6 7 Nf3 Nf6 8 Ne5 Bh7 9 Bd3 Bxd3 10 Qxd3 e6 11 Bd2 Nbd7 12 f4 Be7 13 0-0-0 0-0 14 Qe2 c5 15 dxc5

White relinquishes up his d-pawn, but gains a powerful bishop on the long diagonal to aid his kingside attack.

15...Nxc5 16 Bc3 Qc7 17 f5 exf5

A big mistake, bringing another white knight into the vicinity of the black king. With White's bishop already glaring down him, and the white queen soon to join in, Black may already be lost by direct attack.

18 Nxf5 Rfe8 19 Qf3 Bf8 (diagram 1) 20 Nxh6+

Destroying Black's frail defences on the long diagonal.

20...gxh6 21 Ng4 Nxg4 22 Qxg4+ Kh7 23 Qf5+ Kg8 24 Qf6 Kh7 25 Qh8+ Kg6 26 h5+ Black resigns

As mate follows after 26 Qf6+ etc.

TIP: The e5-square can be a very useful outpost for the white pieces, especially a knight.

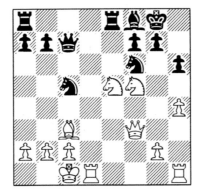

Diagram 1
Black's kingside is vulnerable

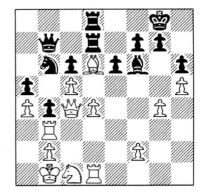

Diagram 2
A clever tactic from Black

Game 50
□ **Glek** ■ **Bareev**
Russian Championship 1998

1 e4 c6 2 d4 d5 3 Nc3 dxe4 4 Nxe4 Bf5 5 Ng3 Bg6 6 h4 h6 7 Nf3 Nd7 8 h5 Bh7 9 Bd3 Bxd3 10 Qxd3 Ngf6 11 Bf4 e6 12 0-0-0 Be7 13 Kb1 0-0 14 Ne5 Rc8

A useful move – both supporting the ...c6-c5 break and defending the c6-pawn so that the b-pawn might also advance.

15 Qf3 Qa5 16 c4 Rfd8 17 Rd3 Qa6 18 Rhd1 b5

Assailing the c4-pawn in order to establish an outpost on d5.

19 c5 b4 20 Ne2 Qb5 21 g4 Nd5 22 Bh2 Nxe5 23 Bxe5 Rd7 24 Rb3 Rcd8 25 Qd3 a6 26 Nc1 Qb7 27 Qc4 a5 28 a4 Bf6 29 Bd6 Nb6 (diagram 2)

A clever move which wins a pawn.

30 Qc2 Nxa4 31 f4 Qb5 32 g5 hxg5 33 fxg5 Bxg5 34 Rg3 Rxd6 35

cxd6 Bh6 36 Qf2

A mistake which allows Black to finish quickly.

36...Nc3+ 37 bxc3 bxc3+ 38 Ka1 Qa4+ White resigns

Game 51
□ **Lautier** ■ **Karpov**
Biel 1997

---

1 e4 c6 2 d4 d5 3 Nc3 dxe4 4 Nxe4 Nd7 5 Ng5 Ngf6 6 Bd3 e6 7 N1f3 Bd6 8 Qe2 h6 9 Ne4 Nxe4 10 Qxe4 c5 11 0-0 Nf6 12 Qh4 cxd4 13 Re1

Although Black's position looks solid he has difficulties because there is no obvious refuge for his king. Castling short is not an option as Bxh6 would destroy the defences immediately, while if Black ever managed to arrange long castling, White would be well prepared to attack there as well.

13...Bd7 14 Nxd4 Qa5 15 Be3 Kf8

This is no real solution to Black's problems as White's next eliminates the dark-square defender, leaving the black king no safer than before.

16 Bf4 Bxf4 17 Qxf4 Rc8 18 Nf3 Ke7 19 Qg3 (diagram 3)

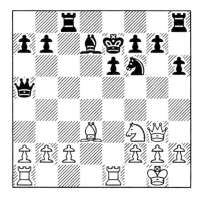
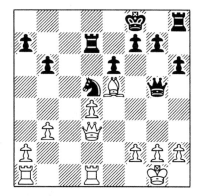

Diagram 3
Black's king is stuck in the centre

Diagram 4
Black has d5 under lock and key

Preventing Black's intended ...Rhd8, ...Kf8 by attacking the g7-pawn. The black king is now stuck in the middle for good.

19...Qb4 20 Ne5 g5 21 c4 Rhd8 22 Qh3 h5 23 Qe3 g4 24 a3 Qxb2 25 Rab1 Qxa3 26 Nxf7

The simplest solution – Black cannot capture 26...Kxf7 as 27 Bg6+ wins the queen.

26...Qc5 27 Nxd8 Qxe3 28 Rxe3 Kxd8 29 Rxb7 a5 30 Ra7 Rc5 31 f4 gxf3 32 Rxf3 Ne8 33 Rf7 Nc7 34 Rh7 Be8 35 Kf2 Kc8 36 Rh8 Kd7 37 Ke3 e5 38 Be2 Bg6 39 Bxh5 Bf5 40 Be2 Be6 41 h4 Kc6 42 Rh6 Kd7 43 h5 Black resigns

WARNING: In many lines of the Caro-Kann, Black has no completely safe hiding place for the king. Black is so solid that there is usually a satisfactory solution to this problem but he should be careful to address this difficulty sooner rather than later.

Game 52
☐ **Sadvakasov** ■ **Karpov**
Wijk aan Zee 1999

1 e4 c6 2 d4 d5 3 Nd2 dxe4 4 Nxe4 Nd7 5 Ng5 Ngf6 6 Bd3 e6 7 N1f3 Bd6 8 Qe2 h6 9 Ne4 Nxe4 10 Qxe4 Qc7 11 Qg4 Kf8

The best way to defend g7, not giving White any kingside targets. Here ...Kf8 is more acceptable than in Lautier-Karpov since White cannot control the dark squares. The only drawback being that it will be a long time before the king's rook can play an active role.

12 0-0 c5 13 Qh4 b6 14 Be4 Rb8 15 Rd1 c4 16 Ne5 Nf6 17 Bf3 Bb7 18 Bxb7 Rxb7 19 b3

A mistake – White opens the c-file but removes support for his d-pawn. By careful manoeuvring Karpov prevents White from achieving anything on the c-file, while the d-pawn drops off on move 40.

19...cxb3 20 cxb3 Nd5 21 Bf4 Qe7 22 Qg3 Bxe5 23 Bxe5 Qg5 24 Qd3 Rd7 (diagram 4)

Black's powerful central knight and superior pawn structure are more important than his poor king's position. He can slowly improve the situation of his king, whereas the White central weaknesses will never go away.

25 Rac1 Qd8 26 Qa6 Ne7 27 Qc4 Kg8 28 Bc7 Qa8 29 Qa4 Qe8 30 Bb8 Kh7 31 Bc7 Nd5 32 Be5 Qe7 33 Qc4 Qg5 34 Qd3+ Qg6 35 Qe2 Rhd8

That these positions require a lot of patience from Black is highlighted by the career of Black's king's rook, which only now makes its first move.

36 h4 h5 37 Rd3 Qg4 38 Qd2 f6 39 Bg3 Ne7 40 Qe3 Rxd4 41 Rxd4 Rxd4 42 f3 Nf5 43 Qxe6 Qxg3 44 Qxf5+ Kh6 45 Qc2 Qxh4

Black finally wins a pawn and with it the game.

46 Rd1 Qf4 47 Rd3 h4 48 Kh1 g6 49 Qc3 Rxd3 50 Qxd3 h3 51 gxh3 Qg3 52 Qd2+ Kh5 53 Qe3 Qxh3+ 54 Kg1 Qf5 55 Qe2 Qe5 56 Qd1 Kh4 57 Kf2 Qh2+ 58 Ke3 Qe5+ 59 Kf2 f5 60 a4 Qg3+ 61 Ke3 Qe5+ 62 Kf2 Qh2+ 63 Ke3 g5 64 Qd5 Qg1+ 65 Ke2 Kg3 0-1

The Advance Variation

1 e4 c6 2 d4 d5 3 e5

In the Advance Variation against the Caro-Kann White adopts a similar strategy to that used in the Advance Variation against the French. He seizes space on the kingside and prevents Black from developing his king's knight to its usual post at f6. In the Caro-Kann the cramping effect of e4-e5 is less severe, though, as Black is able to develop the queen's bishop outside the pawn chain at f5 (or sometimes g4) before playing ...e7-e6. Strategically Black should have few problems.

However, Black's development is slow and the natural break ...c7-c5 will cost Black a tempo since he has already played ...c7-c6. Also, while Black's light-squared bishop is more active after the usual 3...Bf5, it is also more exposed and White can harass it with such moves as Ne2-g3, Nf3-h4 or g2-g4, gaining time for other objectives.

What is White's Strategy?

After the usual 3...Bf5 White has two strategies. He can either use the bishop to build a quick initiative – in the sharpest lines (after 4 Nc3 e6 5 g4) this necessitates White playing very energetically as his central position is insecure. Otherwise White can simply develop his pieces and support his centre with c2-c3 or Bc1-e3. While this initially poses Black fewer problems, White has more flexibility in his choice of plans.

What is Black's Strategy?

Black's foremost target is the d4-pawn which he will attack by ...c6-c5. Further pressure can be applied by ...Qd8-b6, ...Nb8-c6, ...Ng8-e7-f5 and ...Bc8-g4. If g2-g4 has been played Black can also strike with ...h7-h5, aiming to take control of the kingside dark squares.

Tactical/Strategic/Dynamic?

The Advance Variation can be either tactical or strategic depending on choice. 4 Nc3 e6 5 g4 Bg6 6 Nge2 leads to wild complications as White has to follow up vigorously to justify his ambitious pawn advances. The system with 4 Nf3 and 5 Be2 is more strategic as White awaits developments before deciding how to proceed.

Theoretical?

As with most sharp variations 4 Nc3 has been investigated in depth with White trying to prove an advantage by brute force. If Black comes to the board unprepared he can be swept aside. With 4 Nf3 variations are less important, though Black needs at least to have a plan as otherwise his position may soon become lifeless.

How Popular is it?

3 e5 is a common response to the Caro-Kann. Although always popular at club level, it had been disdained by strong grandmasters for a while as the lines with Nc3 and g2-g4 were considered too crude against well prepared opposition. However, now that players such as Nigel Short have demonstrated that a more restrained approach with Nf3 and Be2 is possible, it has regained popularity at a high level.

Illustrative Games

Game 53
□ **Jankowicz** ■ **Pyrich**
1st Email Olympiad 2000

1 e4 c6 2 d4 d5 3 e5 Bf5 4 Nc3 e6 5 g4 Bg6 6 Nge2 c5 7 h4 cxd4 8 Nxd4 h5

Black tries to exploit White's pawn advances and strikes at the kingside light squares. Unfortunately White's pieces become very active and by f4-f5 he is able to open lines for a near decisive attack.

9 Bb5+ Nd7 10 f4 hxg4 11 f5 Rxh4 12 Rf1 exf5 13 e6 fxe6 14 Qe2 Qe7 15 Bg5! (diagram 5)

Black's once solid central pawn formation has been undermined by the sacrifices f4-f5 and e5-e6. Now White throws in a piece to decoy the black queen and brings the black king into the firing line.

15...Qxg5 16 Bxd7+ Kxd7 17 Qxe6+ Kd8 18 Qxd5+ Kc8 19 Qe6+ Kb8 20 Qe5+ Kc8 21 Nd5 Qd8 22 Nxf5 Bf7 23 0-0-0 Rh6 24 Nde7+ Black resigns

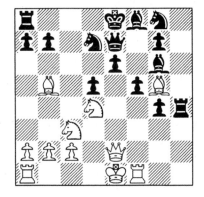

Diagram 5
White's initiative is too strong

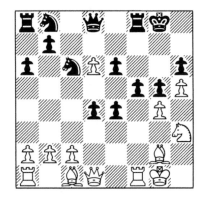

Diagram 6
Black has a huge centre

Game 54
□ **Topalov** ■ **Anand**
Linares 1999

1 e4 c6 2 d4 d5 3 e5 Bf5 4 Nc3 e6 5 g4 Bg6 6 Nge2 Ne7 7 Nf4 c5 8 h4 cxd4 9 Nb5 Nec6 10 h5 Be4 11 f3

In a reversal of the previous game, here it is Black who gives up a piece; in return he gains a large and menacing mobile pawn centre.

11...a6 12 Nd6+ Bxd6 13 exd6 g5 14 Nh3 h6 15 fxe4 dxe4 16 Bg2 f5 17 0-0 0-0 (diagram 6) 18 c3 Qxd6 19 gxf5 exf5 20 Qb3+ Kh8 21 Bxe4 fxe4 22 Rxf8+ Qxf8 23 Qe6 Nd7

On move 21 White returned the piece to lessen the approaching pawn storm, but now Black sacrifices another one to give it fresh impetus.

24 Qxd7 Rd8 25 Qg4 e3 26 b3 Ne5 27 Qe4 Qf6 28 Kg2 e2 29 Bxg5 hxg5 30 cxd4 Qc6

With White having returned the piece for a second time Black now liquidates into a winning endgame.

31 d5 Qxd5 32 Qxd5 Rxd5 33 Re1 Rd2 34 Kf2 Rxa2 35 Rxe2 Nd3+ 36 Ke3 Rxe2+ 37 Kxe2 g4 38 Ng5 Nc1+ 39 Ke3 Nxb3 40 h6 a5 41 Kf4 Nd4 42 Kxg4 a4 43 Kh5 Nc6 White resigns

WARNING: Under no circumstances should you try to combat the Advance Variation by relying solely on general principles.

Game 55
□ **Short** ■ **Yudasin**
Yerevan Olympiad 1996

1 e4 c6 2 d4 d5 3 e5 Bf5 4 Nf3 e6 5 Be2 Ne7 6 0-0 Bg6 7 c3 Nd7 8 Nh4 c5 9 Nd2 Rc8 10 Nxg6 hxg6 11 Nf3 Qb6 12 Rb1 a6 13 b4 cxd4 14 cxd4

White has the advantage, having consolidated his space advantage and gained the bishop pair.

14...Nf5 15 g4 Nh4 16 Nxh4 Rxh4 17 b5 a5 18 Be3 (diagram 7) 18...f5

Black tries to create some counterplay but it backfires.

19 Rc1 Rb8 20 Bg5 Rh7 21 gxf5 exf5

This is very undesirable as the d5-pawn becomes weak. Unfortunately 21...gxf5 would lose immediately to 22 Bh5+.

22 Bf3 Be7 23 Qd2 Bxg5 24 Qxg5 Rh6 25 Qf4 Rd8 26 Bxd5

Not so much winning a pawn as clearing the way for his own army.

26...Nf8 27 Rc5 Nd7 28 Rc2 Nf8 29 Rc5 Nd7 30 Rc4 Qxb5 31 Bg8

Rh8 32 Qg5 Rxg8 33 Qxg6+ Ke7 34 Qd6+ Ke8 35 Qe6+ Kf8 36
Rfc1 Qb6 37 Qxf5+ Ke7 38 d5 Qh6 39 d6+ Ke8 40 e6 Nf6 41 Rc8
Qh5 42 Rxd8+ Kxd8 43 e7+ Ke8 44 Rc8+ Black resigns

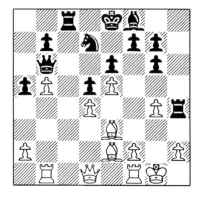

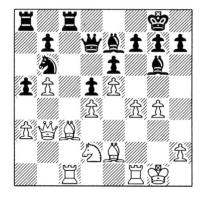

Diagram 7
White has a useful space advantage

Diagram 8
Black has good minor pieces

Game 56
□ **Lutz** ■ **Dautov**
Bundesliga 1998

1 e4 c6 2 d4 d5 3 e5 Bf5 4 Nf3 e6 5 Be2 Nd7 6 0-0 Bg6 7 c3 Nh6

By taking his knight via h6 rather than e7, Black maintains control
over h4 with his queen, thus preventing White from attacking the
bishop with Nf3-h4.

**8 Re1 Nf5 9 Nbd2 Be7 10 b3 0-0 11 Bb2 c5 12 a3 Rc8 13 Rc1 a6
14 b4 cxd4 15 cxd4 Nb6 16 Qb3 Qd7 17 b5 a5 18 Bc3 Ra8 19 Rf1
Rfc8 20 g4 Nh4 21 Nxh4 Bxh4 22 f4 Be7 (diagram 8)**

Although superficially similar to Short-Yudasin, Black has several
advantages over that game. He has managed to avoid weaknesses
while keeping both his light-squared bishop and control of the c-file.

23 Bb2 Rxc1 24 Rxc1 Rc8 25 Rxc8+ Qxc8 26 Qc3 Qxc3 27 Bxc3 a4

Ensuring that White's pawns remained weak and disjointed.

**28 Bb2 Bc2 29 Kf2 f6 30 exf6 gxf6 31 Ke3 Bd6 32 h4 h6 33 Bf3
Kf7 34 Be2 Nc8 35 Bf3 Ne7 36 h5 Nc8 37 Be2 Be7 38 Nf3 Nd6 39
Ne1 Bb3 40 Bc1 Bc4 41 b6 Bxe2 42 Kxe2 Nc4 43 Nd3 Nxb6 44
Nc5 Bxc5 45 dxc5 Nd7 46 f5 e5 47 Bxh6 Nxc5 48 Bd2 Ne4 49 Ba5
b5 50 Be1 d4 51 Bb4 Nc3+ 52 Kd3 Nd5 53 Bd2 b4 54 axb4 a3 55
Kc2 e4 56 Bc1 Nxb4+ 57 Kd1 a2 58 Bb2 d3 59 g5 e3 60 h6 Nc2 61
g6+ Kf8 62 h7 e2+ 63 Kd2 e1Q+ 64 Kxd3 Nb4+ 65 Kc4 Qh4+
White resigns**

Chapter Six

1 e4: Other Defences

 Alekhine's Defence

 The Scandinavian Defence

 The Pirc and Modern Defences

The four responses to 1 e4 considered so far (the Sicilian, 1...e5, the French and the Caro-Kann) are all what might loosely be termed 'classical openings', in that Black immediately fights for a share of the centre, either by preventing a quick d2-d4 or by establishing a pawn on d5. The defences considered in this chapter are different as Black either allows White, for the moment at least, to control the centre, or accepts a loss of time to prevent this.

All the openings considered in this chapter are less popular than the 'classical' Black defences, but are nevertheless perfectly sound and are perhaps more likely to lead to less well charted middlegame positions. All of these are good choices to throw an opponent onto their own resources at as early a stage as possible.

Alekhine's Defence

1 e4 Nf6

Alekhine's Defence is very provocative. Rather than staking a claim in the centre with his pawns, Black not only allows the white pawns to achieve dominance in that sector, but actively encourages them to do so by making a target of his own knight. Since defending the e4-pawn offers White little chance of an advantage, he generally takes up the challenge with 2 e5 Nd5 3 d4.

However, with the pawn on e5 White's centre is further forward than he might wish, as this enables Black to assault it both from the side (...c7-c5) and the front (...d7-d6). The adjacent light squares (d5, f5) are also potential stations for Black's minor pieces.

Routine development is often ineffective for White. Take, for example, 4 Nf3 dxe5 5 Nxe5 Nd7 when White's best chance for advantage is the piece sacrifice 6 Nxf7. In general, Alekhine's Defence creates unusual problems for both sides, requiring imaginative solutions. If White doesn't feel up to this he should play e5xd6.

What is White's Strategy?

White has two main strategies: he can either fully accept the challenge laid down by 1...Nf6 and construct a large pawn centre by 2 e5 Nd5 3 d4 d6 4 c4 Nb6 5 f4 (the Four Pawns Attack), with the aim of suffocating his opponent or throttling him by a timely d4-d5. Otherwise White can simply develop his pieces, 4 Nf3, contenting himself with having gained a tempo or two and a modicum of space.

What is Black's Strategy?

Having lured the white pawns forward Black's plan is to attack them – to show that, unsupported, the big centre is as much a weakness as a strength. In the Four Pawns Attack Black may attack the d4-pawn with ...c7-c5 or solely with pieces, or confront the e5-pawn again with ...f7-f6. In the positional 4 Nf3 variations Black mostly concentrates on e5, having many ways to apply the pressure: ...Bc8-g4, ...Bf8-g7, ...Nb8-c6, ...Nb8-d7.

Tactical/Strategic/Dynamic?

Alekhine's Defence is a strange mixture. The basic challenge of the opening – centre vs counter-attack – might be a strategic one, but in pursuit of their respective objectives both players may undertake strange tactical measures.

Theoretical?

The Four Pawns Attack is quite theoretical and both sides need to know how to continue: White because his central position may otherwise end up as a wreck; Black since otherwise he may be suffocated. The positional lines with 4 Nf3 do not put as much strain on White's game; however, if he wants an opening advantage White still needs some theoretical knowledge, since natural moves often fail to impress.

How Popular is it?

Although the Alekhine has a few devoted adherents it is seen only infrequently. Many of the strongest players have tried it at one time or other, but generally only as a surprise weapon.

Illustrative Games

Game 57
□ **Van der Wiel** ■ **Vaganian**
Ter Apel 1993

1 e4 Nf6 2 e5 Nd5 3 d4 d6 4 c4 Nb6 5 f4 dxe5 6 fxe5 Nc6 7 Be3 Bf5 8 Nc3 e6 9 Nf3 Bg4

Black targets the d4-pawn with his pieces, preparing to remove the defending knight and then double on the d-file.

10 Be2 Bxf3 11 gxf3 Qd7 12 f4 Rd8 13 d5 Bb4 (diagram 1)

White's 12th was a mistake, but only because of this unexpected trick. The point is that taking the knight loses material after 14 dxc6 Qxc6.

14 Bxb6 axb6 15 Bf3 exd5 16 cxd5 Qh3

Threatening ...Qh4+ and ...Qxf4.

17 Ke2 0-0 18 Qd3 Ne7 19 Qc4 Bxc3 20 bxc3 b5 21 Qxb5 c6

Opening more lines against the enemy king in the centre. White quickly succumbs.

22 dxc6 bxc6 23 Qc4 Ng6 24 Rag1 Qf5 25 Rg4 Qc2+ 26 Ke3 Qd2+ 27 Ke4 Rd5 White resigns

TIP: The Four Pawns Attack is a dangerous weapon but leaves great holes in the white position. Both players should be on the lookout for tactics which can exploit these.

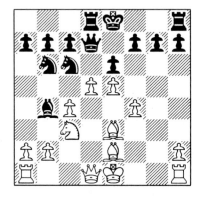

Diagram 1
White's centre is vulnerable

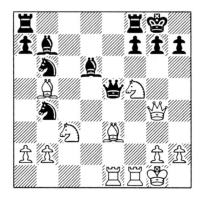

Diagram 2
White's attack is too strong

Game 58
□ **Morozevich** ■ **Bratchenko**
Novgorod 1997

---

1 e4 Nf6 2 e5 Nd5 3 d4 d6 4 c4 Nb6 5 f4 dxe5 6 fxe5 Nc6 7 Be3 Bf5 8 Nc3 e6 9 Nf3 Be7 10 d5 exd5 11 cxd5 Nb4 12 Nd4 Bc8

This allows White to accelerate his development. Instead, the main line runs 12...Bd7 13 e6 fxe6 14 dxe6 Bc6 15 Qg4 Bh4+ 16 g3 Bxh1 with obscure complications.

13 Bb5+ c6 14 dxc6 0-0 15 0-0 Qc7 16 cxb7 Bxb7 17 Qg4

Returning the extra pawn for a dangerous initiative.

17...Qxe5 18 Rae1 Bd6 19 Nf5 (diagram 2)

White ignores the threat to h2 and continues building his own attack which is swiftly decisive. If 19...Qxh2+ 20 Kf2 g6 21 Rh1 wins a piece.

19...Bc8 20 Nh6+ Kh8 21 Qh4 Bc5 22 Nxf7+ Black resigns

Game 59
□ **Short** ■ **Timman**
Tilburg 1991

---

1 e4 Nf6 2 e5 Nd5 3 d4 d6 4 Nf3 g6 5 Bc4 Nb6 6 Bb3 Bg7 7 Qe2 Nc6 8 0-0 0-0

White aims to maintain his pawn on e5 to keep Black's fianchettoed bishop quiet. To this end his next move prevents the pinning ...Bc8-g4.

9 h3 a5 10 a4 dxe5 11 dxe5 Nd4 12 Nxd4 Qxd4 13 Re1 e6 14 Nd2 Nd5 15 Nf3 Qc5 16 Qe4 Qb4 17 Bc4

White intends to attack with Qh4 and Bh6, so he does not want queens exchanged. To prevent the trade he is willing to sacrifice his queenside pawn structure.

17...Nb6 18 b3 Nxc4 19 bxc4 Re8 20 Rd1 Qc5 21 Qh4 b6 22 Be3 Qc6 23 Bh6 Bh8 24 Rd8 Bb7 25 Rad1 Bg7 26 R8d7 Rf8 27 Bxg7 Kxg7 28 R1d4 Rae8 29 Qf6+ Kg8 30 h4 h5 (diagram 3)

White's attack seems to have reached an impasse. The dark squares around the black king are fatally weak but White's queen cannot deliver mate on her own and his rooks and knight are otherwise engaged. However, White's king is not doing anything so he brings this into the attack instead. Black is helpless.

31 Kh2 Rc8 32 Kg3 Rce8 33 Kf4 Bc8 34 Kg5 Black resigns

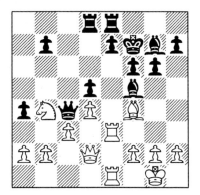

Diagram 3
How can White complete the attack?

Diagram 4
Black is about to play ...e7-e5

Game 60
□ **Adams** ■ **Agdestein**
Oslo 1994

1 e4 Nf6 2 e5 Nd5 3 d4 d6 4 Nf3 dxe5 5 Nxe5 g6 6 Bc4 c6 7 0-0 Bg7 8 Nd2 Nd7 9 Ndf3 Nxe5 10 Nxe5 0-0 11 Re1 Be6

Without doing anything remarkable Black has already equalised. He continues to play natural moves and takes control of the game while White struggles to find something to do.

12 Bb3 a5 13 c3 Qc7 14 Nd3 Bf5 15 Bg5 Rfe8 16 Qd2 a4 17 Bxd5

cxd5 18 Nb4 Rad8 19 Bf4 Qc4 20 Re3 f6 21 Rae1 Kf7 (diagram 4) 22 b3

White sacrifices a pawn to prevent Black's intended expansion with ...e7-e5, but Black is happy to accept the material.

22...axb3 23 axb3 Qxb3 24 c4 Qxc4 25 Rc1 Qb5 26 Rc5 Qa4 27 h3 Bf8 28 Nxd5 b6 29 Nxb6 Qxd4 30 Qa2+

A final mistake as White now loses more material.

30...e6 31 Rc7+ Kg8 32 Rc4 Qxb6 33 Rb3 Rd1+ 34 Kh2 Qd8 35 Rb8 Qe7 White resigns

The Scandinavian Defence

1 e4 d5

In the French and Caro-Kann ...d7-d5 is only played after a preliminary pawn move. In the Scandinavian, however, Black makes the thrust with the d-pawn immediately. The drawback is that after 2 exd5 Qxd5 White can gain time attacking the black queen with 3 Nc3, while if 2...Nf6 White has a choice between supporting the extra pawn or gaining time on the *knight* by 3 d4 Nxd5 4 c4.

Because of this time-loss the Scandinavian is often regarded as inferior. Nevertheless, the 2...Qxd5 lines create a pawn structure similar to the Caro-Kann, which gives Black a solid position. Furthermore, by challenging in the centre immediately Black negates White's alternative systems such as e4-e5, making it simpler for Black to learn the opening.

2...Nf6 is more akin to Alekhine's Defence. If White allows the recapture 3...Nxd5 he can use the knight to gain space by c2-c4. Alternatively White can try to hang on the pawn by either 3 Bb5+ (intending 3...Bd7 4 Bc4), or 3 c4 which usually transposes to the Caro-Kann after 3...c6 4 d4 cxd5, although 3...e6 is an interesting gambit.

What is White's Strategy?

There are two facets to White's position. Firstly, White's d4-pawn, which, as in Caro-Kann, gives him a space advantage and control of e5. Secondly, White has a time advantage which he can use to build an initiative. This may involve harassing Black's light-squared bishop (again as in the Caro-Kann), or the black queen should Black play 2...Qxd5 3 Nc3 Qa5.

What is Black's Strategy?

By move two Black has already achieved his main objective – the elimination of White's e-pawn. Having done that Black is able to develop his pieces smoothly and aim for a solid position in the middlegame.

Tactical/Strategic/Dynamic?

The Scandinavian is combination of all three. White has a small strategic plus based on the d4-pawn in the 2...Qxd5 lines, while both sides can develop without much trouble thus creating dynamic possibilities; and tactics can certainly arise after 2...Nf6. But the positions can very often simplify so that there is not much left for either side to play for.

Theoretical?

One of the appeals of the Scandinavian is that Black can usually get through the opening without needing to know too much. There are a few lines after 2...Nf6 that require some preparation – in particular those in which White tries to keep the pawn by 3 Bb5+ or 3 c4 – but with a little knowledge Black can hope to reach the middlegame unscathed.

How Popular is it?

In the repertoire of leading masters the Scandinavian appears only as an occasional defence, probably because, although the opening is quite solid, it is also rather one-dimensional. Black is slightly worse with few chances to unbalance the position and play for a win.

Illustrative Games

Game 61
□ **Anand** ■ **Lautier**
Biel 1997

1 e4 d5 2 exd5 Qxd5 3 Nc3 Qa5 4 d4 Nf6 5 Nf3 c6 6 Bc4 Bf5 7 Ne5 e6 8 g4 Bg6 9 h4

As in the Caro-Kann White uses the exposed position of Black's light-squared bishop to take the initiative on the kingside.

9...Nbd7 10 Nxd7 Nxd7 11 h5 Be4 12 Rh3 Bg2 13 Re3 Nb6 14 Bd3 Nd5 15 f3

A strong move. White is willing to give up material on c3 or e3 since he will pick up the trapped bishop on g2.

15...Bb4 16 Kf2 Bxc3 17 bxc3 Qxc3 18 Rb1 Qxd4 19 Rxb7 Rd8 20 h6 gxh6 21 Bg6 (diagram 5)

A devastating blow. Black cannot take the queen as he gets mated by 21...Qxd1 22 Rxe6+ Kf8 23 Bxh6+ Kg8 24 Bxf7 – which was the reason for White's preparatory move 20 h6. Instead Black trades off the attacking pieces but loses material as his bishop is still trapped on g2.

21...Ne7 22 Qxd4 Rxd4 23 Rd3 Rd8 24 Rxd8+ Kxd8 25 Bd3 **Black resigns**

WARNING: A benefit of the Centre Counter is that Black retains the possibility to develop the light-squared bishop outside the pawn chain. However, because White has a good lead in development this piece can often become a target.

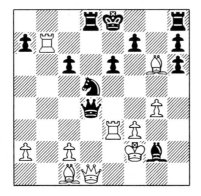

Diagram 5
A brilliant tactic from White

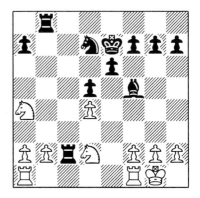

Diagram 6
Black holds all the trumps

Game 62
□ **Wedberg** ■ **Emms**
Harplinge 1998

1 e4 d5 2 exd5 Qxd5 3 Nc3 Qa5 4 d4 Nf6 5 Bc4 c6 6 Qe2 Bf5 7 Nf3 e6 8 Bd2 Bb4 9 Bb3 Nd5 10 Bxd5 cxd5 11 Qb5+

Planning to exploit the weakened dark squares should Black exchange queens. Instead Black offers the b7-pawn to rush his pieces into play.

11...Nd7 12 Qxb7 Rb8 13 Qc6 Ke7 14 0-0 Rhc8 15 Qa4 Qxa4 16 Nxa4 Bxd2 17 Nxd2 Rxc2 (diagram 6)

Already Black has regained the pawn and has a huge advantage with more active pieces and weak white pawns to attack at b2 and d4.

18 Nf3 Rbc8 19 Rfd1 Nb6 20 Nxb6 axb6 21 b3 Bg4 22 a4 Bxf3 23 gxf3 Rb2 24 Rab1 Rxb1 25 Rxb1 Rc3 26 Kf1 Rd3 27 Ke2 Rxd4

Now Black is a pawn ahead and has a winning rook endgame.

28 Ke3 e5 29 b4 g5 30 a5 bxa5 31 bxa5 Ra4 32 Rb7+ Ke6 33 Rb6+ Kf5 34 a6 Ra3+ 35 Ke2 h5 36 h3 e4 37 fxe4+ dxe4 38 Rc6 h4 39 Rb6 f6 40 Kf1 Ke5 41 Kg2 f5 42 Rg6 Kf4 43 Rh6 Ra2 44 Re6 Ra4 45 Rf6 Ra1 46 Rg6 Ra2 47 Re6 g4 48 hxg4 Kxg4 49 Rg6+ Kf4 50 Rh6 Kg5 51 Re6 h3+ 52 Kg3 h2 53 f4+ Kh5 White resigns

Game 63
☐ **Nataf** ■ **Boric**
European Cup 1997

1 e4 d5 2 exd5 Nf6 3 d4 Nxd5 4 c4 Nb6 5 Nf3 g6 6 Nc3 Bg7 7 h3 0-0 8 Be3 Nc6 9 Qd2 e5

Black challenges in the centre and on the long a1-h8 diagonal.

10 d5 Na5 11 b3 e4 12 Ng5 f5 13 Rc1 h6 14 Ne6 Bxe6 15 dxe6 Qxd2+ 16 Bxd2 c5 17 e7 Rf7 18 Nb5 Nc6 19 Nc7 Rxe7 20 Nxa8 Nxa8 (diagram 7)

White has managed to win the exchange but in return Black has an impressive kingside pawn mass and outposts for his knights at d4 and e5.

21 g4 Nc7 22 gxf5 gxf5 23 Rg1 Kh7 24 Be2 Ne6 25 Kf1 Bf6 26 Rd1 Ncd4 27 Bh5 Bg5 28 h4 Bxd2 29 Rxd2 Nf4 30 Bd1 a5 31 Rg3 Ng6 32 h5 Ne5 33 a3 b6 34 Re3 Kg7 35 Be2 Kf6 36 Rg3 Rg7 37 Rxg7 Kxg7 38 b4 axb4 39 axb4 Kf6 40 b5

A decisive mistake as now the black pawns advance. White had to activate his rook by 40 bxc5 bxc5 41 Ra2.

40...f4 41 f3 exf3 42 Bd3 Kg5 43 Kg1 Kh4 44 Bf1 Kg3 45 Rh2 Ne2+ 46 Bxe2 Ng4 47 Rh3+ Kxh3 48 Bxf3 Kg3 49 Be2 Nf6 50 Kh1 f3 51 Bd3 Nxh5 52 Kg1 Nf6 53 Kh1 Ng4 54 Kg1 Kf4 White resigns

TIP: A powerful central pawn is often more than enough compensation for the exchange.

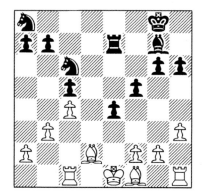

Diagram 7
Black has excellent outposts

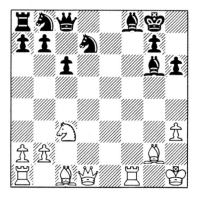

Diagram 8
Black is too uncoordinated

Game 64
☐ **Svidler** ■ **Dreev**
Russian Championship 1997

1 e4 d5 2 exd5 Nf6 3 Nf3 Nxd5 4 d4 Bg4 5 h3 Bh5 6 c4 Nb6 7 Nc3 e5 8 g4 exd4 9 Nxd4 Bg6 10 Bg2 c6 11 0-0 Be7 12 f4

White's play is very direct. With simple moves White keeps his opponent under pressure – as soon Black answers one threat he is faced with another and is given no time to organise his forces.

12...h6 13 f5 Bh7 14 c5 N6d7 15 g5 0-0 16 g6 fxg6 17 Ne6 Qc8 18 Nxf8 Bxc5+ 19 Kh1 Bxf8 20 fxg6 Bxg6 (diagram 8)

Again Black has two pawns for the exchange but his forces are undeveloped and uncoordinated. White accelerates his initiative by offering a piece.

21 Bxh6 Ne5

If 21...gxh6 then 22 Qg4 gains more time attacking the bishop and the white rooks swiftly enter into the action with decisive effect. Hence Black declines the bishop but then remains at a material disadvantage.

22 Bf4 Nbd7 23 Ne4 Qe8 24 Qb3+ Qf7 25 Qg3 Bxe4 26 Bxe4 Nf6 27 Bg2 Nh5 28 Qg5 Nd3 29 Be5 Qe7

Black shortens the game with an error.

30 Qxh5 Qxe5 31 Qf7+ Kh8 32 Rf5 Nf2+ 33 Kg1 Nxh3+ 34 Kf1 Black resigns

The Pirc and Modern Defences

1 e4 d6 2 d4 Nf6 3 Nc3 g6 or 1 e4 g6 2 d4 Bg7

In a sense, the Pirc Defence throws down the gauntlet to White. Black is declining to stake an immediate claim in the centre and challenges White to set out an ambitious stall. Black hopes that if White adopts such a strategy then his mighty central fortress may later come crashing down with the help of some well-timed counter-thrusts from Black.

Though the Modern Defence purports to grant White temporary dominance in the centre in order that Black can attack it, in truth the kingside fianchetto does not commit Black to any particular plan. He might strike at the centre from the side by ...c7-c5, but he might also stake a belated claim there himself with ...e7-e5 or even ...d7-d5, or concentrate wholly on the flank and advance his queenside pawns.

Both lines have the possibility of creating unusual middlegame positions and this is what attracts many creative players to them.

What is White's Strategy?

With Black's forces yet to engage in battle White is free to adopt whatever strategy he feels like. He can build a large centre with f2-f4 and/or c2-c4, or a solid centre with c2-c3; he develop rapidly and attack straightaway, or develop quietly and postpone the battle until the middlegame. Of course the big centre and the quick attack are the most ambitious strategies and put Black under most pressure. The key move for White is the advance e4-e5. As there is often a black knight on f6 (it goes there on move 2 in the Pirc), this can gain time and lead to a big gain of space in the centre or possibly a quick attack with e5-e6.

What is Black's Strategy?

Black hopes that White will over-extend himself in the centre and that injudicious advances in that sector will create the opportunity for powerful undermining blows. Having fianchettoed the king's bishop, Black is mainly looking for dark-square counterplay, most usually with the move ...c7-c5 – often the antidote to White's more ambitious plans. However, if White adopts an unassuming set-up, Black may prefer to simply gain some space on the queen's wing with ...c7-c6 and ...b7-b5 and await developments. Black may also find himself obliged to play ...e7-e5 at some point to blunt White's central ambitions.

Tactical/Strategic/Dynamic?

Both the Pirc and Modern Defences lead to strategically rich positions where an understanding of the key themes is of most importance. If White is dead set on solid play then it can be difficult for Black to create tension in the position but, then again, this can be said of most black openings.

Theoretical?

The king's fianchetto is relatively non-theoretical and has the practical advantage for Black that it can be played against anything. The one drawback is that, if White is content with a solid position, it can be difficult for Black to generate winning chances. There are, of course, lines where White attempts to blow Black away and a clear theoretical knowledge of certain moves and principles are important in these variations.

How Popular is it?

The ...g7-g6 defences – that is the Modern and Pirc combined – are currently about as popular as the Caro-Kann, though relatively few Grandmasters play this way full time. For those who do play the

Modern regularly, it is often because it saves Black from having to learn too much – as English Grandmaster David Norwood has confessed.

Illustrative Games

Game 65
☐ **Gelfand** ■ **Azmaiparashvili**
Dortmund 1990

1 d4 g6 2 e4 Bg7 3 c4 d6 4 Nc3 Nc6 5 d5 Nd4 6 Be3 c5 7 Nge2 Qb6 8 Na4 Qa5+ 9 Bd2 Qd8 10 Bc3 e5 11 dxe6 Nxe6 12 Bxg7 Nxg7 13 Qd2

This is almost a standard position, yet with White in total control of the d-file things already look dismal for Black.

13...Nf6 14 f3 Be6 15 Nf4 Qe7 16 0-0-0 Rd8 (diagram 9)

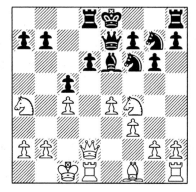 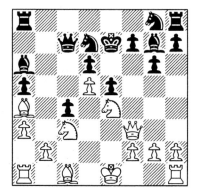

Diagram 9
White has a good central grip

Diagram 10
White is about to launch a big attack

Black manages to defend the d-pawn but White now increases his grip on d5 and advances on the kingside.

17 Nc3 0-0 18 g4 Nd7 19 h4 Nb6 20 b3 f6 21 Nfd5 Nxd5 22 exd5

Black's defences have proved adequate on the d-file so White switches to the e-file, taking control of e6, and begins an attack on the kingside.

22...Bc8 23 h5 gxh5 24 Re1 Qf7 25 Bd3 Kh8 26 Qh6 f5 27 gxh5 Qf6 28 Qxf6 Rxf6 29 h6 Ne8 30 Re7 Rg6 31 Ne2 Nf6 32 Nf4 Rg3 33 Rh3 Rgg8 34 Ne6 Rd7 35 Rg7

The threat of 35 Bxf5 forces Black to give up the exchange after which the result is inevitable.

35...Rgxg7 36 hxg7+ Rxg7 37 Nxg7 Kxg7 38 Rg3+ Kf7 39 Kd2
Bd7 40 Rg1 Ng8 41 Rh1 Kg7 42 Rb1 Ne7 43 b4 cxb4 44 Rxb4 b6
45 a4 Nc8 46 a5 Kf6 47 f4 Ke7 48 Rb1 bxa5 49 Rh1 Kf6 50 Rxh7
Ne7 51 Ke3 Be8 52 Rh8 Bd7 53 Rd8 Bc8 54 Rxd6+ Kf7 55 Bc2
Ng6 56 Rc6 Bd7 57 Rc7 Ke8 58 Rxd7 Black resigns

**WARNING: In provocative openings such as the Modern it is
important for Black to play with a plan. White has a 'natural'
advantage and if Black sits around hoping for the best, he will
probably get squashed.**

Game 66
☐ **J.Polgar** ■ **Shirov**
Amsterdam 1995

---

1 e4 g6 2 d4 Bg7 3 Nc3 c6 4 Bc4 d6 5 Qf3

A very direct system for White. The attack against f7 forces Black to
make another small pawn move as 5...Nf6 would lose to 6 e5.

5...e6 6 Nge2 b5 7 Bb3 a5

This queenside expansion is a typical theme in the Modern Defence
but it is a little slow here and White quickly goes on to the attack.

**8 a3 Ba6 9 d5 cxd5 10 exd5 e5 11 Ne4 Qc7 12 c4 bxc4 13 Ba4+
Nd7 14 N2c3 Ke7 (diagram 10)**

Preparing the consolidating development ...Ngf6 but White refutes it
by sacrificial means.

**15 Nxd6 Qxd6 16 Ne4 Qxd5 17 Bg5+ Ndf6 18 Rd1 Qb7 19 Rd7+
Qxd7 20 Bxd7 h6 21 Qd1 Black resigns**

Game 67
☐ **Ioseliani** ■ **Svidler**
Lucerne 1997

**1 e4 g6 2 d4 Bg7 3 Nc3 d6 4 Be3 a6 5 Qd2 Nd7 6 f3 b5 7 h4 Ngf6
8 g4 h6 9 Nh3 Nb6 10 0-0-0 b4 11 Nb1 a5 12 Nf4 Nfd7 13 Bb5 Bb7
14 d5 c5**

A very strong move. At first sight it appears to lose a piece but Black
has foreseen a tactical solution.

15 dxc6 Bxc6 (diagram 11) 16 Qe2

If 16 Bxc6 then 16...Nc4 forces White to give up her queen as 17 Qd3
Bxb2 is mate.

16...Rc8 17 Bxc6 Rxc6 18 Nd5 0-0 19 Bd4 Bxd4 20 Rxd4

White removes the powerful fianchettoed bishop but Black's queenside attack remains strong.

20...e6 21 Ne3 Nc5 22 Nc4 Nxc4 23 Rxc4 d5 24 exd5 exd5 25 Rd1 Nd3+

Winning the exchange and the game.

26 Qxd3 Rxc4 27 Nd2 Rc6 28 h5 Qg5 29 hxg6 fxg6 30 Kb1 Rfc8 31 Nb3 Rxc2 32 f4 Qxf4 33 Qxg6+ Kh8 34 Rh1 Rh2 White resigns

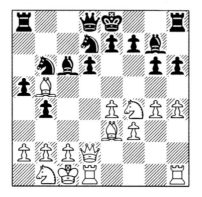

Diagram 11

Black's g7-bishop is very strong

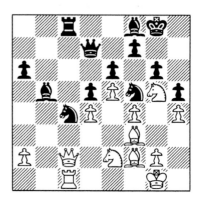

Diagram 12

Black has all the fun on the queenside

Game 68
□ **Forster** ■ **Bacrot**
Bermuda 1999

---

1 e4 g6 2 d4 Bg7 3 Nc3 d6 4 f4 a6 5 Nf3 b5 6 Bd3 Nd7 7 e5 c5

The Modern Defence reverses classical precepts. Traditionally play on the flanks is met by play in the centre. Here Black responds to White's central ambitions by attacking on the flanks.

8 Be4 Rb8 9 Be3 b4 10 Ne2 Nh6 11 h3 0-0 12 c3 Nb6 13 Bf2 bxc3 14 bxc3 Nc4 15 0-0 Qc7 16 Rb1 Bd7 17 Rxb8 Rxb8 18 Qd3 Bb5 19 Qc2 Qd7 20 Ng5 Nf5 21 Re1 e6 22 Bf3 cxd4 23 cxd4 Rc8 24 Rc1 d5 25 h4 h6 26 Nh3 h5 27 Ng5 Bf8 (diagram 12)

White's play in the centre and on the kingside has been closed down while Black's queenside play continues apace.

28 Qd1 Nb2 29 Qd2 Nd3 30 Rxc8 Qxc8 31 Ng3 Nxg3 32 Bxg3 Qc4 33 Qe3 Ba3

The bishops intended return to the long diagonal (...Bb2) is decisive. White tries to resurrect his attack with a piece sacrifice but Black wins through more quickly.

34 Bxh5 gxh5 35 Qf3 Qxd4+ 36 Kh2 Bc5 37 Qxh5 Qg1+ 38 Kh3 Qh1+ 39 Kg4 Nf2+ 40 Bxf2 Qxg2+ White resigns

Chapter Seven

The King's Indian Defence

- The Classical Main Line
- The Sämisch Variation
- The Four Pawns Attack

The King's Indian Defence is the classic counter-attacking system. Black challenges White to construct a big centre or to accept extra space in the hope that his middlegame counterattack will lead White to regret his expansionist plans.

In the early part of the 20th century it was considered essential for Black to stake a claim in the centre at an early stage, otherwise it was assumed that he would be swamped there and would never gain any freedom for his pieces. However, in the 1940s and 1950s, dynamic, imaginative players such as David Bronstein began to demonstrate that it was perfectly possible to allow White a free hand early on and to snipe against White's position from the wings. Nowadays the King's Indian is a perfectly respectable mainstream opening.

White has three major responses to Black's challenge. He can acquire a modest space advantage with the classical, he can bolster his centre with the Sämisch, or he can try to blow Black off the board with the Four Pawns Attack. We shall consider each of these possibilities here.

The Classical Main Line

1 d4 Nf6 2 c4 g6 3 Nc3 Bg7 4 e4 d6 5 Nf3 0-0 6 Be2

The King's Indian is characterised by these first five moves for Black: ...Nf6, ...g6, ...Bg7, ...d6 and ...0-0. The Main Line Classical is White's most natural response: d4, c4, Nc3, e4, Nf3 and Be2. White constructs a pawn centre and then develops his minor pieces in a natural fashion. In this way he supports and protects the pawn front with his pieces.

Players of the King's Indian with Black have the philosophy that White can spend his time building his pawn edifice but have confidence that a few well timed counter-strikes will bring it tumbling down. The opening is often likened to a coiled spring, which once released expands with great power. Black first concentrates on getting his kingside developed but will then seek a stake in the centre, usually with ...e7-e5 (but sometimes preferring ...c7-c5) in order to combat the white space advantage.

White has two distinct approaches to meet Black's counter: either he keeps the tension or he advances with d4-d5. The first method, keeping the tension, hopes to exploit a more comfortable development afforded by having more space, whereas the second method, involving a closed centre, reinforces his space pull and usually prepares a general queenside advance.

What is White's Strategy?

With white pawns on c4, d5 and e4 facing down black pawns on c7, d6 and e5, White generally aims for a c4-c5 advance. This can be achieved with the support of b2-b4 or uniquely with pieces Ra1-c1, Bc1-e3 (or a3) and typically with the manoeuvre Nf3-e1-d3. By playing c4-c5, White hopes to open up a highway into the black camp.

In the case of White retaining the d-pawn on d4 his byword is flexibility: he may wish to play d4-d5 later under better circumstances, toy with the option of d4xe5 opening the d-file or provoke Black to give ground with ...e5xd4. In each case White hopes that his well-centralised pieces gives him good play whatever may crop up.

What is Black's Strategy?

With a closed centre, based around the advanced pawn on d5, Black will counter with ...f7-f5 hitting at e4. If White overprotects his centre, perhaps supporting e4 with the f-pawn (f2-f3 after moving his king's knight away), Black typically switches to an all-out king side assault with ...f5-f4, ...g7-g5 and ...h7-h5, supported by a mass of pieces as Black abandons the queenside to its fate.

If White keeps the tension in the centre then he has to be ready for ...e5xd4 at any moment, when the fianchettoed bishop is opened up on the long diagonal. Despite having less space, Black's pawns are less of a target than White's and pressure against the c4- and e4-pawns can create problems in the White camp.

Another approach is to at first keep as flexible as possible, with moves such as ...c7-c6, ...Nb8-d7 (or ...Nb8-a6) and only switch to other plans once White has shown his hand.

Tactical/Strategic/Dynamic?

The unbalanced positions which arise are very rich and dynamic with good practical counterchances for Black. Allowing White a significant space advantage is strategically somewhat risky and sometimes Black never frees his game. One of the aspects that appeals to King's Indian advocates is that White never has everything totally under control and that Black has more hope of creating counterplay and thus winning chances, than in a more solid system like the Queen's Gambit.

Theoretical?

Although some of the lines have been deeply analysed, it is more important to understand ideas rather than learn great reams of analysis. The two players rarely indulge in immediate contact so there are few early traps for the unwary.

Familiarity with a few illustrative games should enable anyone to be able to play and enjoy this opening. Some players play the King's Indian set-up against White systems with 1 c4 and 1 Nf3 so it can prove to be an economical choice.

How Popular is it?

A popular choice at all levels but particularly in Open tournaments where winning with Black is a necessary aim. Many top players have at some point been on the white side and some use it regularly, as it's considered totally correct by the top echelon. The Main Line Classical is often chosen by positional players as White, who like to have a space advantage. Black players have a wide choice of counters depending on style.

Illustrative Games

Game 69
☐ **Atalik** ■ **Nikolaidis**
Halkida 1997

1 d4 Nf6 2 c4 g6 3 Nc3 Bg7 4 e4 0-0 5 Nf3 d6 6 Be2 e5 7 0-0 Nc6 8 d5 Ne7 9 Ne1 Nd7 10 Be3 f5 11 f3 f4 12 Bf2 g5

Black expands on the kingside with the intention to attack. Meanwhile White prepares the c4-c5 advance to open up the c-file and create play on the whole wing.

13 Rc1 Rf6 14 b4 a6 15 c5 Rh6 16 cxd6 cxd6 17 Nd3 Nf6 18 Na4 Qe8 19 Nb6 Qh5 (Diagram 1)

Black abandons the queen's wing and goes all out for mate.

20 h4 Bf5 21 Nxa8 Ng6 22 Qe1 g4 23 exf5 Nxh4 24 Rc8+ Bf8 25 Bxh4 g3 26 Nf2 Qxf5 27 Rxf8+ Kxf8 28 Bxf6 Rxf6 29 Nh3

White saves his king and wins easily on material.

29...Rh6 30 Qb1 Qc8 31 Rc1 1-0

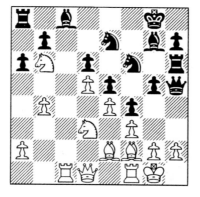

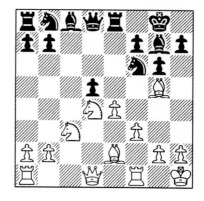

Diagram 1
Black has gone 'all-in' on the kingside

Diagram 2
White has a good initiative

Game 70
☐ **Tal** ■ **Spassky**
Montreal 1979

1 Nf3 Nf6 2 c4 g6 3 Nc3 Bg7 4 e4 d6 5 d4 0-0 6 Be2 e5 7 0-0 exd4

Black aims to open the centre and seek counterplay there.

8 Nxd4 Re8 9 f3 c6 10 Kh1 d5 11 cxd5 cxd5 12 Bg5 (Diagram 2)

Black has eliminated the white centre but lags in development. White is able to maintain the initiative with the opening of the f-file.

12...dxe4 13 fxe4 Nbd7 14 Ndb5 Re5 15 Bf4 Nxe4

The complicated struggle that follows favours White, who has a clear material advantage in the form of an extra exchange.

16 Bxe5 Bxe5 17 Nxe4 Qh4 18 h3 Qxe4 19 Qb3 Nf6 20 Bc4 Qh4 21 Bxf7+ Kh8 22 Rf3 Bf5 23 Nc3 Ne4 24 Nxe4 Bxe4 25 Qc4 Rd8 26 Raf1 Kg7 27 Be6 Rd2 28 Qc5 Bxf3 29 Qxe5+ Qf6 30 Qxf6+ Kxf6 31 Bg4 Rxb2 32 Bxf3 1-0

 WARNING: Although Black can often equalise the game by opening the centre, he should be very wary of going down this route if he is behind in development. This is not just a feature of the King's Indian but applies to all openings.

Game 71
☐ **Piket** ■ **Kasparov**
Tilburg 1989

1 d4 Nf6 2 Nf3 g6 3 c4 Bg7 4 Nc3 0-0 5 e4 d6 6 Be2 e5 7 0-0 Nc6 8 d5 Ne7 9 Ne1 Nd7 10 Be3 f5 11 f3 f4 12 Bf2 g5 13 b4 Nf6 14 c5 Ng6 15 cxd6 cxd6 16 Rc1 Rf7

White has already opened the c-file and is preparing to invade on the flank. Kasparov takes a time out to bolster the weak points c7 and d6 before getting the attack under way.

17 a4 Bf8 18 a5 Bd7 19 Nb5 g4

The thematic pawn advance. Black will use the kingside pawns to scythe his way into the white king's position.

20 Nc7 g3 (Diagram 3)

Material is becoming of less importance than the initiative. Black is concerned with his attack and is not willing to take time out just to save a dormant rook. Kasparov's judgement in this respect proves to be faultless.

21 Nxa8 Nh5 22 Kh1 gxf2 23 Rxf2 Ng3+ 24 Kg1 Qxa8 25 Bc4 a6 26 Qd3 Qa7 27 b5 axb5 28 Bxb5 Nh1 0-1

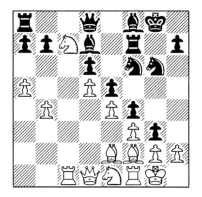

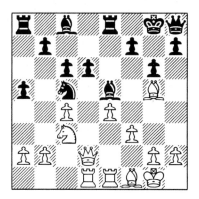

Diagram 3

Black is not worried about his rook...

Diagram 4

Black has good control

Game 72
□ **Lalev** ■ **Ivanchuk**
Lvov 1988

1 c4 Nf6 2 Nf3 g6 3 Nc3 Bg7 4 e4 d6 5 d4 0-0 6 Be2 Nbd7 7 0-0 e5 8 Re1 c6

Black temporarily keeps the centre flexible, waiting for White to show his hand.

9 Bf1 exd4

Ivanchuk judges that this is a good moment to switch plans.

10 Nxd4 Ng4 11 Qxg4 Bxd4

The exchanges have released Black's position and left White with a clumsy set-up.

12 Be3 Nc5 13 Qd1 Be5 14 Qd2 Re8 15 f3 a5

White organises his forces and defends his centre but Black's pieces are well dug in.

16 Rad1 Qf6 17 Bg5 Qh8 (Diagram 4) 18 f4

An error but White was already short of good ideas.

18...Bxc3 19 bxc3 Nxe4 20 Rxe4 Rxe4 21 Qxd6 Bg4 22 Rd4 Re6 23 Qc7 Rae8 24 c5 Be2 0-1

TIP: In many lines of the King's Indian exchanges can favour Black. White is usually playing the game with more space but a large territory needs a large army to defend it, otherwise it can become vulnerable to flanking manoeuvres.

The Sämisch Variation

1 d4 Nf6 2 c4 g6 3 Nc3 Bg7 4 e4 d6 5 f3

The Sämisch is defined by White's set-up d4, c4, Nc3, e4 and f3. The key move f3 supports the e4-pawn and enables a bishop to come to e3 without any harassment involving ...Nf6-g4. White can thus continue aggressively with Be3, Qd2, 0-0-0 and then h2-h4 and g2-g4. His space advantage and central control are thus used to prepare a kingside attack.

Another, more restrained, plan is to aim for kingside castling and play on the queenside, as in the Main Line Classical. The e4-pawn is better protected but development of the kingside pieces is not always straightforward as the knight is denied it's natural square and on e2 it gets in the way of the bishop.

The central tension can be maintained for a while, especially if Black plays ...e7-e5 and White reacts with Ng1-e2. Here the white king tends to be left in the centre for longer, and so Black can consider the line opening counter of ...e5xd4 followed by ...c7-c6 and ...d6-d5, when the pawns are sometimes swept away from the central arena.

What is White's Strategy?

Aggressive intentions on the kingside may not always lead to mate but instead force Black to react quickly in the centre where White is often well-placed to pounce.

The quieter plan of queenside pressure and kingside castling is frequently met by ...f7-f5 but here the move f3 holds things together well and Black is less likely to find the time for the pawn-roller with ...f5-f4 etc. White sometimes reacts to ...f7-f5 by exchanging on f5 when the pawn on f3 covers some useful squares and the opening up of the position may favour the more actively developed player.

If Black doesn't get some sort of a grip in the centre he may be faced with an uncomfortable e4-e5 creating havoc for his cramped pieces.

What is Black's Strategy?

Counterattack is necessary before White is fully developed. Hitting back at the centre with ...e7-e5 or ...c7-c5, concentrating attention on the sensitive d4-point is one approach, and expanding quickly on the queenside with ...c7-c6, ...a7-a6 and ...b7-b5 is another.

If the centre becomes closed after ...e7-e5 with d4-d5 then either ...f7-f5 or ...c7-c6 is required to keep White on his toes and for Black to obtain some play for his pieces. If after ...c7-c5 White chooses to close things with d4-d5 then ...e7-e6 and ...e6xd5, opening the e-file, yields counterplay.

One of the most dynamic methods is to play ...Nc6 with ideas of ...e5 (again concentrating efforts against d4) and ...a6, ...Rb8 with ...b7-b5 in mind.

Tactical/Strategic/Dynamic?

This is another variation of the King's Indian that can be described as dynamic as there is a clash of strategies and styles in view. There is much individual choice as to how aggressively the struggle will be pursued.

Theoretical?

Except for a few of the sharper lines, where White goes all out for a kingside assault, most lines require a knowledge of plans and ideas. Black's strategy needs to be able to cope with both the positional and attack-minded opponent and so knowledge of illustrative games is the best method to understand the clash of ideas.

How Popular is it?

Spassky used to play it aggressively and Botvinnik positionally, but nowadays it's less popular at the top level.

Club players are often attracted to a mating attack, but this is a double-edged strategy and stronger grandmasters generally prefer something less risky with the white pieces. Karpov has been known to handle it positionally for White.

Illustrative Games

Game 73
☐ **Spassky** ■ **Evans**
Varna 1962

1 d4 Nf6 2 c4 g6 3 Nc3 Bg7 4 e4 d6 5 f3 c6 6 Be3 a6 7 Qd2 b5

A slower system that is not bad in itself, it's just that Black has to create some problems for White in order to catch up with development.

8 0-0-0 bxc4 9 Bxc4 0-0 10 h4 d5

White intends a direct attack against which Black counters in the centre. However Spassky just keeps playing for mate.

11 Bb3 dxe4 12 h5 exf3 13 hxg6 hxg6 14 Bh6 fxg2 (Diagram 5) 15 Rh4

White has ditched several pawns to keep the attack going, but Black's king is lacking cover as his undeveloped queenside is not helping the defence.

15...Ng4 16 Bxg7 Kxg7 17 Qxg2 Nh6 18 Nf3 Nf5 19 Rh2 Qd6 20 Ne5 Nd7 21 Ne4 Qc7 22 Rdh1 Rg8 23 Rh7+ Kf8 24 Rxf7+ Ke8 25 Qxg6 Nxe5 26 Rf8+ 1-0

A crushing attack.

WARNING: White has various attacking schemes in the Sämisch which look terribly crude, but they can be very dangerous against inaccurate defence.

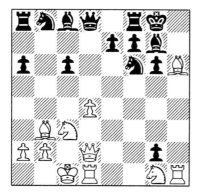

Diagram 5
Black's king is suffering

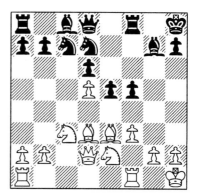

Diagram 6
White must break up Black's pawns

Game 74
□ **Vyzmanavin** ■ **Kozul**
Debrecen 1992

1 d4 Nf6 2 c4 g6 3 Nc3 Bg7 4 e4 d6 5 f3 0-0 6 Be3 e5 7 d5 c6 8 Bd3

This move is associated with kingside castling. White keeps his space advantage and is ready for counterplay on either flank.

8...cxd5 9 cxd5 Ne8 10 Qd2 f5 11 exf5

Here opening of the centre suits the better mobilised player.

11...gxf5 12 Nge2 Nd7 13 0-0 Kh8 14 Kh1 Nc7 (Diagram 6) 15 f4

A typical King's Indian theme to force the central pawns to make a decision. If Black opts for ...e5-e4 then, after retreating the bishop, White will aim for an early g2-g4 to crack open the centre and pick up the e-pawn. Black is not yet well enough developed to counter the white initiative.

15...Nb6 16 fxe5 Bxe5 17 Nf4 Ne8 18 Rf3 Nf6 19 Raf1

White is in no hurry. He just improves his pieces and bears down on the isolated f-pawn.

19...Qe8 20 h3 Bd7 21 Qf2 Rg8 22 Bd4

Exchanging off Black's best defensive piece.

22...Bxd4 23 Qxd4 Qe5 24 Qf2 Rae8 25 Qh4 Qe7 26 Qh6 Rg7 27 R3f2 Qf7 28 Ne6 Rg6 29 Qh4 Nfxd5 30 Rxf5

The defences are breached.

30...Qxe6 31 Rf7 h6 32 Bxg6 Qxg6 33 Nxd5 Nxd5 34 Rxd7 1-0

Game 75
☐ **Timman** ■ **Kasparov**
Reykjavik 1988

---

1 d4 Nf6 2 c4 g6 3 Nc3 Bg7 4 e4 d6 5 f3 0-0 6 Be3 e5 7 d5 c6 8 Bd3 b5

A flank blow to loosen White's hold on the centre.

9 cxb5 cxd5 10 exd5 e4

A highly thematic pawn sacrifice to open up the long diagonal for the King's Indian bishop.

11 Nxe4 Nxd5 12 Bg5 Qa5+ 13 Qd2 Qxd2+ 14 Bxd2 Bxb2 15 Rb1 Bg7 16 Ne2 Nd7 17 Nxd6 Nc5

Black has active piece play for his pawn.

18 Bc2 Be6 19 Ne4 Rac8 20 0-0 Nxe4 21 Bxe4 f5 22 Bd3 (Diagram 7) 22...Nb6

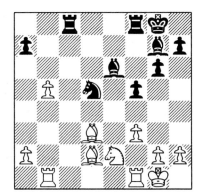 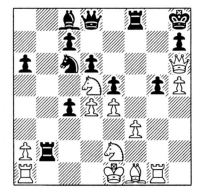

Diagram 7
It is hard to cope with Black's active play

Diagram 8
A complete mess!

The white pieces are unable to find satisfactory squares and something eventually has to give.

23 Nc1 Rfd8 24 Bg5 Rd7 25 Re1 Kf7 26 Be2 h6 27 Bh4 Nd5 28 Bd1 Bd4+ 29 Bf2 Bxf2+ 30 Kxf2 Nc3 31 Bb3 Bxb3 32 Rxb3 Nd1+ 33 Rxd1 Rxd1 34 Nd3 Rd2+ 35 Ke3 Rxg2 36 Ra3 Re8+ 37 Kd4 Re7 38 Ne5+ Kf6 39 Nc6 Rd7+ 40 Kc4 Rc2+ 41 Kb4 Rxh2 42 Ra6 Kg5 43 a4 h5 44 Rxa7 Rxa7 45 Nxa7 0-1

TIP: In the King's Indian Black's dark-squared bishop is the key piece in his armoury. When it gets working it can wreak havoc and it is often worth giving up a pawn to activate it.

Game 76
☐ **Bagirov** ■ **Gufeld**
USSR 1973

---

1 d4 g6 2 c4 Bg7 3 Nc3 d6 4 e4 Nf6 5 f3 0-0 6 Be3 Nc6 7 Nge2 Rb8 8 Qd2 a6 9 Bh6

This plan of exchanging the dark-squared bishops weakens Black's king and is often the prelude to a direct attack.

9...b5 10 h4 e5

Black cannot sit around and so counters quickly in the centre and on the queenside.

11 Bxg7 Kxg7 12 h5 Kh8 13 Nd5

Intending to exchange off another defender.

13...bxc4 14 hxg6 fxg6 15 Qh6 Nh5

Blocking the h-file to gain breathing space for his king.

16 g4 Rxb2 17 gxh5 g5 18 Rg1 (Diagram 8) 18...g4

The struggle has become completely chaotic. Black eventually wins a fine game but the complications are, for a long time, totally unclear.

19 0-0-0 Rxa2 20 Nef4 exf4 21 Nxf4 Rxf4 22 Qxf4 c3 23 Bc4 Ra3 24 fxg4 Nb4 25 Kb1 Be6 26 Bxe6 Nd3 27 Qf7 Qb8+ 28 Bb3 Rxb3+ 29 Kc2 Nb4+ 30 Kxb3 Nd5+ 31 Kc2 Qb2+ 32 Kd3 Qb5+ 0-1

The Four Pawns Attack

1 d4 Nf6 2 c4 g6 3 Nc3 Bg7 4 e4 d6 5 f4

In the Four Pawns Attack, White unashamedly builds a wide pawn front, developing as follows: d4, c4, Nc3, e4, f4. In an ideal world he would like to sweep away the black knight with e4-e5 and then push through in the centre, or even, if Black is too passive, on the kingside.

Black has to react assuredly in the centre and a struggle between advancing pawns and countering pieces ensues. The lines are forcing and sharp. Black's most consistent strategy is to play ...c7-c5 and, after d4-d5 by White, to open the e-file with ...e7-e6 and ...e6xd5.

It is not possible to stop the e4-e5 advance by White for long, but this is often made under double-edged circumstances; the d-pawn becomes passed but often a well-prepared black force can round up this pawn.

What is White's Strategy?

The pawns are advanced quickly and as far as possible to cause fear and disruption in the black army. White plays for an immediate initiative, even before completing rudimentary development and Black has to concentrate on coping with immediate threats. The threats of e4-e5, opening of the f-file and tactical play against uncoordinated defences are dangerous.

If Black counters with an early ...e7-e5, then white reacts with f4xe5, and after ...d6xe5 with the advance d4-d5. Here he has a majority on the left-hand side of the centre and play may involve a queenside advance. Essentially however the advanced d-pawn is the key to either type of position; White has a d5-pawn in other lines of the King's Indian but here, for better or worse, it's more likely to advance to d6.

What is Black's Strategy?

The King's Indian itself can be described as a provocative opening and in the Four Pawns White allows himself to be egged-on into advancing his centre. Black hopes that the pawns will become targets and that White will regret rushing into battle without due preparation.

The main approach is to open the e-file and bear down on the poorly supported e-pawn with ...Rf8-e8. This sometimes involves the preliminary ...Bc8-g4 and ...Nb8-d7 to first restrain the advance to e5 before concentrating efforts onto the e4-point.

Another approach is to play Benko-style with a rapid ...b7-b5, even if it sacrifices a pawn, because White, who is behind in development, will have difficulty keeping control of a widening battle front.

Tactical/Strategic/Dynamic?

This is a very tactical line with hand-to-hand fighting occurring earlier and more frequently than in other lines of the King's Indian.

Theoretical?

Because of the forcing nature of the lines, the Four Pawns is highly theoretical and the main variations can be very long and tricky. The better prepared player often wins.

Some strong players have preferred an early ...Nb8-a6 followed by ...e7-e5 approach where less detailed knowledge is required. This is the exception where knowledge of illustrative games is more important than memory work.

> **NOTE: In most openings it is more important to have a good grasp of the general themes than to memorise specific moves. However, the Four Pawns is an exception. Knowledge of general ideas is of little help if you find yourself on the wrong side of a mating attack.**

How Popular is it?

The French grandmaster Vaisser has increased its popularity and some top players such as Lautier have occasionally given it a try. Most, however, give it a miss, as for them the main lines are analysed out to equality. It's interesting for White to have the initiative but a well-prepared King's Indian player should have nothing to fear.

It's not that popular lower down either, but a few club players who like to bully their opponent or those that simply like to win by provoking an opening blunder are attracted to this type of opening, so care is certainly required to handle the black position.

Illustrative Games

Game 77
□ **Vaisser** ■ **Berthelot**
France 1992

1 d4 Nf6 2 c4 g6 3 Nc3 Bg7 4 e4 d6 5 f4 0-0 6 Nf3 c5 7 d5 e6 8 Be2 exd5 9 cxd5 Re8 10 e5

White advances immediately in the centre to obtain a passed d-pawn and good tactical play even if it means giving up a pawn or two.

10...dxe5 11 fxe5 Ng4 12 Bg5 Qb6 13 0-0 Nxe5 14 Nxe5 Bxe5 15 Bc4 Qxb2 16 d6 Rf8 17 Bxf7+ Kg7 18 Bd5 Qxc3 19 Rxf8 Kxf8 20 Qf1+ Bf5 21 Rd1 Nd7 22 g4 Kg7 23 gxf5 Qc2 24 Rd2 Qxf5 (Diagram 9)

Black has survived the attack and exchanges queens but even here the advanced d-pawn is a thorn in Black's side.

25 Qxf5 gxf5 26 Be7 Bd4+ 27 Kf1 Ne5 28 Rg2+ Ng6 29 h4 Kh8 30 Rxg6 hxg6 31 Bxb7 Rb8 32 d7 c4 33 d8Q+ Rxd8 34 Bxd8 Kg7 35 Bg5 c3 36 Ke2 1-0

Game 78
□ **Lautier** ■ **Rogers**
Yerevan 1996

1 c4 Nf6 2 Nc3 g6 3 e4 d6 4 d4 Bg7 5 f4 0-0 6 Nf3 c5 7 d5 e6 8 Be2

exd5 9 cxd5 b5

A counter on the flank that is met by the thematic e5.

10 e5 Nfd7 11 Bxb5 dxe5 12 0-0 Qb6 13 a4 exf4 14 Bxf4 a6 15 a5 Qb7 16 Bxd7 Nxd7 17 Qd2 Nf6 18 Be5 Bg4 19 Ra4 Bxf3 20 Rxf3 Qe7 21 Bxf6 Bxf6 22 d6 Qe5 (Diagram 10) 23 Re4

Exchanges have not simplified the defensive task.

23...Qg5 24 Qxg5 Bxg5 25 Re5 Bc1 26 Na4 Rfd8 27 Rxc5 Bd2 28 Rd5 Bb4 29 d7 Ra7 30 Rb3 Be7 31 Nb6 Kf8 32 Rc3 1-0

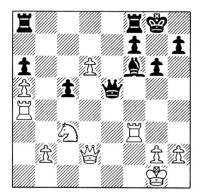

| **Diagram 9** | **Diagram 10** |
| The d-pawn remains powerful | Again the d-pawn is strong |

NOTE: In the Four Pawns even if Black succeeds in exchanging off some of White's pieces, this doesn't always solve all his problems.

Game 79
☐ **Djuric** ■ **Ilincic**
Yugoslavia 1998

1 d4 Nf6 2 c4 g6 3 Nc3 Bg7 4 e4 d6 5 f4 0-0 6 Nf3 Na6 7 Be2 e5 8 0-0 exd4 9 Nxd4 Re8 10 Bf3 Nc5

If the central pawns are not threatening to go forwards they are just targets to be hit.

11 Re1 Bg4 12 Nc2 Bxf3 13 Qxf3 c6 14 Rb1

White is becoming tangled up and cannot develop normally.

14...Qe7 15 e5 dxe5 16 Rxe5 Qd6 (Diagram 11)

The exchange of White's e-pawn has not helped much as he still has holes that are difficult to cover. He thus sacrifices a pawn to free his game but he never obtains enough compensation.

17 Be3 Rxe5 18 fxe5 Qxe5 19 Bd4 Qe7 20 Re1 Ne6 21 Bf2 Qc7 22

h3 Nd7 23 Rd1 Ne5 24 Qe2 Rd8 25 Rxd8+ Qxd8 26 Bxa7 Nd3 27
Ne3 Ndf4 28 Qf2 Qa5 29 Bb8 Nd3 30 Qd2 Nxb2 31 Qxb2 Bxc3 32
Qe2 Be5 33 Bxe5 Qxe5 34 Qd2 Qd4 35 Qe1 f5 36 Kh1 Kf7 37 Qc1
Nf4 38 c5 Ne2 39 Qc4+ Qxc4 40 Nxc4 Ng3+ 41 Kh2 Ne4 42 g4
fxg4 43 hxg4 Ke6 44 Kg2 Nxc5 45 Kf3 Kd5 46 Nb6+ Kd4 47 a4
Ne6 48 Nd7 c5 49 Nf6 c4 50 Ke2 c3 51 Kd1 Kd3 52 Nd7 c2+ 53
Kc1 Nd4 54 Nc5+ Kc4 55 Ne4 h5 56 gxh5 gxh5 57 a5 h4 0-1

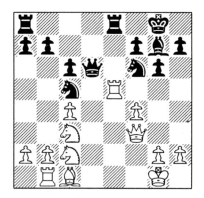

Diagram 11
White's centre has disintegrated

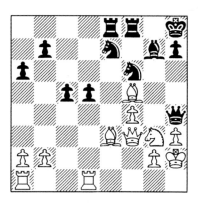

Diagram 12
The open lines favour Black

Game 80
□ **Monin** ■ **Shchekachev**
St Petersburg 1994

**1 d4 g6 2 c4 Nf6 3 Nc3 Bg7 4 e4 d6 5 f4 0-0 6 Nf3 c5 7 d5 e6 8 Be2
exd5 9 cxd5 Bg4 10 0-0 Nbd7 11 h3 Bxf3 12 Bxf3 Rb8 13 Re1 Ne8
14 Bg4 f5**

Reducing the potential of White's centre and freeing the black game.

**15 exf5 gxf5 16 Be2 a6 17 Bd3 Nc7 18 Qc2 Qf6 19 Ne2 Rbe8 20
Rd1 Qh4 21 Kh2 Nf6**

Black's forces are more harmoniously deployed than White's and thus
he takes the initiative.

22 Bxf5 Ncxd5 23 Ng3 Kh8 24 Qf2 Ne7 25 Qf3 d5 26 Be3 (Diagram 12)

Only now does White find the moment to develop this piece, but this
unfortunately allows a neat combination.

**26...Qxg3+ 27 Qxg3 Nxf5 28 Qg5 Nxe3 29 Re1 Ne4 30 Qh5 d4 31
Rac1 c4 32 Qf3 Rxf4 33 Rxe3 Rxf3 0-1**

Chapter Eight

The Indian Defences

- The Nimzo-Indian with 4 e3
- The Nimzo-Indian with 4 Qc2
- The Nimzo-Indian with 4 a3 or 4 f3
- The Queen's Indian Defence
- The Bogo-Indian Defence

In this chapter we will be looking at the so-called Indian defences which revolve around the move ...e7-e6 for Black (note that the King's Indian Defence features the move ...g7-g6). The most popular of these is the Nimzo-Indian Defence (1 d4 Nf6 2 c4 e6 3 Nc3 Bb4), which is a very popular opening, especially at the higher levels, as it is very rich strategically.

The Nimzo gives rise to positions which encompass many of the major strategic battles which are played out in chess. For example it is easily possible for any of the following themes to arise.

1) Isolated queen's pawn: White has the structural weakness of an isolated queen's pawn, but has active piece play to balance this.

2) The bishop pair: White often obtains the bishop pair in the Nimzo but in compensation Black usually has a solid position or a slight lead in development.

3) Doubled pawns: White can easily end up with doubled c-pawns which will usually make endgames unattractive for him. However, he will often have an initiative and a big centre and will hope to turn this into a winning attack long before the endgame is reached.

Therefore, even if you do not wish to feature the Nimzo-Indian Defence in your repertoire, an understanding of some of the key positions in this opening will invariably be useful for your chess education.

 TIP: The Nimzo-Indian Defence is always worthy of study even if you do not intend to play it.

This chapter also features the Queen's Indian Defence (1 d4 Nf6 2 c4 e6 3 Nf3 b6) and the Bogo-Indian Defence (1 d4 Nf6 2 c4 e6 3 Nf3 Bb4+). Both these openings are close relations of the Nimzo-Indian Defence and share many of the same themes.

Nimzo-Indian with 4 e3

1 d4 Nf6 2 c4 e6 3 Nc3 Bb4 4 e3

In the Nimzo-Indian Defence (1 d4 Nf6 2 c4 e6 3 Nc3 Bb4), White's attempt to advance with e2-e4 is restrained by the pin against his knight. The 4 e3 variation gives up for the moment any ideas of an early e2-e4. White instead intends to develop his kingside and castle before reviewing the possibility of playing for any further central pawn advances.

The queen's bishop is temporarily hemmed in by 4 e3 and this piece often takes time to get into play. Black then has some time to decide how to continue developing while at the same time building his own stake in the centre.

Black can play with ...c7-c5, or ...d7-d5 or even both, in order to counteract the white central pawns. The queen's bishop is frequently fianchettoed, so ...b7-b6 is often high on Black's list of possibilities.

Play in the opening is often dominated by the resolution of the characteristic pin on White's queen's knight. At some point the bishop will make a decision as to what to do, either voluntarily, or after being attacked by a2-a3. If Black retreats then the pressure is off the white centre, if Black captures on c3 then White obtains the bishop pair. This involves doubled pawns if White typically recaptures with the b-pawn or a loss of time if White organises the recapture with a piece.

What is White's Strategy?

White will rapidly castle kingside and then prepare to resolve problems in the centre. By then his central pawn front d4 and c4 will have been challenged by Black, and White will need to react accordingly.

Although a wide variety of pawn structures are possible, White's late opening/early middlegame considerations will revolve around the dark-squared bishops: the question of how to cope with the bishop on b4 eyeing the knight on c3, followed by a plan to find a route and a role for the White queen's bishop.

If the Nimzo-bishop retreats then White may be able to play for e4 or even d5 to open a diagonal for his problem bishop. If Black captures on c4 and doubles the pawns then White may first need to overprotect his weakened structure before looking to promote his bishop pair.

What is Black's Strategy?

This can be summarised as restraint of the White pawns and then, after giving up the Nimzo-bishop, limiting the power of White's bishops. To these ends, combined piece and pawn pressure is required to bear down on White's centre. Black typically yields the bishop pair in order to obtain comfortable development, a stake in the centre and pressure against the c4 or d4 points.

If ...Bb4xc3 is met by b2xc3 then the white c4-point is denied pawn support and Black is sometimes able to play a plan with ...b7-b6, ...Bc8-a6 and ...Nc6-a5. The Nimzo-Indian Defence is a rich opening and Black has a wide choice of plans. For example he can play an early ...c7-c5 and ...d7-d5, exchange these off and leave White with easy development but an isolated d-pawn. Alternatively, he can play a quick ...c7-c5, ...Bb4xc3, ...d7-d6 and ...e6-e5, (known as the Hübner variation) where he gladly gives up his dark-squared bishop and plays for a rock-solid centre which White's bishops may have difficulty in breaching.

Tactical/Strategic/Dynamic?

The variation is a strategic struggle between lovers of the bishop pair and centre (White) and those who like to have comfortable development and a good pawn structure (Black).

The interesting but difficult question of which piece is superior (knight or bishop?) frequently needs to be asked throughout the game. A good choice for strategic players looking for a complex but not overly tactical struggle.

TIP: The Nimzo-Indian Defence is an ideal battleground if your strengths are strategic rather than tactical.

Theoretical?

Many of the lines have been well examined, but in general not much theoretical knowledge is required. One should be aware of the main strategic ideas, gleaned from instructive examples, but plans are more important here than memorising variations.

How Popular is it?

Once the most popular line due to players such as Botvinnik and Korchnoi, it has lost it's shine in recent years. An occasional choice at the top level, but Black has a wide choice of reasonable lines. The annoying Hübner variation has frustrated many white players to move away from 4 e3. Club players tend to prefer a more lively struggle early on.

Illustrative Games

Game 81
□ **Botvinnik** ■ **Ragozin**
Moscow 1947

1 d4 Nf6 2 c4 e6 3 Nc3 Bb4 4 e3 Qe7 5 Nge2 b6 6 a3 Bxc3+ 7 Nxc3 Bb7 8 d5

White obtains the bishop pair and expands his central grip. Black cannot use his lead in development.

8...d6 9 Be2 Nbd7 10 0-0 0-0 11 e4 exd5 12 exd5 (Diagram 1)

In symmetrical positions knights can be the equal of bishops but here they lack any outposts. Black is unable to find any counterplay.

12...Rfe8 13 Be3 a6 14 Qc2 Ne5 15 Rae1 Bc8 16 Bd4 Bd7 17 f4 Ng6 18 g4

White has sufficient control to be able push forward with his kingside pawns. The knights have nowhere to run and one is soon lost.

18...Qd8 19 g5 Ng4 20 Qd2 h6 21 f5 N6e5 22 h3 Nf6 23 gxf6 Qxf6 24 Qf4 Re7 25 Kh1 c5 26 Bg1 g6 27 fxg6 Qxf4 28 Rxf4 fxg6 29 Rf6 Bf5 30 Rxd6 Nxc4 31 Re6 Rxe6 32 dxe6 Bxe6 33 Bf3 1-0

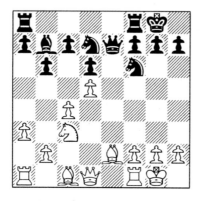
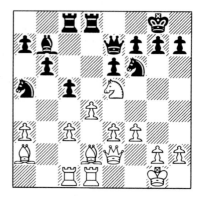

Diagram 1	**Diagram 2**
White's bishops are very strong	White's position has great potential

Game 82
☐ **Gulko** ■ **Gruenfeld**
Philadelphia 1991

1 d4 Nf6 2 c4 e6 3 Nc3 Bb4 4 e3 0-0 5 Bd3 c5 6 Nf3 d5 7 0-0 Nc6 8 a3 Bxc3 9 bxc3 dxc4 10 Bxc4 Qc7

The main line. Black has pressure against the centre and it's difficult for White to free his dark-squared bishop as e3-e4 will require considerable preparation.

11 Ba2 Rd8 12 Qc2 Na5 13 Qe2 Nd5 14 Bd2 b6 15 Rac1 Bb7 16 Ne5 Nf6 17 f3

White threatens to achieve his positional aim; e3-e4.

17...Qe7 18 Rfd1 Rac8 (Diagram 2) 19 Be1

Finally unravelling with Be1-h4 or e3-e4 in mind. Black decides that waiting is no longer viable but releasing the tension only helps White.

19...cxd4 20 exd4 Nd5 21 c4 Nf4 22 Qe3 Nh5 23 Bb4 Qe8 24 Bxa5

Cashing in: Ceding the dark-squared bishop to cripple Black's pawns.

24...bxa5 25 Rb1 Rc7 26 Qd2 a4 27 Qa5 Re7 28 Nxf7 Rxf7 29 Qxh5 g6 30 Qe5 Qe7 31 c5 Bc8 32 Rb8 Rf5 33 Bxe6+ 1-0

 WARNING: The latent strength of White's bishop pair should not be underestimated.

Game 83
□ **Balashov** ■ **Vaganian**
Odessa 1989

1 d4 Nf6 2 c4 e6 3 Nc3 Bb4 4 e3 c5 5 Bd3 Nc6 6 Nf3 Bxc3+ 7 bxc3 d6 8 0-0 e5

The Hübner variation. Black builds a defensive wall of pawns on the dark squares. As White's structure is compromised it's hard for him to challenge it's solidity.

9 Nd2 0-0 10 d5 Ne7 11 e4 h6 12 Re1 Nh7 13 Nf1 f5 14 exf5 Bxf5

The way to negate the bishop pair is to exchange a pair of bishops.

15 Ng3 Bxd3 16 Qxd3 Qd7 17 a4 Rf7 18 a5 Raf8 (Diagram 3)

Black has full deployment and no easy targets for White's army.

19 f3 Nf5 20 Nxf5 Rxf5 21 Rb1 R8f7 22 Rb2 Qd8

White's inferior pawn structure starts to become a problem. The following exchanges only help Black who is generally better in the ending when White has such damaged pawns.

23 Rxb7 Rxf3 24 gxf3 Rxb7 25 f4 Qh4 26 Qg3 Qxg3+ 27 hxg3 e4 28 f5 Rb1 29 Kf1 Kf7 30 g4 Nf6 31 Bf4 Rxe1+ 32 Kxe1 Nxg4 33 Bxd6 a6 34 Bxc5 Ne5 35 Bd4 Nxc4 36 Kf2 g6 37 fxg6+ Kxg6 38 Bb6 Kf6 39 Bc7 h5 40 Kg3 Kf5 41 Kf2 h4 0-1

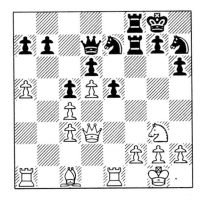

Diagram 3
White has horrible pawn weaknesses

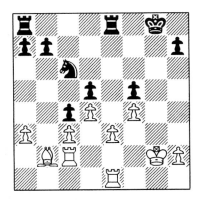

Diagram 4
White's bishop is terrible

Game 84
□ **Lautier** ■ **Kramnik**
Tilburg 1997

1 d4 Nf6 2 c4 e6 3 Nc3 Bb4 4 e3 0-0 5 Bd3 c5 6 Nf3 d5 7 0-0 Nc6 8

a3 Bxc3 9 bxc3 Qc7 10 cxd5 exd5 11 Nh4

White hopes to free his bishop with an eventual e4 or c4. Meanwhile the knight eyes f5.

11...Qa5 12 Bb2 Re8 13 Re1 c4

Thwarting any hopes of opening the long diagonal.

14 Bc2 Ne4 15 Rc1 Qd8 16 g3 g5

White is in full retreat and the bishop on b2 is dead wood.

17 Ng2 g4 18 f3 Ng5 19 fxg4 Nh3+ 20 Kf1 Qg5 21 Nf4 Bxg4 22 Qd2 Bf5 23 Qg2 Nxf4 24 gxf4 Qxg2+ 25 Kxg2 Bxc2 26 Rxc2 f5 (Diagram 4)

The ending is miserable for White who has a bishop badly blocked in by his own pawns.

27 Kf3 Kf7 28 a4 Rg8 29 Ba3 Ke6 30 Rb1 b6 31 Bb4 Rab8 32 Rcb2 Rb7 33 Rg2 Rxg2 34 Kxg2 Rg7+ 35 Kf3 Rg8 36 Ra1 h5 37 Rb1 h4 38 a5 bxa5 39 Bc5 Rg7

Kramnik carefully avoids counterplay and takes his time; the white bishop is going nowhere.

40 Ba3 h3 41 Rb5 a4 42 Rc5 Nb8 43 Ra5 a6 44 Rxa4 Rg2 45 Bb4 Rxh2 46 Kg3 Re2 47 Kxh3 Rxe3+ 48 Kg2 Nc6 49 Rxa6 Kd7 50 Kf2 Rd3 51 Bc5 Rxc3 52 Rb6 Rb3 53 Ra6 Rd3 0-1

NOTE: The white dark-squared bishop can be a problem piece for White deep into the endgame.

Nimzo-Indian: The Classical 4 Qc2

1 d4 Nf6 2 c4 e6 3 Nc3 Bb4 4 Qc2

With 4 Qc2 White prepares to recapture on c3 with his queen, avoiding the risk of doubled pawns, that would otherwise arise in the case of ...Bb4xc3. He also leaves the c1-h6 diagonal open, enabling a rapid deployment of the queen's bishop. So White hopes to avoid the two main strategic problems associated with the 4 e3 variation and will try to complete his development whilst keeping his central superiority intact.

Lavishing all this care and attention on the queenside is all well and good but the downside is that White's king tends to be left in the centre longer than Black's. White frequently has the bishop pair and no structural weaknesses, but in return Black will have well placed knights, a lead in development and counterchances against the centre.

What is White's Strategy?

By not giving any strategic targets or having any locked-in pieces White hopes to simply get his pieces out whilst holding onto a bigger share of the centre. If he can get through the opening without incurring any structural weaknesses he will probably stand well.

White will often play some of the following typical themes; a2-a3 and Qc2xc3 getting hold of the bishops, Bc1-g5 pinning down the Black forces and e2-e4 supported by f2-f3 building the centre. Castling may be delayed but by then White hopes that the centre is under his control.

What is Black's Strategy?

Arguably, 4 Qc2 can be considered as a loss of time and Black can react with an immediate counterattack against the centre with 4...c5, 4...d5 or even 4...Nc6. Black is hoping that White will have to give away some of his central stake in order to get his pieces out and catch up with his development. The sharpest is move is 4...c5 as White is not well placed to maintain the tension. Then after 5 dxc5 Black will choose to soon recapture with either ...Bb4xc5 or ...Nb8-a6xc5 and continue to pressurise the white centre mainly with piece play.

The most popular approach is to rapidly develop with 4...0-0 and follow up with ...b7-b6 and ...Bc8-b7 first, and only then decide how best to hit back, usually with the appropriate timing of ...d7-d5 and ...c7-c5.

 WARNING: When facing 4 Qc2 in the Nimzo-Indian Defence, Black must do something active early on, or he will simply be worse.

Tactical/Strategic/Dynamic?

Although one or two lines can become sharp, the variation has a reputation for being strategic. The struggle is often between Black's lead in development and White's bishop pair and centre. Players of both colours tend to be positional inclined.

Theoretical?

One or two of the lines have been extensively analysed, but most of the time general considerations and logical plans rule the day.

How Popular is it?

Over the last decade or so, it has become the most popular white line against the Nimzo-Indian. It has been very trendy amongst international players who are interested in a strategic struggle without the risk of being unpleasantly surprised by home analysis. Kasparov has often played White while Kramnik, Karpov and many other strong d4-players have included it in their repertoire with either colour.

It is less popular amongst club players who tend to prefer more direct openings.

Illustrative Games

Game 85
□ **Kasparov** ■ **Timman**
Linares 1993

1 d4 Nf6 2 c4 e6 3 Nc3 Bb4 4 Qc2 0-0 5 a3 Bxc3+ 6 Qxc3 b6 7 Bg5

White obtains the bishop pair without allowing weak pawns.

7...Bb7 8 f3 d5 9 e3 Nbd7 10 cxd5 exd5 11 Bd3 Re8 12 Ne2 h6 13 Bh4 c5 14 0-0 Rc8 15 Qd2 Qe7 16 Bf2

At first White has to regroup but gradually he takes back the initiative.

16...Bc6 17 Nc3 Nf8 18 Rfe1 Ne6 19 Bh4 Ng5 20 Bf5 Bd7 21 Bc2 Bc6 22 Rad1 Qe6 23 Qf2 Rcd8 24 h3 Ngh7 25 dxc5 bxc5 (Diagram 5) 26 e4

The line opening that results enhances the power of the bishops and Black soon drops a pawn.

26...dxe4 27 Rxd8 Rxd8 28 Qxc5 Ng5 29 Bxg5 hxg5 30 Qxg5 Qc4 31 fxe4 Qd4+ 32 Qe3 Qxe3+ 33 Rxe3 Rd2 34 Re2 Rxe2 35 Nxe2 Nxe4 36 Bxe4 Bxe4 37 Kf2 Kf8 38 g3 Ke7 39 Ke3 Bc6 40 h4 Bd7 41 Kf4 Kd6 42 g4 f6 43 h5 Ke7 44 Nd4 Kf7 45 b4 Ba4 46 Nf5 g6 47 Nd6+ Kg7 48 Nc8 a6 49 Nd6 Bd1 50 Ne8+ Kf7 51 Nxf6 Kxf6 52 g5+ Kf7 53 h6 1-0

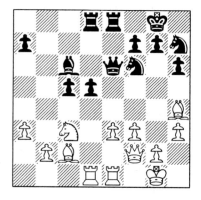

Diagram 5
White opens lines for the bishops

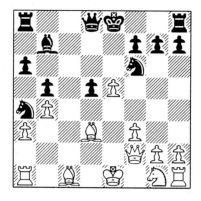

Diagram 6
Black is weak on the dark squares

Game 86
☐ **Bacrot** ■ **Degraeve**
France 1998

1 d4 Nf6 2 c4 e6 3 Nc3 Bb4 4 Qc2 c5 5 dxc5 Na6 6 a3 Bxc3+ 7 Qxc3 Nxc5 8 f3

White restricts the knights and prepares to play b2-b4 and e2-e4 to take control of the centre. Black hopes to use his lead in development to stop White's plans.

8...d5 9 cxd5 b6 10 b4 Na4 11 Qc2 b5 12 e4 a6 13 Bd3 Bb7 14 Qf2 exd5 15 e5 (Diagram 6)

Black's temporary initiative is at an end and White prepares to get his bishops working. White aims for dark square domination.

15...Qe7 16 Qd4 Nd7 17 f4 f6 18 Nf3 0-0 19 0-0 Rae8 20 Re1 fxe5 21 fxe5 Rxf3

Otherwise White's attack, based on e5-e6 and threats against the Black king, is too strong.

22 gxf3 Nxe5 23 Kh1 Bc6 24 Bf4 Nxf3 25 Bxh7+ Kh8 26 Rxe7 Nxd4 27 Rxe8+ Bxe8 28 Bd3 Nb2 29 Be5 Nxd3 30 Bxd4 Bg6 31 Rf1 Kh7 32 h4 Kh6 33 Kg2 1-0

TIP: If you have the bishop pair, look for ways to use pawn moves to prise open the position.

Game 87
☐ **Hauchard** ■ **Shirov**
Santiago 1990

1 d4 Nf6 2 c4 e6 3 Nc3 Bb4 4 Qc2 0-0 5 a3 Bxc3+ 6 Qxc3 b6 7 Bg5 Bb7 8 Nh3 h6 9 Bh4 c5 10 dxc5 bxc5 11 f3 Nc6 12 Bf2 d5

A vigorous reply. White's lag in development becomes a problem if Black wrests the initiative.

13 Bxc5 d4 14 Qd2 Re8 15 e4 e5 16 Nf2 Qc7 17 b4 Nd8 18 Nd3 Ne6 19 Be2 Bxe4

With White's king still in the centre, Black sacrifices a piece to get a deadly pawn roller in motion.

20 fxe4 Nxe4 21 Qc2 N4xc5 22 Nxc5 Nxc5 23 bxc5 e4 24 0-0 Rad8 25 Rad1 Qxc5 26 Kh1 d3 27 Bxd3 exd3 (Diagram 7) 28 Qc3

28 Rxd3 loses to the beautiful 28...Qf5.

28...Re3 29 h3 Qc6 30 Kg1 Re2 31 Rf3 Rc2 32 Qa5 Rd6 33 Qf5 Rg6 34 g4 Rf6 35 Qxd3 Qxf3 36 Qxc2 Qg3+ 37 Qg2 Qe3+ 38 Kh1 Rf2 0-1

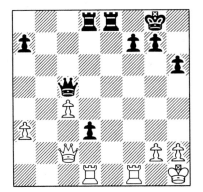

Diagram 7

A clever tactic from Black

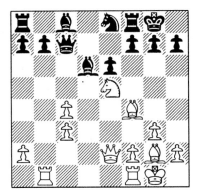

Diagram 8

White has weak pawns

Game 88
□ **Hertneck** ■ **Karpov**
Baden 1992

1 d4 Nf6 2 c4 e6 3 Nc3 Bb4 4 Qc2 0-0 5 Nf3 c5 6 dxc5 Na6 7 g3 Nxc5 8 Bg2 Nce4

White's development is not dangerous and Black has already obtained the positional concession of doubled pawns.

9 0-0 Nxc3 10 bxc3 Be7 11 e4 d6 12 e5 dxe5 13 Nxe5 Qc7 14 Qe2 Bd6 15 Bf4 Ne8 16 Rab1 (Diagram 8) 16...f6

White's advanced knight is repulsed and one of the c-pawns already falls.

17 Nd3 Qxc4 18 Bxd6 Nxd6 19 Rb4 Qc7 20 Nf4 Re8 21 Rd1 a5 22 Rbd4 Ra6 23 Qh5 Rf8 24 g4

White tries to obtain some compensation but Black is too solid.

24...a4 25 c4 Nf7 26 h4 Ra5 27 g5 Rf5 28 Nh3 g6 29 Qe2 fxg5 30 h5 Kg7 31 Be4 Rf6 32 Qg4 gxh5 33 Qxh5 Rh6 34 Qg4 Rh4 35 Qg2 e5 36 R4d3 g4 37 f4 exf4 38 Rd5 Qb6+ 39 c5 Qf6 0-1

Nimzo-Indian with 4 a3 or 4 f3

1 d4 Nf6 2 c4 e6 3 Nc3 Bb4 4 a3/f3

In this line White aims to get in e2-e4 quickly. He does this either with the preparatory f2-f3 or by hitting the bishop as early as possible in order to force the capture on c3 and then to set about getting in e2-e4. The two lines are closely related and the mentality is identical: build the centre and create attacking chances as soon as possible.

Doubled c-pawns are a typical burden (after 4 a3) that White has to bear. Although they are clearly a long-term problem they do help White to build an imposing central pawn mass.

These radical approaches both force Black to react quickly to try to destabilise the white centre before it becomes too well supported. Although Black can try and counter the centre with piece play alone the standard idea is to counter immediately with his own pawns. Play can become tense, particularly as White's king takes time to get safe.

What is White's Strategy?

If White can maintain a pawn on e4, catch up in development and castle then he can count on good chances in the middlegame. A sturdy centre often splits an opponent's forces in two and makes the defence against a kingside attack problematic. So White invests a tempo with a2-a3 and takes positional risks with his structure because he is playing for high stakes.

Black generally reacts quickly with ...c7-c5 and ...d7-d5 to avoid White's ideal set-up, but then after c4xd5 White undoubles the c-pawns. White sometimes tries a more restrained approach with e2-e3 instead of e2-e4, when play can become similar to the 4 e3 variation.

4 f3 tries to build the centre without wasting time on a3, but allowing Black to retain the bishop can prove dangerous.

What is Black's Strategy?

After 4 a3, a quick ...c7-c5 and ...d7-d5 is the typical response. Black generally prefers to meet c4xd5 with ...Nf6xd5, keeping pressure on the White centre and hoping to profit from his lead in development. White's position can look rather clumsy but he has the bishop pair and the position is likely to open up further. Black should keep harassing the white central position with ideas such as ...Qd8-a5 or ...c5xd4 and ...Nb8-c6 and, in the case that White tries to hold the fort with Qd1-d3, with ...b7-b6 and ...Bc8-a6.

Another idea is allow White to build his centre but aim for counterplay by taking direct action against the c4-weakness with ...b7-b6, ...Bc8-a6 and ...Nc6-a5. 4 f3 should be similarly met with either the immediate ...d7-d5 or ...c7-c5, not allowing White an easy time in his construction project.

Tactical/Strategic/Dynamic?

Really a mixture of all three. When one player tries a controversial strategic idea it forces an equally critical response. Play then can then explode into sharp tactical variations bearing little resemblance to the original strategy! White's bishop pair, but a lag in development, leads to a double-edged struggle.

Theoretical?

Although either player may aim to play the variation in a strategic manner, the game can quickly turn sharp and some lines are quite forcing. So some theoretical knowledge is required.

How Popular is it?

Although Shirov popularised 4 f3 in his youth (4 a3 often transposes), neither of these lines are popular at grandmaster level nowadays. They may appeal as an occasional weapon for the tactician but as Black's resources are considered adequate, few are willing to try such risky variations these days. However, at club level these lines can prove much more dangerous and are consequently seen more often.

Illustrative Games

Game 89
□ **Shirov** ■ **Chandler**
Hastings 1991/92

1 d4 Nf6 2 c4 e6 3 Nc3 Bb4 4 f3 d5 5 a3 Bxc3+ 6 bxc3 c5 7 cxd5 Nxd5 8 Qd3 0-0 9 e4 Ne7 10 f4

A risky strategy of building the centre when behind in development.

10...b6 11 Qe3 Ba6 12 Bxa6 Nxa6 13 Nf3 cxd4 14 cxd4 Nc7 15 a4 (Diagram 9) 15...f5

Black now obtains use of the d5-square.

16 Ba3 fxe4 17 Qxe4 Qd5 18 Qc2 Qa5+ 19 Qd2 Qxa4 20 0-0 Qe8

Black has won a pawn but White obtains some practical chances.

21 Rae1 h6 22 d5 Nexd5 23 Bxf8 Qxf8 24 Nd4 Qd6 25 Rc1 Rf8 26 Nc6 a5 27 Ne5 Rd8 28 Rc6 Qb4 29 Qe1 Qd4+ 30 Kh1 Nxf4 31 Nf3 Qd3 32 Rxc7 Ne2 33 Qa1 1-0

TIP: These lines are wonderful for the tactically inclined player as, even when it goes wrong for White, there are usually numerous tactical possibilities to keep the position complex.

Game 90
□ **Speelman** ■ **Karpov**
Linares 1991

1 d4 Nf6 2 c4 e6 3 Nc3 Bb4 4 e3 0-0 5 Bd3 d5 6 a3 Bxc3+ 7 bxc3 dxc4 8 Bxc4 c5 9 Ne2 Nc6 10 0-0 e5

Black's easy development and pressure on the white centre compensate for the potential of the bishop pair.

11 Rb1 Qc7 12 Ba2 Rd8 13 Qc2 b6 14 Ng3 exd4 15 cxd4 cxd4 16 exd4 Be6 17 Bxe6 fxe6 18 Bg5

The bishop is free but the d-pawn is very weak.

18...Rac8 19 Bxf6 gxf6 20 Rbc1 Rxd4 21 Rfe1 Qf7 (Diagram 10) 22 Qc3

Black has an extra pawn but his pieces are tangled and his kingside is draughty.

22...Rdd8 23 Ne4 e5 24 Qg3+ Kh8 25 Qh4 Nd4 26 Rxc8 Rxc8 27 Nxf6 Qg6 28 Ng4 Ne2+ 29 Kh1 Nf4 30 h3 Re8 31 Rd1 Qg7 32 Rd8 Rg8 33 Rxg8+ Qxg8 34 Qf6+ Qg7 35 Qd8+ Qg8 36 Qe7 Ng6 37 Qxa7 Qe6 38 Qb8+ Kg7 39 Qc7+ Kh8 40 Nh6 Qf6 41 Qc8+ Kg7 42 Nf5+ Kf7 43 Qd7+ Kf8 44 g3 h5 45 h4 Kg8 46 Kg2 Nf8 47 Qd5+ Kh7 48 Qb7+ Kg8 49 Ne7+ Kh8 50 Nd5 Qd6 51 Qf7 Ng6 52 Nf6 1-0

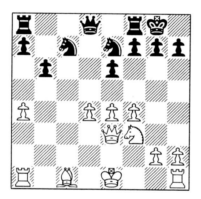

Diagram 9
Can Black undermine White's centre?

Diagram 10
Black's kingside is vulnerable

Game 91
☐ **Yusupov** ■ **Karpov**
Linares 1993

---

1 d4 Nf6 2 c4 e6 3 Nc3 Bb4 4 e3 c5 5 Bd3 Nc6 6 a3 Bxc3+ 7 bxc3 0-0 8 Ne2 b6 9 e4 Ne8 10 0-0 Ba6 11 f4 f5 12 Ng3 g6 (Diagram 11)

Black makes his position as solid as possible, giving White's bishops and central pawns limited scope.

13 Be3 cxd4 14 cxd4 d5

Countering in the centre and forcing the exchange of a pair of bishops.

15 cxd5 Bxd3 16 Qxd3 fxe4 17 Qxe4 Qxd5 18 Qxd5 exd5 19 Rac1 Rc8 20 f5 Nd6 21 fxg6 hxg6

White has a poor bishop and worse pawns.

22 Rxf8+ Kxf8 23 h4 Nc4 24 Bg5 Nxd4 25 h5 gxh5

White gives up a pawn to activate his forces but Karpov is able to squeeze out a win.

26 Rf1+ Ke8 27 Nxh5 Nxa3 28 Ng7+ Kd7 29 Rf7+ Kc6 30 Rxa7 Nac2 31 Bf6 b5 32 g4 b4 33 Ra2 b3 34 Rb2 Kc5 35 Nf5 Rg8 36 Nxd4 Rxg4+ 37 Kf2 Nxd4 38 Bxd4+ Kxd4 39 Rxb3 Re4 40 Ra3 Re8 0-1

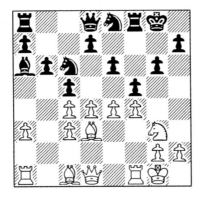

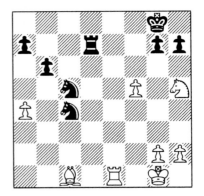

Diagram 11

Black cramps the white bishops

Diagram 12

Black has a good endgame

TIP: Hemming in the white pawns on c4 and f4 (by placing pawns on c5 and f5) can severely limit the scope of his bishops.

Game 92
□ **Piket** ■ **Salov**
Dortmund 1992

1 d4 Nf6 2 c4 e6 3 Nc3 Bb4 4 a3 Bxc3+ 5 bxc3 c5 6 e3 Nc6 7 Bd3 0-0 8 Ne2 b6 9 e4 Ne8

Moving out of harm's way and later coming to d6 to further pressurise the c4-pawn.

10 0-0 Ba6 11 f4 f5 12 Ng3 Nd6 13 Re1 Bxc4 14 Bxc4 Nxc4 15 exf5 cxd4 16 Qd3 N6a5 17 cxd4 Qf6

White has the worse structure and little joy for his bishop.

18 fxe6 dxe6 19 Ra2 Rad8 20 Rae2 Qxd4+ 21 Qxd4 Rxd4 22

Rxe6 Rd7 23 f5 Nb3 24 a4 Nc5 25 Re7 Rf7 26 Re8+ Rf8 27 R8e7 Rfd8 28 Nh5 Rxe7 29 Rxe7 Rd7 30 Re1 (Diagram 12) 30...Kf7

Black consolidates and the a4-weakness must now finally fall.

31 Bg5 Nxa4 32 f6 g6 33 Ng7 Nc5 34 h4 Nd6 35 h5 Nde4 36 hxg6+ hxg6 37 Be3 Nxf6 38 Bxc5 Kxg7 39 Ba3 Ng4 40 Bb2+ Kf7 41 Bc3 Rd3 42 Rc1 Ne3 43 Be1 Ke6 44 Kf2 Ng4+ 45 Ke2 Re3+ 46 Kd2 Ra3 47 Rc6+ Kf5 48 Ke2 Ra2+ 49 Bd2 Ne5 50 Rc8 b5 51 Rc5 Ke4 52 Kd1 Nc4 53 Bc1 a6 54 Rg5 Ne5 55 g3 Rh2 0-1

The Queen's Indian Defence

1 d4 Nf6 2 c4 e6 3 Nf3 b6

After 3 Nf3 Black often prepares the development of his queen's bishop with 3...b6. The king's bishop is kept at home for the moment choosing to come to b4, d6 or e7 depending on circumstances. Black also retains the flexibility to hit back with either ...c7-c5 or ...d7-d5 and sometimes both. From b7, the queen's bishop bears down on the key e4-square. So Black aims to counter in the centre without overly-committing himself too early.

Following 3...b6 White has a variety of ideas, 4 Nc3 Bb4 leads to play akin to the Nimzo, 4 e3 intending Bd3 and 0-0 aims for a restrained quiet game, but the most popular are 4 a3 and 4 g3.

By playing 4 a3 White really shows that he wants to avoid the Nimzo-Indian pin with ...Bb4, so much so that he is willing to spend a tempo to get his knight to c3 without it being harassed. This loss of time is perhaps justified by the slow 3...b6 which doesn't immediately threaten the white central pawns.

The fianchetto line with 4 g3 hopes to challenge any of Black's intentions along the diagonal, such as occupying e4 with a knight. A bishop on g2 has indirect influence on the e4-square and White can sometimes expand in the centre due to a tactical point or after the exchange of light-squared bishops.

What is White's Strategy?

White would like to achieve a broad pawn centre without enduring any of the risks associated with a Nimzo-Indian. In most lines this involves completing the kingside development first and only then getting down to thinking about the e4-square where Black has his greatest central influence.

After 4 e3 the bishop is developed to d3 and, once castling has been achieved, Nb1-c3 can be played without any pin. In order to then stop a white e3-e4 advance Black will generally play ...d7-d5, when White's best is to just keep the tension with b2-b3 and Bc1-b2, aiming to complete development and see what turns up.

The fianchetto with 4 g3 again leads to kingside development preceding aims for e2-e4. Once castling is achieved White plays moves such as Nb1-c3, Qd1-c2 or Rf1-e1 with e2-e4 in mind.

After 4 a3 Bb7 5 Nc3 Black reacts with 5...d5 and after the capture has to choose between 5...exd5, bolstering the centre but blocking the bishop behind a pawn, or 5...Nxd5 keeping the long diagonal open but lacking the same central control. In either case White forces a decision before committing his king's bishop.

What is Black's Strategy?

The queen's bishop, Black's problem piece in many queen's pawn openings, is found an immediate role. Either it comes to b7 observing the e4-square, or to a6 hitting the c-pawn and thus gaining a tempo to enable rapid development elsewhere.

Control of e4 is a temporary strategic gain and Black will soon need to follow-up with ...d7-d5 or ...Nf6-e4 to frustrate White's efforts to play his own pawn to e4. Once White is denied his primary aim Black can set about completing his development, especially his queen's knight which needs to find a role where it doesn't hinder the light-squared bishop's role.

Tactical/Strategic/Dynamic?

Although essentially strategic, the struggle is quite complex and gives rise to rich and varied play. Black can generally obtain a solid game, but the Queen's Indian Defence lacks the double-edged nature of the Nimzo as there is no imbalance in material or structure. For tacticians it is a little dull as it's virtually a non-contact opening.

Theoretical?

Many of the lines have been well analysed but as there are rather few tactical points the opening requires little detailed knowledge. Black players need to prepare a sensible system of development against each of the White tries, in order to take on the opening with any confidence. A good example of an opening requiring 'understanding' of what's going on rather than memorisation.

How Popular is it?

Popular at all levels, largely because it's solid enough to avoid any major surprises. Nimzo players need to have an opening choice ready to meet 3 Nf3 and this is the favourite choice, especially at higher levels.

Illustrative Games

Game 93
□ **Kasparov** ■ **Portisch**
Niksic 1983

1 d4 Nf6 2 c4 e6 3 Nf3 b6 4 Nc3 Bb7 5 a3

White is ready for d4-d5 gaining territory. Black must immediately react in the centre.

5...d5 6 cxd5 Nxd5

6...exd5 7 g3 blocks in the light-squared bishop. If Black follows up with ...c5 then after d4xc5 White will create play against Black's exposed central pawns.

7 e3 Nxc3 8 bxc3 Be7 9 Bb5+ c6 10 Bd3 c5 11 0-0 Nc6 12 Bb2 Rc8 13 Qe2 0-0 (Diagram 13) 14 Rad1

Now that he is ready, White will expand in the centre with e4 or c4 to increase the range of his bishop battery.

14...Qc7 15 c4 cxd4 16 exd4 Na5 17 d5

The white centre is under attack but, more importantly, Black's king is lacking in defensive cover.

17...exd5 18 cxd5 Bxd5 19 Bxh7+ Kxh7 20 Rxd5 Kg8 21 Bxg7 Kxg7 22 Ne5 Rfd8 23 Qg4+ Kf8 24 Qf5 f6 25 Nd7+ Rxd7 26 Rxd7 Qc5 27 Qh7 Rc7 28 Qh8+ Kf7 29 Rd3 Nc4 30 Rfd1 Ne5 31 Qh7+ Ke6 32 Qg8+ Kf5 33 g4+ Kf4 34 Rd4+ Kf3 35 Qb3+ 1-0

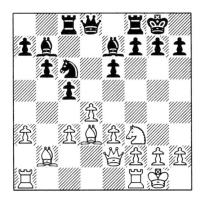

Diagram 13
White is ready to expand?

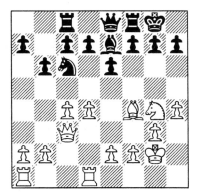

Diagram 14
White will expand in the centre

The advance d4-d5 can often herald a quick kingside attack in this type of position.

Game 94
□ **Beliavsky** ■ **Petrosian**
Vilnius 1978

1 d4 Nf6 2 c4 e6 3 Nf3 b6 4 g3 Bb7 5 Bg2 Be7 6 Nc3 Ne4 7 Qc2

White must not allow Black to get too comfortable on the e4-outpost.

7...Nxc3 8 Qxc3 0-0 9 0-0 Be4 10 Bf4 Bf6 11 Rfd1 Nc6

Black controls e4 and bears down his pieces on the d4-pawn. However White has more space and the time to defuse the tension.

12 Ne5 Bxg2 13 Kxg2 Rc8 14 h4 Qe8 15 Ng4 Be7 (Diagram 14) 16 d5

Forcing Black on the back foot whilst expanding the centre.

16...Nd8 17 h5 f6 18 h6

White keeps his central pressure and softens up Black's kingside, creating future targets.

18...g6 19 Bxc7 Rxc7 20 d6 Bxd6 21 Rxd6 Qe7 22 Rad1 Nb7 23 R6d4 d5 24 Qd3 Nd6 25 cxd5 e5 26 Rb4 f5 27 Ne3 Rfc8 28 Ra4 Qg5 29 Qa3 Qe7 30 b3 Kf8 31 Qb2 Rc5 32 Nc4 Nf7 33 Qa3 b5 34 Rxa7 Qf6 35 Ra6 Qe7 36 Ra7 Qd8 37 Na5 Qb6 38 Nb7 b4 39 Nxc5 1-0

Game 95
□ **Polugaevsky** ■ **Korchnoi**
Evian 1977

1 d4 Nf6 2 c4 e6 3 Nf3 b6 4 g3 Bb7 5 Bg2 Be7 6 0-0 0-0 7 Nc3 Ne4 8 Qc2 Nxc3 9 Qxc3 f5

Ensuring some influence on e4.

10 b3 Bf6 11 Bb2 Nc6 12 Rad1 Ne7 13 Ne1 Bxg2 14 Nxg2 g5

Black is not yet sure what he wants to do with his central pawns and advances there may merely lead to weaknesses. So, instead, he gains space on the wing and awaits developments.

15 Qc2 Ng6 16 e4 f4

Guaranteeing a double-edged struggle ahead.

17 e5 Bg7 18 Qe4 Qe7 19 Rd3 Rad8 20 Re1 d5 (Diagram 15)

Using a tactical point to hit back at White's centre.

21 exd6 Qxd6 22 Red1 Qe7 23 Ne1 Qf6 24 R1d2 Qf5 25 Qxf5 exf5 26 Ng2 g4 27 Nxf4 Nxf4 28 gxf4 Bh6 29 Re2 Bxf4 30 Re6 Rfe8 31 Rf6 Re1+ 32 Kg2 Rf8 33 Rxf8+ Kxf8 34 d5

White finally advances to open up his bishop, but Black's active pieces enable his majority to be the most significant.

34...Bd6 35 Bc3 Rc1 36 Bd2 Rc2 37 a4 f4 38 h3 f3+ 39 Kf1 h5 40 hxg4 hxg4 41 Ke1 0-1

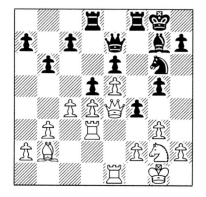

Diagram 15

Black attacks the white centre

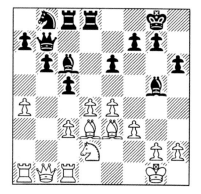

Diagram 16

Provoking White to over-extend

Game 96
□ **Vaganian** ■ **Timman**
Rio de Janeiro 1979

1 d4 Nf6 2 c4 e6 3 Nf3 b6 4 a3 Bb7 5 Nc3 d5 6 cxd5 Nxd5 7 e3 Be7 8 Bb5+ c6 9 Bd3 0-0 10 Qc2 h6 11 Bd2 Nd7

Allowing White to freely play e3-e4 but then relying on his superior development to hit back at the centre.

12 e4 Nxc3 13 bxc3 c5 14 0-0 Rc8 15 Qb1 Qc7 16 a4 Rfd8 17 Rc1 Bc6 18 Be3 Qb7

Black's forces are fully mobilised and White finds it hard to expand his pawn front further.

19 Nd2 Nb8 20 f3 Bg5 (Diagram 16)

Provoking White to over-extend his pawns.

21 f4 Be7 22 Nc4 cxd4 23 cxd4 Na6 24 Ne5 Nb4 25 Nxc6 Rxc6 26 Qb3 Rdc8 27 Rxc6 Rxc6 28 Bd2 Qd7

Continuing to harass the centre.

29 d5 Nxd3 30 Qxd3 exd5 31 Kh1 Rc4 32 exd5 Rc5

The centre is finally killed off.

33 Be3 Rxd5 34 Qc2 Rd3 35 Bg1 Qd5 36 Re1 Rd2 37 Qc8+ Kh7 38 Qg4 f5 39 Qh3 Bf6 40 Rf1 Qe4 41 a5 bxa5 42 Bxa7 Rd3 0-1

The Bogo-Indian Defence

1 d4 N6 2 c4 e6 3 Nc3 Bb4+

The Bogo-Indian Defence is another standard way for Black to play when White is keen on avoiding the Nimzo-Indian Defence. The opening is not considered a particularly ambitious one by Black, who is happy to simply 'get his pieces out' on sensible squares and accept a slight inferiority in the centre.

As White usually develops before aiming to expand, Black has time to castle and after the exchange of his bishop to be well entrenched around any white centre.

What is White's Strategy?

He hopes for a comfortable life, limiting the effectiveness of the bishop check. The early exchange of bishops with 4 Bd2 enables both camps to more or less complete their development without any further contact. White typically follows up with the fianchetto of his king's bishop, early castling and then a bid for extra space with e2-e4, and when forced to, d4-d5.

More challenging is the rarer 4 Nd2, allowing a pin, but preparing to hit back with a3. Just as in the Nimzo-Indian, White plays for the bishop pair but here without giving any free targets for his opponent. However, the knight is a little clumsy on d2 and this gives Black counterchances.

What is Black's Strategy?

After 4 Nd2 Black needs to take some ground in the centre as, similarly to the Nimzo-Indian, he will probably be soon playing against the bishop pair. Fortunately the follow-up 4 a3 is time-consuming and Black has plenty of time to get his knights and central pawns in place.

After 4 Bd2 keeping the tension temporarily with 4...Qe7, 4...a5 or even 4...c5 are generally considered very solid. The typical exchange of dark-squared bishops, at some point, means that any space disadvantage is less cramping than in other openings where all the pieces are on the board.

As his opponent has no immediate threats Black has time to prepare ...d7-d6 and ...e6-e5, putting his pawns on dark-squares allowing plenty of scope for his remaining light-squared bishop. If White's central pawns eventually become fixed on light-squares then Black may have the better bishop despite a space disadvantage.

Tactical/Strategic/Dynamic?

Very much a strategic opening, where the central question is resolved slowly over time, almost in slow motion. Even the lines involving 4 Nd2 seeking the bishop pair are like a Nimzo-Indian without the sharp corners.

Theoretical?

Not at all really, Black's solid strategy is fairly straightforward as there are no tactical ideas to cross his plans. One of the simplest of the major openings to put into practice.

How Popular is it?

A bit tame for club players the line has become popular amongst strategic and solid players of international standard. Top players such as Adams, Gelfand, Korchnoi, Yusupov have all include it in their repertoire as it's hard to surprise and just so solid!

TIP: The Bogo-Indian is a rock-solid defence and the middlegame play is highly strategic. It is unusual for the stronger player to lose on either side of the Bogo.

Illustrative Games

Game 97
□ **Yakovich** ■ **Makarov**
Elista 2001

1 d4 Nf6 2 c4 e6 3 Nf3 Bb4+ 4 Nbd2 b6 5 a3 Bxd2+ 6 Qxd2 Bb7

White has the bishop pair and a solid position.

7 e3 0-0 8 Be2 a5 9 b3 d6 10 0-0 Nbd7 11 Bb2 Qe7 12 Rfd1 Rfd8 13 b4 axb4 14 axb4 Qe8 15 Qc2 Rxa1 16 Bxa1 Ra8 17 Nd2 c5 18 Bc3 Qc8 19 Qb2 (Diagram 17)

There is little to bite on in the black camp, but there is no hurry; Black has no counterplay and slowly but surely the bishops come to the fore.

19...h6 20 f3 cxd4 21 exd4 Qc7 22 Nb3 Rc8 23 Be1 Nf8 24 Bf1 Ng6 25 Bf2 Ra8 26 Nd2 Bc6 27 Nb1 e5 28 Nc3 exd4 29 Bxd4 Ne5 30 Qf2 Rb8 31 Re1 Ned7 32 Qg3 Re8 33 Ra1

Retaining the rooks improves the chances of getting at the sensitive points b6 and d6.

33...Nh5 34 Qf2 Nf4 35 Be3 Ne6 36 Nd5 Bxd5 37 cxd5 Ng5 38 Bb5 Rf8 39 Rc1 Qd8 40 Bd4 Ne5 41 Kh1 Qa8 42 Bxe5 dxe5 43 d6 Qa3

44 Qd2 Ne6 45 d7 g5 46 h3 Kg7 47 Rc8 Qa1+ 48 Kh2 e4 49 Rxf8
Kxf8 50 d8Q+ Nxd8 51 Qxd8+ Kg7 52 Qe7 exf3 53 Bc4 Kh8 54
Qf8+ 1-0

Diagram 17
White's bishop pair will prove useful

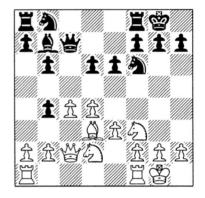

Diagram 18
White has more central control

Game 98
□ **Livshits** ■ **Dizdar**
Moscow Olympiad 1994

1 d4 Nf6 2 c4 e6 3 Nf3 Bb4+ 4 Bd2 c5 5 Bxb4 cxb4

White's central pawns are not that easy to advance as White is denied
the c3-square for his knight.

**6 e3 0-0 7 Bd3 b6 8 Nbd2 Bb7 9 0-0 d6 10 Qc2 Qc7 (Diagram 18)
11 a3**

A promising plan now that White has completed his development.
The rook proves to be useful on the third rank.

**11...bxa3 12 Rxa3 Nc6 13 Qc3 a5 14 Bb1 Rfc8 15 Rc1 d5 16 e4
Qf4 17 exd5 exd5 18 Qe3 Qg4**

White is also more active after the exchange of queens.

19 h3 Qd7 20 Ne5 Qd8 21 Re1

Switching to attack mode.

**21...dxc4 22 Ndf3 Qd5 23 Qg5 Re8 24 Rae3 h6 25 Qh4 Red8 26
Ng4 Nxg4 27 hxg4 Qd6 28 g5 Kf8 29 Qe4 1-0**

**WARNING: Even in solid openings such as the Bogo it is important
to come up with an active plan at some point. The point of playing a
solid opening with Black is that White is allowed fairly free development but this *laissez faire* attitude must not last for the entire game!**

Game 99
□ **Piket** ■ **Anand**
Wijk aan Zee 1996

1 d4 Nf6 2 c4 e6 3 Nf3 Bb4+ 4 Bd2 Qe7 5 g3 Nc6 6 Nc3 d6 7 Bg2 Bxc3 8 Bxc3 Ne4 9 Rc1 Nxc3 10 Rxc3 e5 11 d5 Nb8 12 e4

The exchange of two pairs of minor pieces gives Black sufficient room despite his space disadvantage. Note that White's pawns are fixed on the same colour complex as his bishop.

12...0-0 13 Nh4 a5 14 0-0 Na6

Restraining any prospect of a general queenside pawn advance by White.

15 Qe1 g5 16 Nf5 Bxf5 17 exf5 Nc5 18 Be4 Qf6 19 f3 Rfe8 20 Qe3 Kg7 21 Kg2 (Diagram 19) 21...h5

With the centre blocked Black seeks chances on the flanks particularly as he has the superior minor piece.

22 Rh1 Rg8 23 h3 h4 24 g4 Rgb8 25 Rhc1 b5 26 cxb5 Rxb5 27 R1c2 Rab8 28 Qd2 Qd8 29 b3 Qe7 30 Rc4 R8b6 31 Kf1 Qd8 32 Ke2 Kf6 33 Qc1 Qb8 34 Qe3 Ra6

Black dominates proceedings. White thus decides to try and complicate matters now before Black plays his intended ...a5-a4.

35 Bd3 Ra7 36 f4 gxf4 37 g5+ Kg7 38 f6+ Kg8 39 Rxc5 fxe3 40 Rxb5 Qe8 41 Rc6 e4 42 Bc2 Ra8 43 Rb7 Qe5 44 Rbxc7 Qf4 0-1

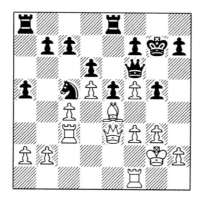

Diagram 19
Black has the better minor piece

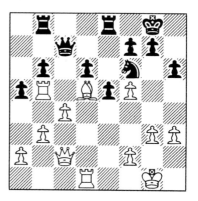

Diagram 20
Black is very solid

NOTE: White's light-squared bishop is often an inferior piece to a black knight, even if the position is not completely closed.

Game 100
□ **Ehlvest** ■ **Adams**
New York 1994

1 d4 Nf6 2 Nf3 e6 3 c4 Bb4+ 4 Bd2 Qe7 5 Nc3 Bxc3 6 Bxc3 Ne4 7 Rc1 0-0 8 g3 d6 9 Bg2 Nxc3 10 Rxc3 e5 11 0-0 Re8 12 e4 Bg4 13 d5

Black has comfortable development and White will be unable to keep the tension for long.

13...a5 14 Qc2 Na6 15 Nh4 Nc5 16 Re3 c6 17 Nf5

White waits until Black is committed to ...c7-c6 before making this move. This way the bishop ensures an open diagonal.

17...Qc7 18 h3 Bxf5 19 exf5 cxd5 20 Bxd5 Nd7 21 Rb3 Rab8 22 Rb5 Nf6 23 Rd1 h6 24 b3 b6 (Diagram 20)

By putting his forces on dark squares the bishop is still denied much influence.

25 Qd2 e4 26 Qf4 Re5 27 g4 Rbe8 28 Qe3 Nd7 29 a3 h5 30 b4 axb4 31 axb4 hxg4 32 hxg4 Rb8

Black intends ...Nf6, increasing the pressure.

33 Bxe4 Qxc4 34 Rxe5 Nxe5 35 f3 Qxb4 36 Qd4 Qxd4+ 37 Rxd4 b5

The advanced b-pawn leads to a win.

38 Rxd6 b4 39 Kf2 b3 40 Rd1 b2 41 Bb1 Nc4 42 Ke2 Na3 43 g5 Kf8 44 f6 gxf6 45 gxf6 Ke8 46 Ke3 Rb6 47 f4 Rxf6 48 Ke4 Re6+ 49 Kf5 Ke7 50 Ba2 Rb6 51 Re1+ Kf8 52 Bb1 Nxb1 53 Rxb1 Ke7 0-1

Chapter Nine

The Queen's Gambit Declined

- The Classical Main Lines
- The Slav Defence
- The Semi-Slav Defence

Playing 1...d5 against White's 1 d4, with the intention of maintaining, for the moment at least, this pawn in the centre, is the classical way to defend against the queen pawn opening. Conducting the defence in this way is completely sound, if a little unambitious. All the great champions have been prepared, at some point in their career, to take on the black side of the Queen's Gambit Declined. The QGD is the 'safety first' approach against 1 d4. When all the complicated stuff like the King's Indian Defence, the Nimzo-Indian Defence or the various Benoni systems are not getting results, you often find the best players rushing for the security blanket of the QGD.

The main lines of the Queen's Gambit are extremely solid for Black but it is also possible to play 1...d5 more dynamically, by adopting either the Slav (1 d4 d5 2 c4 c6) or the Semi-Slav (1 d4 d5 2 c4 e6 3 Nc3 Nf6 4 Nf3 c6) Defences, both of which we consider in this chapter. The Slav leaves the route open for Black to develop the queen's bishop and often intends a capture on c4 to create some imbalance in the position. Play in these lines tends to be highly strategic. The Semi-Slav, on the other hand, can become a ferociously complex opening. Given the chance Black again intends to make the capture ...d5xc4 but usually with the idea of holding onto this pawn with a quick ...b7-b5. White will be allowed to advance with e2-e4-e5 and wild complications often ensue.

The Classical Main Lines

1 d4 d5 2 c4 e6

This is often the first opening that people come across in answer to 1 d4 and some stick with it. With 1...d5 Black lays claim to his share of the centre and after 2 c4 e6 he shows his intention to maintain it. White may typically lay siege to this strongpoint with the knight on c3 and bishop on g5. Black stubbornly intends to hold onto d5 through thick and thin.

The danger of such an approach is that Black's game is a mite passive and lacks dynamism.

What is White's Strategy?

With Black primarily concerned with defence of his centre, White is able to develop more actively; his queen's bishop outside of the pawn chain for instance. White can then complete his development without making any major decisions about the central pawns. Typically he may keep the central tension, inviting Black to make his decision and rely on his well placed pieces to keep the better chances whatever Black's choice.

Another approach is to play an early c4xd5 when Black's ...e6xd5 leads to a fixed structure in the centre. Black has less options with his pawns but his queen's bishop is no longer blocked in by the e-pawn. Play then involves completing the development of both wings before deciding where to seek the initiative. Because White has the slightly freer game it is he who decides the arena of battle.

What is Black's Strategy?

After ensuring the future of the d5-bastion, Black has to think about his other forces. None of his pieces is that active, and his queen's bishop is locked in behind his central light-squared pawns. If Black doesn't find a solution to this bishop then he will remain passive well into the middlegame.

The traditional method is to complete development of the kingside before timing ...d5xc4 and ...e6-e5. Thus Black gives up the strong-point to look for a more fluid centre where his bishop will find a role along the c8-h3 diagonal.

Another plan is to move the king's knight with ...Nf6-e4 to first exchange some minor pieces, giving Black more space to manoeuvre before freeing the light-squared bishop. The more modern Tartakower defence involves kingside development followed by ...b7-b6 and ...Bc8-b7; in this case Black can hold onto d5 and even increase his central presence with ...c7-c5.

Tactical/Strategic/Dynamic?

Most lines have very little tactical engagement. The Orthodox Queen's Gambit is considered to be strategic, but far too simplistic for those seeking a dynamic struggle. Tartakower's ...b6 retains the solidity of the black encampment but adds some dynamism, but the Queen's Gambit has never shaken off it's reputation of being solid but passive.

Theoretical?

Although some lines are deeply analysed, because of the number of games played over the years, anyone can quickly learn the first stage of development. So it doesn't require much knowledge to give it a try.

In order to be successful, those intending to play with the black pieces should particularly appreciate the various techniques to free the queen's bishop.

How Popular is it?

In Capablanca's time, it was the most popular defence, despite it being somewhat dull. Nowadays, although it's played by some grandmasters looking for a rock solid game, it tends to be particularly popular with weaker club players who haven't the confidence or knowledge to play anything else. The problem for them is that it's often difficult to complete development of the queenside and obtain counterplay, so it isn't necessarily that easy to play.

Illustrative Games

Game 101
☐ **Fischer** ■ **Spassky**
Reykjavik 1972

1 c4 e6 2 Nf3 d5 3 d4 Nf6 4 Nc3 Be7 5 Bg5 0-0 6 e3 h6 7 Bh4 b6 8 cxd5 Nxd5 9 Bxe7 Qxe7 10 Nxd5 exd5 11 Rc1 Be6 12 Qa4 c5 13 Qa3

Pressurizing Black's centre and creating difficulties for his opponent to complete development. Note that White has very solid pawns.

13...Rc8 14 Bb5 a6 15 dxc5 bxc5 16 0-0 Ra7 17 Be2 Nd7 18 Nd4 Qf8 19 Nxe6 fxe6 (Diagram 1) 20 e4

Battering away at the centre. Black must either allow it to become very loose and exposed to further attack or cede some squares.

20...d4 21 f4 Qe7 22 e5 Rb8 23 Bc4 Kh8 24 Qh3 Nf8 25 b3 a5 26 f5

White blocks Black's centre and actively uses his majority to create threats elsewhere.

26...exf5 27 Rxf5 Nh7 28 Rcf1 Qd8 29 Qg3 Re7 30 h4 Rbb7 31 e6 Rbc7 32 Qe5 Qe8 33 a4 Qd8 34 R1f2 Qe8 35 R2f3 Qd8 36 Bd3 Qe8 37 Qe4 Nf6 38 Rxf6 gxf6 39 Rxf6 Kg8 40 Bc4 Kh8 41 Qf4 1-0

TIP: In classical Queen's Gambit positions the black pawns are often slightly loose. Therefore it can pay White to simplify the position with piece exchanges when these weaknesses may begin to tell.

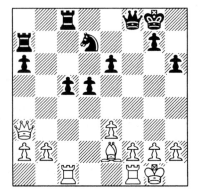

Diagram 1	**Diagram 2**
White will attack the black centre	Black's pawns are weak

Game 102
☐ **Capablanca** ■ **Lasker**
Havana 1921

1 d4 d5 2 Nf3 e6 3 c4 Nf6 4 Bg5 Nbd7 5 e3 Be7 6 Nc3 0-0 7 Rc1 Re8 8 Qc2 c6 9 Bd3 dxc4 10 Bxc4 Nd5

Black hopes to free his game by exchanging some minor pieces. He hopes to avoid unnecessarily moving his pawns which may create potential weaknesses.

11 Bxe7 Rxe7 12 0-0 Nf8 13 Rfd1 Bd7 14 e4 Nb6 15 Bf1 Rc8 16 b4

Increasing space and avoiding the freeing ...c7-c5 break. Black hasn't yet solved the problem of his light-squared bishop and thus slips into a passive position.

16...Be8 17 Qb3 Rec7 18 a4 Ng6 19 a5 Nd7 20 e5

Not just expanding his space bind, White also creates an outpost for a knight on d6.

20...b6 21 Ne4 Rb8 22 Qc3 Nf4 23 Nd6 Nd5 24 Qa3 (Diagram 2) 24...f6

Black intends to liberate his game with ...Bh5, so White simplifies to leave Black with loose pawns.

25 Nxe8 Qxe8 26 exf6 gxf6 27 b5 Rbc8 28 bxc6 Rxc6 29 Rxc6 Rxc6 30 axb6 axb6

White needs to limit the scope of Black's forces and exchange the central knight in order to fully expose the weak pawns to attack.

31 Re1 Qc8 32 Nd2 Nf8 33 Ne4 Qd8 34 h4 Rc7 35 Qb3 Rg7 36 g3 Ra7 37 Bc4 Ra5 38 Nc3 Nxc3 39 Qxc3 Kf7 40 Qe3 Qd6 41 Qe4 Ra4 42 Qb7+ Kg6 43 Qc8 Qb4 44 Rc1 Qe7 45 Bd3+ Kh6 46 Rc7 Ra1+ 47 Kg2 Qd6 48 Qxf8+ 1-0

Game 103
☐ **Bobotsov** ■ **Petrosian**
Lugano 1968

1 d4 Nf6 2 c4 e6 3 Nf3 d5 4 cxd5 exd5 5 Nc3 c6 6 Bg5 Be7 7 Qc2 g6 8 e3 Bf5

In the exchange variation Black does well to play ...Bf5 if possible. He thus has influence on the e4-square and also covers the b1-square, making a White queenside pawn advance more difficult to support. If White exchanges the light-squared bishops then Black is rid of his problem piece.

9 Bd3 Bxd3 10 Qxd3 Nbd7 11 Bh6 Ng4 12 Bf4 0-0 13 0-0 Re8 14 h3

An imperceptible weakening of his king.

14...Ngf6 15 Ne5 Nb6 16 Bg5 Ne4 17 Bxe7 Qxe7 18 Qc2 Nd6

An ideal square for a knight in this variation. Naturally e4 is covered (to be ready for any central action by White) but also c4 so that if White pushes his b-pawn Black obtains an outpost on this square.

19 Na4 Nbc4 20 Nxc4 Nxc4 21 Nc5 Nd6 22 Rac1 Qg5 23 Qd1 h5 (Diagram 3)

Black is ready to gradually develop threats against the white king. There is no counterplay so he can take his time.

24 Kh1 Re7 25 Nd3 Ne4 26 Nc5 Nd6 27 Nd3 Qf5 28 Ne5 f6 29 Nf3 Rg7 30 Nh2 Re8 31 Kg1 Ne4 32 Qf3 Qe6

Black's attack is much stronger with queens on.

33 Rfd1 g5 34 Qxh5 f5 35 Re1 g4 36 hxg4 fxg4 37 f3 gxf3 38 Nxf3 Rh7 39 Qe5 Qc8 40 Qf4 Rf8 41 Qe5 Rf5 0-1

NOTE: If Black can exchange off the light-squared bishop without making any serious concessions, he should not have any problems.

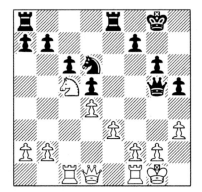

Diagram 3
Black can build up on the kingside

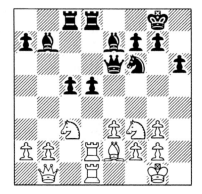

Diagram 4
Black's 'hanging pawns' are strong

Game 104
□ **Korchnoi** ■ **Karpov**
Merano 1981

1 c4 e6 2 Nc3 d5 3 d4 Be7 4 Nf3 Nf6

Notice the unusual move-order leading to a Queen's Gambit.

5 Bg5 h6 6 Bh4 0-0 7 e3 b6 8 Rc1 Bb7 9 Be2 Nbd7 10 cxd5 exd5 11 0-0 c5 12 dxc5 bxc5

Black has so-called 'hanging pawns'. These can come under attack but with a crowded board they control important squares and thus cramp the opponent.

13 Qc2 Rc8 14 Rfd1 Qb6 15 Qb1 Rfd8 16 Rc2 Qe6 17 Bg3 Nh5 18 Rcd2 Nxg3 19 hxg3 Nf6 (Diagram 4)

The pawns now prove to be difficult to put under pressure.

20 Qc2 g6 21 Qa4 a6 22 Bd3 Kg7 23 Bb1 Qb6 24 a3 d4

A thematic advance, cutting the White forces in two.

25 Ne2 dxe3 26 fxe3 c4 27 Ned4 Qc7

White now has significant weaknesses on the dark squares, a direct consequence of not being able to cope with the expansion of the hanging pawns.

28 Nh4 Qe5 29 Kh1 Kg8 30 Ndf3 Qxg3 31 Rxd8+ Bxd8 32 Qb4 Be4 33 Bxe4 Nxe4 34 Rd4 Nf2+ 35 Kg1 Nd3 36 Qb7 Rb8 37 Qd7 Bc7 38 Kh1 Rxb2 39 Rxd3 cxd3 40 Qxd3 Qd6 41 Qe4 Qd1+ 42 Ng1 Qd6 43 Nhf3 Rb5 0-1

The Slav Defence

1 d4 d5 2 c4 c6

As in the Orthodox Queen's Gambit, Black defends his d5-point with ...e7-e6. Here, however, Black plays instead ...c7-c6, leaving the c8-h3 diagonal open for the quick development of the light-squared bishop. One of the attractions of the Slav is that if Black can get away with this whilst maintaining the centre intact then the rest of his forces can easily find satisfactory squares.

The Slav player is looking for free minor piece play, which he generally obtains, but he is often obliged to cede the d5-point in the process. So the Slav is characterised by ...d5xc4 releasing the pressure and gaining time in order to obtain good prospects for his pieces.

What is White's Strategy?

White will generally try to achieve the advance e2-e4 when his central superiority will begin to show. If Black captures on c4 (for example 1 d4 d5 2 c4 c6 3 Nf3 Nf6 4 Nc3 and here 4...dxc4) White can immediately occupy the centre with 5 e4 and even threaten further expansion with e4-e5. Black will continue with 5...b5 holding onto the pawn and gambit-style play ensues, White relying on his initiative for compensation.

White's main strategy is to recapture with a piece on c4 even if it involves a preliminary a2-a4 to dissuade ...b7-b5.

Capturing with the king's knight (involving the manoeuvre Nf3-

e5xc4) frees the f-pawn and prepares f2-f3 followed by e2-e4. Taking back instead with the bishop (after e2-e3 and Bf1xc4) leads to play involving Qd1-e2 to support the e2-e4 advance.

Some players who prefer a simple game will play 3 cxd5 which leads to symmetrical pawns and easy piece development for both sides.

What is Black's Strategy?

With the queen's bishop developed actively to f5 (eyeing e4) or to g4 (with a possible pin), the path is clear for Black to play ...e7-e6 and then develop the other bishop. If ...d5xc4 has been played then White has a slight majority in the centre (d- and e-pawns against a sole e-pawn) and Black will aim for ...c7-c5 to negate this central plus. In some lines, this idea occurs in the opening, but Black will generally deploy his forces first and only play for the central break when he feels ready, often into the middlegame.

If White meets ...d5xc4 with a2-a4 Black will typically occupy the b4-square with a minor piece, an advanced square that can be no longer attacked by a white pawn.

Another, more recent plan is to hold onto the d5-point and play an early ...a7-a6 to follow-up with ...b7-b5 and ...Bc8-f5 or ...Bc8-g4. In this way Black hopes for a solid centre and easy piece development.

Tactical/Strategic/Dynamic?

Overall, Black's attempts to play dynamically. Lines involving 3 cxd5 are rather sterile and this puts some players off, but others can be quite sharp, especially if White employs a gambit. Lines where White quickly threatens to occupy the centre with e2-e4, provoke Black to react aggressively and some tactical fights can then occur.

Theoretical?

Some of the critical variations are sharp and have become very theoretical and some memory work is required. If, on the other hand, White reacts quietly then Black can develop his forces without much contact and these lines can be handled using general principles.

How Popular is it?

The Slav has become popular over the last twenty years and remains popular at all levels. The ...a7-a6 variations have added an extra weapon to Black's Slav armoury with many of the world's elite playing both versions.

Illustrative Games

Game 105
□ **Euwe** ■ **Alekhine**
Holland 1937

1 d4 d5 2 c4 c6 3 Nf3 Nf6 4 Nc3 dxc4 5 a4 Bf5 6 Ne5 Nbd7 7 Nxc4 Qc7 8 g3

White has regained his pawn and Black is ready to somewhat free his game with ...e7-e5, so White prepares an annoying pin.

8...e5 9 dxe5 Nxe5 10 Bf4 Nfd7 11 Bg2 f6 12 0-0 Rd8 13 Qc1 Be6 (Diagram 5) 14 Ne4

White ties down his opponent with piece pressure.

14...Bb4 15 a5 0-0 16 a6

Undermining the solidity of Black's queenside.

16...bxa6 17 Nxe5 Nxe5 18 Nc5 Bxc5 19 Qxc5 g5 20 Be3 Bd5 21 Rxa6

Black has not been able to avoid just being left with weak pawns. It's not surprising that he eventually finds himself a pawn down in an ending.

21...Bxg2 22 Kxg2 Rf7 23 Rfa1 Qd6 24 Qxd6 Rxd6 25 Rxa7 Rxa7 26 Rxa7 Nc4 27 Bc5 Re6 28 Bd4 Rxe2 29 Bxf6 g4 30 Kf1 Rc2 31 Rg7+ Kf8 32 Rxg4 Nxb2 33 Bxb2 Rxb2 34 Rc4 Rb6 35 Ke2 Kf7 36 Rh4 Kg6 37 Rf4 Rb3 38 Rc4 Rb6 39 Ke3 Kf5 40 g4+ Ke6 41 f4 Kd5 42 Rd4+ Ke6 43 f5+ Ke7 44 Re4+ Kf7 45 h4 Rb1 46 Kf4 Rc1 47 Ra4 h6 48 Ra7+ Kg8 49 g5 Rc4+ 50 Ke5 1-0

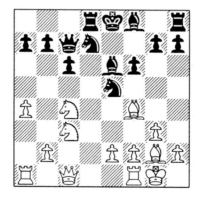

Diagram 5
Black is struggling to develop

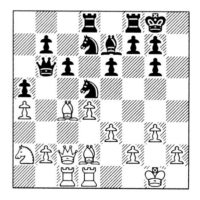

Diagram 6
White advances in the centre

Game 106
□ **Kasparov** ■ **Timman**
Amsterdam 1988

1 d4 d5 2 Nf3 Nf6 3 c4 c6 4 Nc3 dxc4 5 a4 Bf5 6 Nh4 Bc8 7 Nf3 Bf5 8 e3 e6 9 Bxc4 Bb4

Whilst White spends time regaining his pawn, Black is able to find good squares for his pieces.

10 0-0 Nbd7 11 Qb3 a5 12 Na2 Be7 13 Nh4

Trying to dislodge Black's grip on the e4-square.

13...Bg6 14 g3 Qc7 15 Nc3 0-0 16 Nxg6 hxg6 17 Rd1 Bb4 18 Qc2 Rad8 19 Na2 Be7 20 Bd2 Qb6 21 Rac1 Nd5 (Diagram 6) 22 e4

Finally achieving this key central advance and enabling the dark-squared bishop to take on a more active posting.

22...N5f6 23 Be2 e5 24 Be3 exd4 25 Bxd4 Qc7 26 f4

The freely advancing pawns, supported by the bishop pair, give White the better game.

26...g5 27 e5 Nd5 28 Qe4 N7b6 29 Bd3 g6 30 f5 f6 31 fxg6 f5

The resulting complications leave Black with problems as his king is more prone to attack.

32 Qe2 Kg7 33 Qh5 Rh8 34 Qf3 Nf4 35 Bxf5 Rxd4

A forlorn sacrifice of the exchange to get some play.

36 Rxd4 Qxe5 37 Re4 Bc5+ 38 Kh1 Qxf5 39 gxf4 Bd6 40 Qc3+ Kxg6 41 Qd3 Be7 42 fxg5 Qd5 43 Qe2 Rh4 44 Nc3 Rxe4 45 Nxe4 Nxa4 46 Rd1 Qe6 47 Qc2 Qf5 48 Qxa4 Qf3+ 49 Kg1 Qg4+ 50 Kf2 Qf4+ 51 Ke2 Qg4+ 52 Kd3 Bb4 53 Qc2 Qf3+ 54 Kd4 Kg7 55 Ke5 1-0

WARNING: It is imperative for Black to find an active plan at some point in the Slav, otherwise the white advantages in the position will gradually make themselves felt.

Game 107
□ **Novikov** ■ **Khalifman**
Lvov 1990

1 d4 d5 2 c4 c6 3 Nf3 Nf6 4 Nc3 dxc4 5 a4 Bf5 6 Ne5 e6 7 f3 Bb4 8 e4

A theoretical line where Black sacrifices a piece for three pawns. He has little choice as otherwise he loses all influence in the centre.

8...Bxe4 9 fxe4 Nxe4 10 Bd2 Qxd4 11 Nxe4 Qxe4+ 12 Qe2 Bxd2+ 13 Kxd2 Qd5+ 14 Kc2 Na6 15 Nxc4 0-0 16 Qe5

Black has approximate material equality and a solid game in return for the piece.

16...Rfd8 17 Be2 f6 18 Qxd5 cxd5 19 Na5 Rdc8+ 20 Kb3 Nc5+ 21 Ka3 (Diagram 7) 21...b6

This ending is fine for Black who can easily defend any potential weaknesses.

22 Nb3 Kf7 23 Rac1 Nxb3 24 Kxb3 a5 25 Ka3 Ke7 26 b4 Kd6 27 bxa5 bxa5 28 Rxc8 Rxc8 29 Rb1 Rc3+ 30 Rb3 Rxb3+ 31 Kxb3 f5 32 h4 Ke5

Black's more active king now gives him the winning chances.

33 Kc3 Ke4 34 Kd2 Kf4 35 Bf3 Kg3 36 h5 g5 37 hxg6 hxg6 38 Ke2 g5 39 Kf1 g4 40 Be2 f4 41 Bb5 f3 42 Bc6 d4 43 gxf3 gxf3 44 Ke1 e5 45 Bb5 e4 46 Bc6 e3 47 Be4 Kg2 0-1

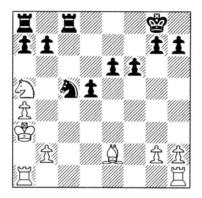

Diagram 7
Black has full compensation

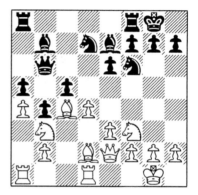

Diagram 8
Black frees his game

Game 108
□ **Reshevsky** ■ **Smyslov**
USA-USSR Radio Match 1945

1 d4 d5 2 c4 c6 3 Nf3 Nf6 4 Nc3 dxc4 5 e3

A temporary gambit. Black would like to hold onto the pawn but his queenside pawns come under attack.

5...b5 6 a4 b4 7 Na2 e6

Returning the pawn to enable normal development. Note that the knight on a2 is now out of play and White will have to spend some time to redeploy it

8 Bxc4 Be7 9 0-0 0-0 10 Qe2 Bb7 11 Rd1 a5 12 Bd2 Nbd7 13 Nc1 Qb6 14 Nb3 c5 (Diagram 8)

The freeing break is achieved (improving his light-squared bishop's prospects and counterattacking the central majority) and Black can count on a comfortable game.

15 Be1 Rfd8 16 Bb5 Bd5 17 Nbd2 Qb7 18 Nc4 Nb6 19 Nce5 Ne4 20 dxc5 Nxc5 21 Nd4 Rdc8 22 f3 Nb3 23 Nxb3 Bxb3 24 Rd3 Bc2 25 Rd2 b3 26 Bf2 Bb4 27 Rd4

White has not been able to develop in peace and Black has an annoying initiative.

27...Nd5 28 Nd3 e5

A neat combination to exploit White's tangled army. Black wins material by force.

29 Nxe5 Bc3 30 Nc4 Bxd4 31 exd4 Qc7 32 Bg3 Qa7 33 Qe4 Nb4 34 Nd6 Rf8 35 Qe3 Rad8 36 Qc3 Qe7 37 Re1 Qg5 38 Qe3 Qg6 39 Ne4 Bxe4 40 Qxe4 Nc2 41 Qxg6 hxg6 42 Rc1 Nxd4 43 Bc7 Rd5 44 Bc4 Rc8 45 Ba6 Re8 46 Kf1 Nc2 47 Kg1 Re1+ 48 Rxe1 Nxe1 49 Kf2 Nc2 50 Ke2 Rc5 51 Bg3 Nb4 52 Bd3 g5 53 Be4 Rc4 54 Be1 Kf8 55 Bc3 f6 56 g4 Ke7 57 Kd2 Kd6 58 Ke2 Nd5 59 Bxa5 Rxa4 60 Be1 Ra2 61 Kd3 Rxb2 62 Kc4 Re2 63 Bg3+ Nf4 64 Kxb3 Rxe4 65 fxe4 Ke5 66 h4 Kxe4 67 hxg5 fxg5 68 Kc4 Kf3 69 Be1 Kxg4 70 Kd4 Kf3 71 Ke5 g4 0-1

The Semi-Slav Defence

1 d4 d5 2 c4 e6 3 Nc3 Nf6 4 Nf3 c6

Black plays ...c7-c6 as in the Slav, and ...e7-e6 as in an Orthodox Queen's Gambit, so the Semi-Slav (where Black plays both ...c7-c6 and ...e7-e6) has similarities to both systems.

The light-squared bishop is locked inside the pawn chain (à la Queen's Gambit Declined) but here Black intends to do something about it quickly. The bishop will generally be developed to b7, often after ...d5xc4 and ...b7-b5, and this frequently occurs before Black has got round to castling.

What is White's Strategy?

The three main ideas are e2-e3 with Bf1-d3, e2-e3 with a preliminary Qc2 or finally, the aggressive Bc1-g5.

The immediate e2-e3 followed by Bf1-d3 already prepares the space-gaining e2-e4. If this is achieved Black is left with a passive game and therefore the threat of this provokes Black into action. This usually involves giving up the d5-strongpoint to gain time for development. This is known as the Meran Variation. White can then use his d- and e-pawns to advance rapidly in the centre.

The flexible e2-e3 with Qd1-c2 system allows a wide choice of set-ups; some are quite aggressive and they all have the advantage of avoiding the robust Meran.

The sharpest try is 5 Bg5 when White hopes to develop actively as in a Queen's Gambit. Black can react with 5...h6 obtaining the two bishops, but allowing White a comfortable time in the centre, but if he chooses the critical 5...dxc4 then White has e2-e4-e5. The resulting pin on the h4-d8 diagonal forces sharp uncompromising play.

What is Black's Strategy?

Black starts out with a solid hold on the d5-point. He may then develop his kingside before his queen's bishop as in a Queen's Gambit, especially if White indulges in cautious development, but the Semi-Slav set-up offers more dynamic possibilities. The most active way of handling Black is to time ...d5xc4, and if White recaptures on c4, ...b7-b5 gaining time by attacking the bishop and then ...Bc8-b7.

The bishop finds a potentially interesting diagonal. However to further this piece's ambitions the c-pawn will need to advance to c5, preceded by ...b5-b4 or ...a7-a6 to safeguard the b-pawn. All this takes time and Black has to be aware of central action by White. Black is usually willing to leave his king temporarily in the centre in order to guarantee a rosy future for his queen's bishop.

If White prefers Bc1-g5 then Black's most ambitious approach is to capture the c-pawn and support it with ...b7-b5. Black will again be able to play ...Bc8-b7 and this time have a queenside majority but this line leads to compensating tactical chances for White.

Tactical/Strategic/Dynamic?

This opening starts out with noble strategic intentions but often degenerates into tactical hand-to-hand fighting. Although each side has the opportunity to steer the game into quieter channels, the most important lines are double-edged and invariably treacherous for the unwary.

Theoretical?

Some plans that avoid the main theoretical discussions don't test the opponent that much. The exception are the Qd1-c2 lines which require understanding and general considerations as well as some theory. The sharper Meran and razor-edge 5 Bg5 gambit (named after Botvinnik) are two of the most fascinating and ultra-theoretical variations around.

How Popular is it?

At the top end of the chess world, very much so. Kramnik in particular has added his name to a long list of regular users. For club players the weight of theory tends to put many off, and practitioners tend to concentrate on the less theoretical lines. For lesser international players the Qd1-c2 lines are attractive, as there is plenty of scope for the individual touch without having to learn too much theory.

Illustrative Games

Game 109
□ **Epishin** ■ **Brenninkmeijer**
Wijk aan Zee 1992

1 d4 Nf6 2 c4 c6 3 Nc3 d5 4 Nf3 e6 5 e3 Nbd7 6 Qc2

A flexible and versatile method of developing.

6...Bd6 7 Be2 0-0 8 0-0 dxc4 9 Bxc4 a6 10 Rd1 Qc7 11 Ne4 Nxe4 12 Qxe4 e5 13 Qh4

White's queen clearly has attacking potential, mainly because Black's forces take time to get organised.

13...Nf6 (Diagram 9) 14 e4

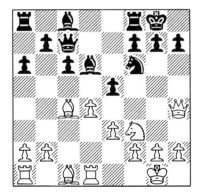

Diagram 9
White will free the c1-bishop

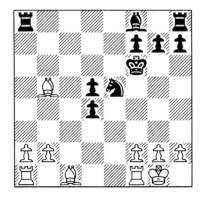

Diagram 10
White's queenside pawns are strong

Preparing to bring the dark-squared bishop into play.

14...exd4 15 e5

An ambitious sacrifice leading to complications.

15...Bxe5 16 Re1 Bd6 17 Bd3 Qa5 18 Bg5 Bf5 19 Bxf6 Bxd3 20 Bxg7 Kxg7 21 Qxd4+ Kg8 22 Qxd6 Rad8 23 Qg3+ Bg6 24 h4 Rfe8 25 Kh2 Kg7 26 Rad1 Rxe1 27 Rxe1 Rd5 28 a3 Qd8 29 Re5 Rxe5 30 Nxe5 h5 31 b4 Qd4 32 Nf3

The queen and knight continue the pressure on the black camp.

32...Qd7 33 Qf4 f6 34 Nd4 b6 35 Qe3 Kf7 36 Ne2 Qd6+ 37 Nf4 c5 38 bxc5 bxc5 39 Qg3 Bf5 40 Nxh5 Qxg3+ 41 Kxg3 c4 42 Kf3 c3 43 Ke3 Ke7 44 Ng3 Bh7 45 Ne2 c2 46 Kd2 1-0

TIP: In many forms of the Queen's Gambit White ends up with an extra centre pawn (often having d- and e-pawns while Black has only an e-pawn). This central superiority can sometimes create the basis for a kingside attack.

Game 110
□ **Speelman** ■ **Ribli**
Subotica 1987

---

1 d4 d5 2 Nf3 Nf6 3 c4 c6 4 Nc3 e6 5 e3 Nbd7 6 Bd3 dxc4 7 Bxc4 b5 8 Bd3 a6 9 e4 c5

The sharp Meran variation.

10 e5 cxd4 11 Nxb5 Ng4 12 Qa4

The clash of strategies leads to a tactical mêlée.

12...Ngxe5 13 Nxe5 Nxe5 14 Nd6+ Ke7 15 Nxc8+ Rxc8 16 Bxa6 Ra8 17 Qb5 Qd5 18 Qxd5 exd5 19 Bb5 Kf6 20 0-0 (Diagram 10)

Black has survived to the ending but his central pawns are not as strong as White's queenside.

20...Bb4 21 Bf4 Rhc8 22 a4 Nc4 23 Rad1 Nxb2 24 Rxd4 Bc3 25 Rxd5 h6 26 Rd6+ Ke7 27 Rd7+ Kf8 28 Ra1 Bf6 29 g3 Kg8 30 Ra3 Rc5 31 Rb7 Bd4 32 Be3 Bxe3 33 Rxe3 Nxa4 34 Ra3 1-0

Game 111
□ **Wells** ■ **Dreev**
Cappelle la Grande 1992

---

1 d4 d5 2 c4 c6 3 Nf3 Nf6 4 Nc3 e6 5 e3 Nbd7 6 Bd3 dxc4 7 Bxc4 b5 8 Bd3 Bb7 9 0-0 a6 10 e4 c5 11 d5

Another double-edged approach by White. The advance of the d-pawn creates a central majority whereas Black has counterplay with his queenside. Black again lags in development, but his pieces have no problem finding active squares.

11...c4 12 dxe6 fxe6 13 Bc2 Qc7 14 Qe2 Bd6 15 Ng5 Nc5 16 f4 h6 17 Nh3 e5 18 a4 0-0 (Diagram 11)

Black finally gets his king into safety and now has the more active game. White wins a pawn but loses control of events in the centre.

19 axb5 Ne6 20 bxa6 exf4 21 e5 f3 22 gxf3 Nd4 23 Qg2 Bxe5 24 Bxh6 Nxc2 25 Qxc2 Bc8 26 Kh1 Bxh3 27 Rg1 Ng4 28 Rxg4 0-1

NOTE: In the Meran Black can often end up with a powerful pair of bishops bearing down on the long diagonals towards the white king.

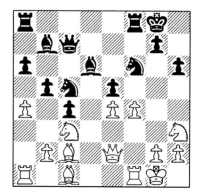

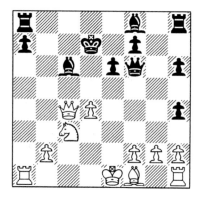

Diagram 11

White's centre is under pressure

Diagram 12

Black's bishops are very important

Game 112
☐ **Van Wely** ■ **Kramnik**
Manila 1992

---

1 d4 d5 2 Nf3 c6 3 c4 Nf6 4 Nc3 e6 5 Bg5

White hopes to continue development as in a Orthodox Queen's Gambit. Black refuses to play passively and takes the pawn on offer, but thus allows White to immediately advance his e-pawn.

5...dxc4 6 e4 b5 7 a4 Bb7 8 e5 h6 9 Bh4 g5 10 exf6

Another line starts with 10 Nxg5. This also leads to highly complex play.

10...gxh4 11 Ne5 Nd7 12 Qh5 Qxf6 13 Nxd7 Kxd7 14 axb5 cxb5 15 Qxb5+ Bc6 16 Qxc4 (Diagram 12)

Material equality is restored and superficially Black has the most exposed king. However, this is more than compensated for by the bishop pair in a very open position.

16...Bd6 17 Ra6 Rhc8 18 Rxc6

Otherwise White finds it hard to develop his kingside.

18...Rxc6 19 Qa4 Qg5 20 Bb5 Qxg2 21 d5

The complications that result favour Black.

21...Qxh1+ 22 Ke2 Kd8 23 Bxc6 Rb8 24 Nb5 exd5 25 Qa5+ Ke7 26 Qxa7+ Kf8 27 Qe3 Kg8 28 h3 Bf8 29 Qf4 Qe4+ 30 Qxe4 dxe4 31 Ke3 Rb6 32 Bd7 Rf6 33 b3 Bc5+ 34 Kxe4 Rxf2 35 Kd5 Bb4 36 Nd4 Kg7 37 Kc4 Rf4 38 Kd5 Kf6 39 Bc8 Rf1 40 Bg4 Bc3 41 Nf3 Kg6 42 Nxh4+ Kg5 43 Nf3+ Kf4 44 Nh4 Rf2 45 Bc8 Kg5 0-1

Chapter Ten

1 d4: Other Defences

In this chapter we consider various other ways for Black to meet 1 d4. All the variations examined here are perfectly respectable but are, on the whole, less popular than the main line defences such as the King's Indian and Nimzo-Indian.

Although the four lines considered here are quite different in their approach, they do have one feature in common. In all cases Black is usually prepared to make some sort of positional concession in order to create dynamic imbalance in the position. This makes them slightly more risky than the lines already considered but it also means that they can be good weapons against a weaker player who you want to try and outplay.

The Queen's Gambit Accepted

1 d4 d5 2 c4 dxc4

White's 2 c4 is met by 2...dxc4. The Queen's Gambit is really a bit of a misnomer. It is not a proper gambit opening at all, as Black cannot hope to mount a successful defence of the extra pawn after 2...dxc4.

In most lines Black immediately returns the pawn in order to get on with his development. Black leaves behind no obvious targets and is flexible, so that for each of White's plans he has an appropriate counter.

White has two central pawns against one but the open nature of the game doesn't allow White to easily get his pawns working for him. Black in return has a slight preponderance on the queenside, and he often plays ...b7-b5 and/or ...c7-c5 to gain space and react quickly before White's centre becomes too imposing.

Both sides can count on easy development for their pieces and this suits players looking for open play. The pawn structure can become symmetrical if Black is able to exchange off his c-pawn for the white d-pawn. In such cases White's may rely on his slight lead in development to obtain something more concrete.

What is White's Strategy?

White wants to advance in the centre with e2-e4 and a later e4-e5, or d4-d5, and hopes to obtain better piece play as a result.

There are three typical ways of trying to achieve this:

1) The immediate 3 e4 which achieves the primary aim, but Black's flexibility permits him to hit back in various ways.

2) The gambits involving a quick e4-e5. A typical sequence here is 1 d4 d5 2 c4 dxc4 3 Nf3 Nf6 4 Nc3 a6 5 e4 b5. White has given up a pawn for good, but has strong play in the centre.

3) Preliminary development with e3, Bxc4 and 0-0 which is the most common plan. White then sometimes switches to an alternative idea of hitting back at Black's pawn front on ...b5 with a2-a4, when White can sometimes use the consequent weakness of the c4-square (if Black advance ...b5-b4) for his pieces.

What is Black's Strategy?

By releasing all pressure on his own centre as soon as possible, Black prepares to hit back with an early ...c7-c5. This counters any White central advantage and yields plenty of space for his future development. Black often plays ...a7-a6 and ...b7-b5 to develop the bishop to b7 where it bears down on e4.

Another option for this piece is to come to g4 and, after ...e7-e6 and then ...Bf8-d6, to obtain good piece emplacements. In such a scenario, Black may prefer to counter with a subsequent ...e6-e5.

In the gambit line Black hopes to hold onto the c4-pawn with ...b7-b5 and ...a7-a6. White does obtain a useful initiative and Black then hopes to simply complete development without falling for anything.

The 3 e4 variation can be met with ...c7-c5 or ...e7-e5, striking back before White has time to support his pawn front. Some prefer to hit back with 3...Nc6, (4 d5 Ne5 is double-edged) with a later ...e7-e5 in mind, or 3...Nf6 so that if 4 e5 Nd5, Black has a permanent hold on the d5-square to compensate for the e5-pawn wedge.

Tactical/Strategic/Dynamic?

The early e4 lines can be quite tactical but overall the QGA is a strategic choice. The most dangerous and tactical, for the unprepared is the real gambit line where Black has to tread carefully and really know his stuff.

The e3 lines allow Black to develop naturally but it's useful to know various set-ups and counters from typical games. A choice for those who like to have good play for their pieces, but note that some of the quieter lines with symmetrical pawns can be a little dull.

Theoretical?

Apart from a few forcing lines, the QGA is less theoretical than the Slav and Semi-Slav and more active than the QGD, so it appeals to some. Some theory is required but most of the time Black can get away with basic knowledge of the general piece set-ups and the standard counters.

How Popular is it?

It has never been as popular as the Slav or Semi-Slav but many of the World's elite employ it occasionally. Nigel Short's successful defence of the QGA in his famous match against Karpov gave it a boost and Anand is another top-level fan of this opening.

Not that popular at a lower level, as the King's Indian or Queen's Gambit have clearer strategies.

Illustrative Games

Game 113
□ **Kasparov** ■ **Piket**
Tilburg 1997

1 d4 d5 2 c4 dxc4 3 e3 Nf6 4 Bxc4 e6 5 Nf3 c5 6 0-0 a6 7 Bb3

A clever prophylactic move. If Black develops a piece then it may commit him and reduces his later options.

7...b5 8 a4 b4

White obtains access to the c4-square which helps his attacking pretensions. If instead ...bxa4 then Black's exposed king and lack of development will please White.

9 Nbd2 Bb7 10 e4

A gambit idea to obtain a rapid deployment of his forces.

10...cxd4 11 e5 Nd5 12 Nc4 Nc6 13 Bg5 Qd7 14 Rc1 h6 15 Bh4 Bc5 (Diagram 1) 16 Nfd2

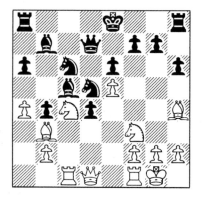

Diagram 1
The extra pawn does not help Black

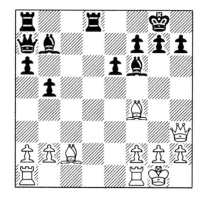

Diagram 2
White has a winning attack

The knight outpost on c4 enables White to play for Ne4-d6.

16...0-0 17 Ne4 Be7 18 Bg3 Qd8 19 Ncd6 Na5 20 Bc2 b3 21 Bb1 Qb6 22 Qd3

With Black tied down to defensive chores in the centre, White switches to the denuded kingside.

22...g6 23 Nc5 Bc8 24 h4 Nc6 25 a5 Qxa5 26 Nxf7 Rxf7 27 Qxg6+ Kf8 28 Nxe6+ Bxe6 29 Rxc6 Bd7 30 Qxh6+ 1-0

NOTE: When the centre has been cleared of the d- and c-pawns and White advances the e-pawn to e5, a double-edged position results. The pawn can be springboard for a powerful attack but if the position is simplified it may become a weakness.

Game 114
□ **Sadler** ■ **Brunner**
Bern 1996

---

1 d4 d5 2 c4 dxc4 3 e3 Nf6 4 Bxc4 e6 5 Nf3 c5 6 Qe2 a6 7 dxc5 Bxc5 8 e4

A symmetrical pawn structure doesn't necessarily mean that the game is drawish. A slight initiative in such positions can easily develop into something significant as the weaker camp lacks targets to hit back. White is the first to get his e-pawn advancing.

8...b5 9 Bb3 Bb7 10 Bc2 Nbd7 11 0-0 Qb8 12 Nbd2 0-0 13 e5

This pawn wedge opens up the b1-h7 diagonal towards the Black kingside. Black is well placed to cope with the pawn, but not the resulting disruption in his camp.

13...Ng4 14 Ne4 Ngxe5 15 Bf4 Nxf3+ 16 Qxf3 Qa7 17 Qh3 Bd4 18 Nc5

A neat tactical sequence that puts Black into difficulty.

18...Nf6 19 Nd7 Rfd8 20 Nxf6+ Bxf6 (Diagram 2) 21 Be3

The attack is too strong. White picks up a couple of pawns and Black's king is left to fend for himself.

21...Bd4 22 Qxh7+ Kf8 23 Qh8+ Ke7 24 Qh4+ Ke8 25 Qh8+ Ke7 26 Bg5+ Bf6 27 Qxg7 Qd4 28 Bg6 Bxg5 29 Qxf7+ Kd6 30 Rad1 Bd2 31 Qxb7 Rh8 32 Qf3 Kc5 33 Rc1+ Bxc1 34 Rxc1+ Kb6 35 Qc6+ Ka5 36 Qc7+ Kb4 37 a3+ Kb3 38 Qc2+ Ka2 39 Qb1+ Kb3 40 Bc2+ Kc4 41 Be4+ Kb3 42 Rc3+ Ka4 43 Qc2+ 1-0

Game 115
□ **Gelfand** ■ **Anand**
Linares 1993

---

1 d4 d5 2 c4 dxc4 3 e4 c5

The attempt to claim the centre immediately is vigorously countered before White can get organised.

4 d5 Nf6 5 Nc3 b5

The sharpest, not giving White an easy time.

6 Bf4 Qa5 7 e5 Ne4 8 Nge2 Na6 9 f3 (Diagram 3) 9...Nb4

Sacrificing a piece to tangle up his opponent. The complications seem fine for Black.

10 fxe4 Nd3+ 11 Kd2 g6 12 b3 Bg7 13 bxc4 Nxf4 14 Nxf4 Bxe5

Black wins his material back with interest.

15 Nfe2 b4 16 Qa4+ Qxa4 17 Nxa4 Bxa1 18 Nxc5 0-0 19 Nd3 a5 20 g3 Bg7 21 Bg2 Ba6 22 c5 Rac8 23 c6 Rfd8

White's central pawns seem to give some hope of compensation for the exchange. However, the Black pieces all strafe the white centre from afar and he retains the advantage.

24 Rc1 Bh6+ 25 Nef4 Bxd3 26 Kxd3 e5 27 Kc4 exf4 28 Re1 fxg3 29 e5 Bf4 30 hxg3 Bxg3 31 Re3 Bf4 32 Re4 Bh2 33 Bh3 Rc7 34 Re2 Bg3 35 Re3 Bf4 36 Re4 g5 37 Kc5 Re7 38 Kd4 f6 39 d6 Bxe5+ 40 Rxe5 Rxd6+ 0-1

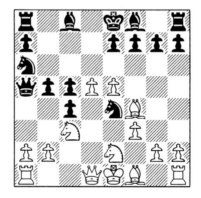

Diagram 3
Black finds an amazing sacrifice

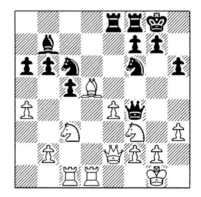

Diagram 4
Black is very solid

Game 116
□ **Djandjava** ■ **Sadler**
Yerevan 1996

---

1 d4 d5 2 Nf3 e6 3 c4 dxc4 4 e3 Nf6 5 Bxc4 c5 6 0-0 a6 7 a4

Stopping Black's intended expansion and holding onto more space, but at the cost of potential weaknesses.

7...Nc6 8 Qe2 Qc7 9 Nc3 Bd6 10 Rd1 0-0 11 h3 b6 12 d5

This is the prelude to e3-e4 and the freeing up of the dark-squared bishop. Meantime Black's pieces find reasonable squares and are ready for anything.

12...exd5 13 Bxd5 Bb7 14 e4 Rae8 15 Be3 Bf4 16 Rac1 h6 17 Bxf4 Qxf4 (Diagram 4) 18 Bxc6

The only try for an advantage, but pawn hunting on the queenside whilst neglecting the centre and other wing is not without risk.

18...Bxc6 19 Qxa6 Nxe4 20 Qxb6 Re6 21 Nxe4 Bxe4 22 Qb3 Rg6 23 Ne1 Rb8 24 Qc4 Rxb2 25 Qf1 Rb3

Black's forces are so active that it's not surprising that something has to give.

26 f3 Bxf3 27 Qf2 Re3 28 Ra1 Kh7 29 a5 Qe4 30 Rd2 Qe5 31 Nxf3 Qxa1+ 32 Kh2 Ra3 33 Qxc5 Rxa5 34 Qc8 Qf6 35 Rd8 Qf4+ 36 Kh1 Ra1+ 37 Ng1 Re6 38 Qc2+ Qe4 39 Qc3 Qe1 40 Qd4 Rg6 0-1

The Grünfeld Defence

1 d4 Nf6 2 c4 g6 3 Nc3 d5

Black combines the dynamic qualities of the King's Indian with a ...d7-d5 counter, immediately seeking play in the centre. White has a wide choice of strategies available depending on personal taste. One of the most popular ideas is to build a big pawn centre and support this with the pieces. This typically occurs after the sequence c4xd5 ...Nxd5 and now e2-e4, or after Qd1-b3 so that ...d5xc4 can be met with Qb3xc4 and then e2-e4.

If White prefers to simply develop quietly and get his king castled before doing anything too ambitious, then Black tends to have a choice of playing actively with ...c7-c5 or just bolstering his d5-point with ...c7-c6. Play in the centre is overseen by the bishop on g7 whose influence extends as far as the white rook on a1.

What is White's Strategy?

The main plan is to capture on d5 and play e2-e4 (the Exchange Variation), i.e. 4 cxd5 Nxd5 5 e4 Nxc3 6 bxc3 when White may continue with Bf1-c4 and Ng1-e2 to avoid a pin with ...Bc8-g4 and help support the centre. Further support with Bc1-e3 and Ra1-c1 is typical.

A similar approach with Ng1-f3, Bf1-e2 and Ra1-b1 (getting off the long diagonal and taking up an active posting on the b-file) is also common.

Once that he has constructed his centre White must be ready to meet

...c7-c5 pressurising d4 in particular, but also indirectly the whole of the long diagonal.

If the centre holds firm then White can switch to ideas of a kingside attack or just try to make use the pawns. This often involves a d4-d5 advance, aiming to cramp Black.

Quieter lines with Bc1-g5, or Bc1-f4 followed by e2-e3 and Ng1-f3, or even e2-e3 with the bishop inside the pawn-chain, are more concerned with just maintaining some tension and developing pieces. With sensible piece deployment White hopes to be ready to meet any ...c7-c5 counter.

What is Black's Strategy?

Black wants to enhance the scope of his dark-squared bishop and an early ...c7-c5 punch in many lines is ideal.

Pressure on dark squares can be increased with such typical moves as ...Nb8-c6 and ...Qd8-a5 and the further ...Ra8-d8 and ...Bc8-g4 are also employed to make the centre creak.

In the critical Exchange Variation, White often feels obliged to sacrifices a queenside pawn or even the exchange to diminish this pressure.

In the quieter lines Black has the choice of the solid but passive ...c7-c6 to hold onto d5, but this lacks sting. More typical is to play ...c7-c5, even if this temporarily sacrifices a pawn, as the dark-squared play that results usually leads to recovery of the pawn with interest.

Tactical/Strategic/Dynamic?

One of the most dynamic defences where Black obtains active pieces and good counterplay against White's centre without leaving any targets. The strategy of actively countering White's central ambitions is an ideal choice for those seeking a lively game.

Theoretical?

Some lines are inevitably theoretical as play can be very forcing. However, most of the time Black can get by with natural moves if they fit in with the various schemes to counterattack White's pawn centre. He also has sufficient alternatives to avoid getting bogged down learning too much theory.

How Popular is it?

A highly respected opening at all levels (another of Kasparov's favourites) but less popular than its close relative, the King's Indian. A serious problem with the Grünfeld is that White can employ various move orders to avoid the opening altogether (delaying Nb1-c3, an early g2-g3, or delaying d2-d4 etc.) that various lower ranked players prefer to simply stick to the King's Indian all the time.

Illustrative Games

Game 117
□ **Karpov** ■ **Kasparov**
London 1986

1 d4 Nf6 2 c4 g6 3 Nc3 d5 4 Bf4

White's early development of his bishop leads to Black counterattacking the queenside dark squares as soon as possible.

4...Bg7 5 e3 c5

The most ambitious counter.

6 dxc5 Qa5 7 Rc1 Ne4 8 cxd5 Nxc3 9 Qd2 Qxa2 10 bxc3

Black can also retain queens. In either case he wins back his pawn and the positional struggle is between White's centre and Black's queenside majority.

10...Qxd2+ 11 Kxd2 Nd7 12 Bb5 0-0 13 Bxd7 Bxd7 14 e4 f5 15 e5 (Diagram 5) 15...e6

Countering the centre as aggressively as possible.

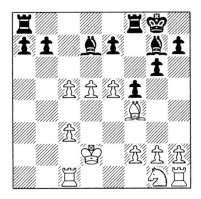

Diagram 5
White has a huge centre

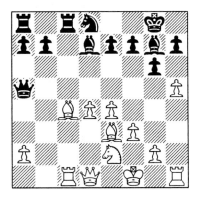

Diagram 6
White has a dangerous attack

16 c4 Rfc8 17 c6

Aiming for a favourable pawn structure.

17...bxc6 18 d6 c5 19 h4 h6 20 Nh3 a5 21 f3 a4

Black's a-pawn creates little discomfort for White who has managed to maintain his big cramping centre. Black is soon left with no activity and a lost ending.

22 Rhe1 a3 23 Nf2 a2 24 Nd3 Ra3 25 Ra1 g5 26 hxg5 hxg5 27 Bxg5 Kf7 28 Bf4 Rb8 29 Rec1 Bc6 30 Rc3 Ra5 31 Rc2 Rba8 32 Nc1 1-0

WARNING: The Grünfeld, in common with many of the more complex replies to 1 d4, allows White free play in the centre, in the hope of creating later play with counterattacking thrusts. However, if these thrusts do not materialise, Black can find himself swamped by the white centre.

Game 118
□ **Shirov** ■ **Kozul**
Biel 1991

---

1 d4 Nf6 2 c4 g6 3 Nc3 d5 4 cxd5 Nxd5 5 e4 Nxc3 6 bxc3 Bg7 7 Bc4 c5 8 Ne2 0-0 9 Be3 Nc6 10 Rc1

Reinforcing the centre is always an important strategy for White in the Grünfeld.

10...cxd4 11 cxd4 Qa5+ 12 Kf1

White accepts a displaced king in order to keep the centre intact and the queens on the board. In these circumstances he can think about a kingside assault.

12...Bd7 13 h4 Rfc8 14 h5 Nd8 15 f3 (Diagram 6) 15...b5

Black counterattacks with his pawn majority on the queenside.

16 Bb3 Rxc1 17 Bxc1 Qb6 18 hxg6 hxg6 19 Qe1 Rc8 20 Bg5 Ne6

Black needs to react quickly to avoid being mated, but being obliged to give up some pawns on the king's wing leads to an inevitable conclusion.

21 Bxe7 g5 22 d5 Nd4 23 Bxg5 b4 24 Be3 Qa6 25 Bxd4 Bxd4 26 Qd2 Bg7 27 d6 Bb5 28 Bxf7+ Kf8 29 Be6 Rc1+ 30 Qxc1 Bxe2+ 31 Kf2 Bd4+ 32 Kg3 Qxd6+ 33 Qf4+ Ke7 34 Rh7+ 1-0

Game 119
□ **Piket** ■ **Ivanchuk**
Tilburg 1989

---

1 d4 Nf6 2 Nf3 g6 3 c4 Bg7 4 Nc3 d5 5 Qb3 dxc4 6 Qxc4 0-0 7 e4 Na6 8 Bf4 c5

This robust counter is a key move in many variations. Black's pieces find active play even if he temporarily sheds a pawn.

9 dxc5 Qa5 10 e5 Nd7 11 a3 Qxc5 12 Nd5 Nb6

A more permanent pawn sacrifice this time, but Black can rely on his enhanced activity to hold onto the initiative.

13 Qxc5 Nxc5 14 Nxe7+ Kh8 15 Rc1 Ne6 16 Be3 Bd7 17 Be2 Rae8 18 Bxb6 axb6 19 Nd5 Bc6 20 Rd1 f6 (Diagram 7)

Further line opening will be too dangerous, so White gives back the pawn to castle and try to exploit the weakened black pawns.

21 0-0 fxe5 22 Bc4 b5 23 Ba2 e4

The bishop pair will soon run riot.

24 Nd2 Bxb2 25 Nxe4 Bxa3 26 Rfe1 Nc5 27 Nef6 Rd8 28 h4 b4 29 Re7 Rxf6 30 Nxf6 Rxd1+ 31 Kh2 Rd7 32 Nxd7 Bxd7 33 h5 Bc1 34 g3 gxh5 35 f4 h4 36 Bb1 hxg3+ 37 Kxg3 b3 38 Rxh7+ Kg8 39 Rh6 Bc6 40 Rh5 Ne4+ 0-1

TIP: When White grabs the centre in the Grünfeld he is often slightly behind in development. Black should always be on the lookout for ways to exploit this even if it means gambiting a pawn.

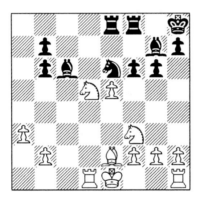

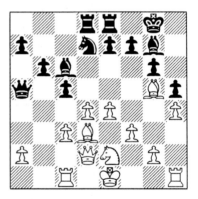

Diagram 7
Black's bishops are coming to life

Diagram 8
White's centre is under great pressure

Game 120
□ **Shaked** ■ **Kasparov**
Tilburg 1997

1 d4 Nf6 2 c4 g6 3 Nc3 d5 4 cxd5 Nxd5 5 e4 Nxc3 6 bxc3 Bg7 7 Be3 c5 8 Qd2 Qa5 9 Rb1

White is ready to exchange queens to hold onto the centre. Black prefers to hit away at the White pawn front before the first player gets his development organised;

9...b6 10 Bb5+ Bd7 11 Be2 Bc6 12 Bd3 Nd7 13 Ne2 Rd8 14 f3 0-0 15 h4 h5 16 Bg5 Rfe8 17 Rc1 (Diagram 8) 17...Bb7

White will have problems on the d-file if he tries to maintain the tension.

18 d5 Ne5 19 Bb1 Nc4

Black takes the initiative and is will soon prepare ...e7-e6 to dissolve the d-pawn. White now blunders but his centre was already creaking.

20 Qf4 Be5 0-1

The Benoni Defences

1 d4 Nf6 2 c4 c5

These defences are characterised by an early ...c7-c5 by Black, usually with the immediate 1 d4 Nf6 2 c4 c5. If White continues with the principled 3 d5, as most do, he immediately obtains a significant space advantage which can endure deep into the middlegame. Black can then react in a number of ways, but must not allow White to have his space free of charge.

One traditional approach, the out-of-favour Czech Benoni, involves 3...e5 when the centre becomes blocked. Both players go in for heavy manoeuvring on the flanks, but Black's problem is that he remains cramped.

More aggressive is the Modern Benoni where Black reacts with a quick ...e7-e6 and ..e6xd5 followed by fianchettoing the King's bishop. White still has his space but Black obtains tactical counterplay.

Perhaps the most attractive choice is the positional Benko Gambit, 3...b5, where Black aims to give up his a- and b-pawns for White's c-pawn in order to obtain pressure down the semi-open a- and b-files. This is augmented by the influence of the king's bishop down the long diagonal. Black often remains a pawn down for a long time but his activity continues into the endgame where White is often unable to make the extra pawn tell.

What is White's Strategy?

The Modern Benoni is characterised by an early ...e7-e6 followed by ...e6xd5. This is met by c4xd5 and Black thus obtains a queenside majority but White in return has an extra pawn in the centre. White has various possibilities in the centre, including pressure against the d6-pawn and the timely advance e4-e5, which can be supported by first moving the f-pawn to f4. The queenside majority will require some restraint, so White often plays an early a2-a4. There is one typical manoeuvre that helps with all these plans: Nf3-d2-c4 which, if conducted successfully, puts Black in difficulty.

The most practical strategy against the Benko is to decline the gambit and continue to develop normally, as White still has a space advantage. If White insists on taking up the gauntlet, then holding the queenside whilst preparing the counter e4-e5 is the soundest approach. It's important not to go too passive.

What is Black's Strategy?

He typically pressurises the e4-pawn with ...Rf8-e8 and needs to keep a firm grip on e5 (to reduce White's chances of getting e4-e5 under favourable circumstances) and his backward pawn on d6. The dark-squared bishop plays a role and moves such as ...Nb8-d7 and ...Qd8-c7 are typical. Black wants to get his queenside rolling with ...b7-b5 and then ...b5-b4 or ...c5-c4 which he can do if the centre can be stabilised for long enough.

The bishop can also be employed more actively with tactical chances along the long diagonal especially if Black can find the moment to move his knight aggressively from f6 to g4 or h5. There are even tactical shots involving ...Nf6xd5 or ...Nf6xe4.

The Benko involves pressure from afar with the rooks and dark-squared bishop bearing down on the white queenside pawns. Black often tries ...Qd8-a5 or ...Qd8-b6 as well as employing manoeuvres such as ...Ne8-c7-b5 to further soften up the queenside. In some lines even ...e7-e6 or ...f7-f5 are used to create threats elsewhere.

Tactical/Strategic/Dynamic?

Both the Modern Benoni and Benko are dynamic defences with good practical chances for the second player. The structural imbalance in the Modern Benoni often provokes sharp play where tactical awareness is an important quality.

The Benko, despite it's gambit label, is strategic by nature. There are however some sharper tactical lines which often come about where White refuses the gambit and prefers to react actively in the centre.

Theoretical?

Both lines have a solid background of theory but whereas the Modern Benoni is naturally sharp and requires precise variations, the Benko can be, and is, played by many who rely on standard plans.

Black has some very sensible methods of development and White has to do something special to try and undo the harmony in the Benko player's camp.

How Popular is it?

The Modern Benoni, has a reputation of being rather risky as White can obtain a significant spatial advantage and good prospects with his central majority. This turns off stronger players and many club players are concerned about being overrun in the centre. However, it is a good choice for tacticians who like living on their nerves!

The Benko is very popular at all levels as White is often the one who has to defend accurately. A dynamic choice for players who like a positionally sound opening which can yield winning chances.

Illustrative Games

Game 121
□ **Kasparov** ■ **Jurtaev**
USSR 1977

1 d4 Nf6 2 c4 c5 3 d5 e6 4 Nc3 exd5 5 cxd5 d6 6 e4 g6 7 Bd3 Bg7 8 Nge2 0-0 9 0-0 Ne8 10 Be3 Nd7 11 f4 a6 12 a3 b6 13 Qd2 Ra7

In the Modern Benoni it is important for Black to look for tactical counterplay or, sooner or later, White will come crashing through in the centre. Here Black has played much too passively and White can build up at his leisure.

14 Rae1 Rc7 15 a4 Ra7 16 Ng3 Qc7 17 Qe2 Qb8 18 Kh1 (Diagram 9) 18...b5

Black is already desperate for counterplay and speculates on a pawn sacrifice. However, White continues with his natural plan.

19 e5 bxa4 20 e6 Nb6 21 f5 fxe6 22 fxg6 hxg6 23 Bxg6 Nf6 24 Bg5

White's central breakthrough has led directly to the decimation of Black's kingside.

24...Nbxd5 25 Nxd5 exd5 26 Nh5 Bg4 27 Nxf6+ Rxf6 28 Qxg4 Rxg6 29 Qh5 Rxg5 30 Qxg5 1-0

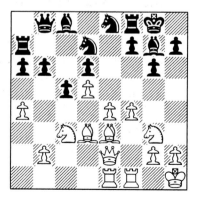

Diagram 9
White has an imposing build up

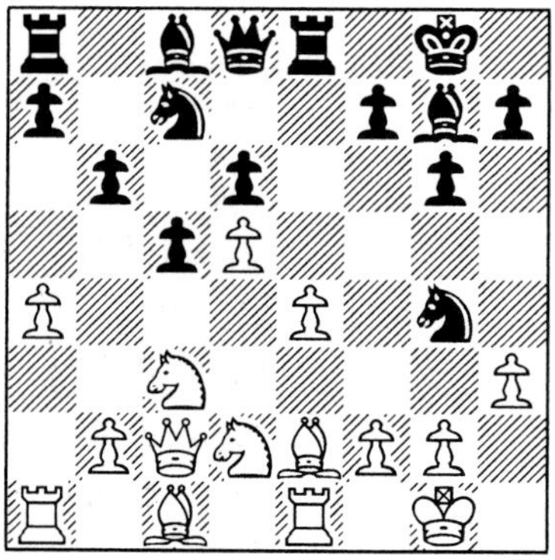

Diagram 10
Tal gambits a piece

Game 122
□ **Gurgenidze** ■ **Tal**
Moscow 1957

1 d4 Nf6 2 c4 c5 3 d5 e6 4 Nc3 exd5 5 cxd5 d6 6 Nf3 g6 7 e4 Bg7 8 Be2 0-0 9 0-0 Re8 10 Nd2 Na6 11 Re1 Nc7 12 a4 b6 13 Qc2 Ng4

This is good active play from Black who is getting his pieces working before White has a chance to complete development.

14 h3 (Diagram 10) 14...Nxf2

A typical Tal gambit.

15 Kxf2 Qh4+ 16 Kf1 Bd4 17 Nd1 Qxh3 18 Bf3

Of course White cannot capture the queen as 18 gxh3 Bxh3 is mate.

18...Qh2 19 Ne3 f5 20 Ndc4 fxe4 21 Bxe4 Ba6 22 Bf3 Re5

Although Black is a piece down, his forces are attacking White from all directions.

23 Ra3 Rae8 24 Bd2 Nxd5 25 Bxd5+ Rxd5 26 Ke2 Bxe3 27 Rxe3 Bxc4+ 0-1

NOTE: The key to Benoni systems is White's advance e4-e5. If White achieves this under favourable circumstances he nearly always stands well. If Black can prevent this advance and generate counterplay elsewhere, the situation is not so clear.

Game 123
□ **Van der Sterren** ■ **Adams**
Ter Apel 1992

1 d4 Nf6 2 c4 c5 3 d5 b5 4 cxb5 a6 5 bxa6 g6 6 Nc3 Bxa6 7 Nf3 d6 8 g3 Bg7 9 Bg2 0-0 10 0-0 Nbd7 11 Qc2 Qa5 12 Rd1 Ng4 13 Bd2 Rfb8 14 b3 Qb6 15 h3 Nge5 16 Nxe5 Nxe5 17 Rab1 Bc8 (Diagram 11)

Although Black is active, White is a pawn ahead and thus holds a small advantage. However, this is the type of position that is very tricky to play for White as it is difficult to keep fending off the black pieces. White's next move is a good idea in the long run but probably a little premature here as it leaves his queenside vulnerable.

18 a4 Bf5 19 e4 Bd7 20 Be3 Qa5 21 f4

This is often a powerful advance for White in Benoni structures, but here it just weakens his centre and leaves his back ranks very exposed.

21...Nc4 22 bxc4 Bxc3 23 Rxb8+ Rxb8 24 Rb1 Rb4 25 Bf1 Qxa4 26 Qxa4 Bxa4 27 Bd3

White's pawns, in particular the c-pawn, are exposed and Black soon rounds one up with a clever bishop manoeuvre.

27...Bb3 28 Kf2 Ba2 29 Rc1 Bb2 30 Rc2 Bb1 31 Rd2 Bxd3 32 Rxd3 Rxc4 33 Rb3 Rb4 34 Rxb4 cxb4 35 Ke2 b3 36 Kd3 Bf6 37 f5 Kf8 38 g4 Ke8 39 Bd2 Kd7 40 Ba5 g5 41 Bd2 Kc7 42 Be3 h6 43 Bd2 Kb7 0-1

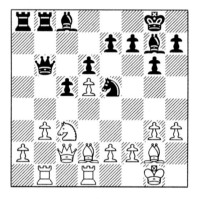

Diagram 11

Black has sufficient play for the pawn

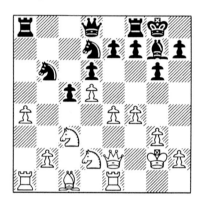

Diagram 12

White has the initiative and an extra pawn

Game 124
□ **Vaisser** ■ **Degraeve**
Narbonne 1997

1 d4 Nf6 2 c4 c5 3 d5 b5 4 cxb5 a6 5 bxa6 d6 6 Nc3 Bxa6 7 Nf3 g6 8 e4 Bxf1 9 Kxf1 Bg7 10 g3 0-0 11 Kg2 Nbd7 12 Re1 Ng4 13 Nd2 Nge5 14 Qe2 Nb6 15 f4 Ned7 16 a4 (Diagram 12)

If White did not time these advances correctly, they could be weakening. Here, however, Black is not yet mobilised on the queenside and White can push forward with impunity.

16...Ra7 17 a5 Qa8 18 a6 Qc8 19 Nb5 Ra8 20 Nf3 c4 21 Nfd4 Rxa6 22 Nc6 Bf6 23 Be3 Qb7 24 Na5 Qb8 25 Nc6 Qb7 26 Rxa6 Qxa6 27 Nc3 Re8 28 Bxb6 Nxb6

Although Black has regained his pawn it has taken him a great deal of time and meanwhile White has been building up ominously in the centre.

29 e5 dxe5 30 fxe5 Bg7 31 Qf3 Nc8 32 Rf1 Rf8 33 Rd1 Qb7 34 d6 exd6 35 exd6

White's central breakthrough in Benoni formation can often lead to a powerful passed pawn such as this one.

35...Nxd6 36 Rxd6 Qxb2+ 37 Ne2 c3 38 Ne7+ Kh8 39 Kh3 h5 40

Nf4 Kh7 41 Nfxg6 fxg6 42 Qe4 Qb5 43 Rxg6 Kh8 44 Rxg7 Qf1+
45 Kh4 Qf6+ 46 Rg5 1-0

The Dutch Defence

1 d4 f5

The advantage of the Dutch is that Black can play 1...f5 against all reasonable moves except 1 e4. So it's not just a queen's pawn defence, but a system that can be used against the English (1 c4) and the Reti (1 Nf3).

The drawback with 1...f5 is that Black shows his hand early and White can develop accordingly.

Control of the e4-square is an obvious point of 1...f5 but, by continuing with kingside development behind the advanced pawn, Black obtains some space on this wing. He may use this fact as a prelude to a kingside attack or keep such ideas in reserve and reinforce the centre first.

The unbalanced central disposition suits players who like to avoid drawish exchange variations.

What is White's Strategy?

The fianchetto of the light-squared bishop is popular against all of Black's set-ups as White's king is given added protection. The bishop has a promising diagonal including influence on the important e4-square.

In those lines where Black plays ...d7-d5, White tries to exchange the dark-squared bishops when Black will have problems with his dark square complex.

If Black prefers the more reserved ...d7-d6 and ...e7-e6 then White will generally play for e2-e4, gaining space and influence and perhaps exposing some soft spots on the e-file.

Against the Leningrad (...g7-g6) White can also play for e2-e4, but usually only after completing development. Another approach is a general advance on the queenside; Ra1-b1 and b2-b4 for instance.

Other types of White development are less common, but the advance e2-e4 is often an important aim.

What is Black's Strategy?

Black has three major ways of interpreting the Dutch Defence.

He can build a 'Maginot Line' with ...c7-c6, ...d7-d5, ...e7-e6 and ...f7-f5, when White is faced with a rock-like structure. This is appropriately named the Stonewall Defence. Traditionally Black would try and hold the centre and switch to a kingside assault, but modern masters find this to be too crude and prefer to complete development with ...b7-b6 and ...Bc8-b7 or ...Bc8-a6, or the laborious but effective manoeuvre ...Bc8-d7-e8-h5. The Stonewall affords some solidity and use of e4 but weakens the whole dark-square complex.

Another approach is to put the central pawns on d6 and e6, which is less weakening. Black can also switch to the kingside with ...Qd8-e8 and ...Qe8-g6 or ...Qe8-h5, but without burning his bridges.

The Leningrad System involves ...g7-g6 and ...Bf8-g7 where Black uses this bishop to influence the centre. Black completes development and then can either play centrally (...e7-e5) or expand on the kingside with ...h7-h6 and ...g7-g5 with ideas of ...f5-f4.

Tactical/Strategic/Dynamic?

The Leningrad is a dynamic modern opening and hard to destabilise. The other systems are considered a little too predictable and rather clumsy, but still work against the unprepared and inexperienced.

There are some tactical lines, but the Dutch has definite strategic aims and the basic set-up is not hard to learn. The closed nature of the position means that move order is not really that important, a definite plus for club players.

Theoretical?

Not particularly but there are few lines that require detailed memory work. The main consideration is getting the development organised and not forgetting to find a role for the queen's bishop.

How Popular is it?

The Leningrad has some strong advocates such as M.Gurevich and club players often enjoy the freedom to develop relatively untroubled by threats but, nevertheless, it's not that popular these days.

Illustrative Games

Game 125
□ **Portisch** ■ **Radulov**
Budapest 1969

1 c4 f5 2 Nf3 Nf6 3 g3 e6 4 Bg2 Be7 5 0-0 0-0 6 d4 c6 7 Qc2 b6 8 Nbd2 d5 9 Ne5 Bb7 10 Nd3

A typical manoeuvre against the Stonewall; White eyes Black's weakness on e5 and frees the bishop to press against the rigid structure.

10...Nbd7 11 b4

Expanding on the wing and making ...c7-c5 difficult to achieve.

11...Re8 12 a4 Bd6 13 Nf3 Ne4 14 c5 bxc5 15 bxc5 Bc7 16 Bf4 (Diagram 13)

Exchanging the dark-squared bishops makes e5 weaker. The black light-squared bishop is ineffective behind his own pawns.

16...Bxf4 17 gxf4 Qc7 18 Nfe5 Nef6 19 Rfb1 a5 20 Nxd7 Nxd7 21 Ne5 Nxe5 22 fxe5 Reb8 23 Rb6

Black has rid himself of White's knights but his remaining pieces are too passive.

23...Ba6 24 Rab1 Rb7 25 Qd2 Rxb6 26 cxb6 Qb7 27 Qxa5 Bb5 28 Qb4 Rxa4 29 Qd6 Kf7 30 e4

A combination that opens up an attack on the e6-square.

30...Qxb6 31 exf5 Qa7 32 Qxe6+ Kf8 33 Bxd5 cxd5 34 Rxb5 Rxd4 35 Qc8+ 1-0

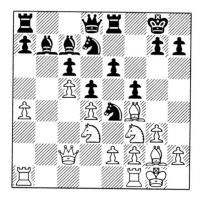

Diagram 13
White takes control of the dark squares

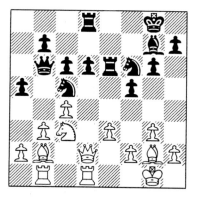

Diagram 14
White needs to open lines

Game 126
☐ **Ribli** ■ **Mestel**
London 1986

1 d4 d6 2 Nf3 g6 3 c4 f5 4 Nc3 Nf6 5 g3 Bg7 6 Bg2 0-0 7 0-0 c6 8 d5 Bd7 9 Rb1 Na6 10 b3 Nc5 11 Bb2

White develops naturally and holds onto his space in the centre.

11...a5 12 Qd2 Qb6 13 Nd4 Rad8 14 Rfd1 Rfe8 15 e3 e5

Aiming for freedom.

16 dxe6 Bxe6 17 Nxe6 Rxe6 (Diagram 14) 18 Na4

Weakening his pawns to open up his bishops and rooks.

18...Nxa4 19 bxa4 Qa6 20 Bd4 Ne4 21 Bxe4 Rxe4 22 Bxg7 Kxg7 23 c5

The exchanges have left Black's king exposed and his pawns also prove to be weaker.

23...Rd7 24 cxd6 Rxa4 25 Qc3+ Kh6 26 Qf6 Qe2 27 Qe6 Rxa2 28 Rf1 Rg7 29 Rbe1 1-0

Game 127
☐ **Smejkal** ■ **Larsen**
Leningrad 1973

---

1 d4 f5 2 g3 Nf6 3 Bg2 e6 4 Nf3 Bb4+ 5 c3 Be7 6 0-0 0-0 7 c4 c6 8 Nc3 d5 9 Qc2 Ne4 10 Ne5 Nd7 11 Nxe4 fxe4 12 Bf4 Bf6 13 Rad1 Bxe5 14 Bxe5 Nxe5 15 dxe5 Qe7 16 Qc3 Bd7

Although Black has a theoretically 'bad' bishop, with his central pawns all being on light squares, it does not really matter here as the white bishop is not really doing a great deal either. With his next move White tries to get this piece working, but only succeeds in weakening his position.

17 f3 exf3 18 exf3 Qc5+ 19 Rd4 a5 20 f4 Qa7 (Diagram 15) 21 f5

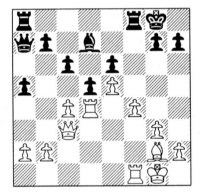

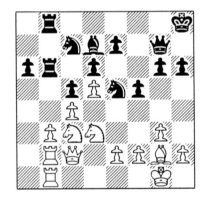

Diagram 15
Black's centre is very solid

Diagram 16
A balanced position

TIP: Black light-squared bishop can appear to be a terrible piece in the Stonewall but it is important to remember that all such assessments are relative and often White's theoretically stronger king's bishop is actually not participating in the game either.

White is trying to take the initiative but this advance actually weakens his centre.

21...Rae8 22 cxd5 cxd5 23 Kh1 Rc8 24 Qd2 Rc2 25 Qxc2 Qxd4 26 Qc3 Qxc3 27 bxc3 Rc8 28 Rd1 Rc5 29 fxe6 Bxe6 30 Kg1 Kf7 31 Rd3 Rb5

Black's active rook gives him all the chances in this endgame.

32 Rd2 a4 33 a3 Rb3 34 Bxd5 Rxa3 35 c4 Rb3 36 Kf2 a3 37 Ke2 Rb2 38 Rxb2 axb2 39 Be4 Bxc4+ 40 Kd2 Ba2 0-1

Game 128
☐ **Cvitan** ■ **Malaniuk**
Forli 1992

---

1 d4 f5 2 g3 Nf6 3 Bg2 d6 4 Nf3 g6 5 0-0 Bg7 6 c4 0-0 7 Nc3 Qe8 8 d5 Na6 9 Rb1 c5 10 Bd2 Bd7 11 Qc1 Nc7 12 Bh6 Qf7 13 b3 Bxh6 14 Qxh6 Qg7 15 Qd2 h6 16 Ne1 Rab8

White has not managed to take the initiative anywhere and Black has a comfortable game.

17 a4 a6 18 a5 b5 19 axb6 Rxb6 20 Nd3 Rfb8 21 Qc2 Kh8 22 Rb2 Ng4 23 Rfb1 Ne5 (Diagram 16)

It was now better for White to play the simple 24 Nxe5 with an approximately equal position. Instead he initiates a tactical sequence which ultimately backfires.

24 Na4 Nxd3 25 Nxb6 Nb4 26 Nxd7 Nxc2 27 Nxb8 Na3

Now White loses too much material

28 b4 cxb4 29 Rxb4 a5 30 Rb7 Nxb1 31 Rxb1 a4

This passed a-pawn proves to be decisive. White manages to stir up some trouble but never enough to alter the outcome.

32 Rb7 Ne8 33 Nc6 Qa1+ 34 Bf1 Nf6 35 Nxe7 Ne4 36 Nxg6+ Kg8 37 Ne7+ Kf8 38 Nxf5 Nd2 39 Rb8+ Kf7 40 Rb7+ Kf6 41 Ne3 a3 42 Rd7 Ne4 43 Ng4+ Kg6 44 f3 Nd2 45 Rxd6+ Kf7 46 Ne3 Qd4 47 Kf2 Nxc4 0-1

Chapter Eleven

The English Opening

The English Opening was for a long time considered to be a poor cousin of the more direct opening moves 1 e4 and 1 d4. This is certainly not the case now and all the best players have, at one time or another, played the English. Indeed, the great Bobby Fischer, who opened 1 e4 almost exclusively throughout his entire career, switched – with great success – to 1 c4 for several games of his famous World Championship against Boris Spassky in 1972.

The idea behind 1 c4 is nearly always to follow up with a fianchetto of the king's bishop and to aim for play against Black's queenside. In fact, White often ends up adopting a strategy similar to that put into practice by Black when defending against the Closed Sicilian, with moves such as Ra1-b1 and b2-b4 being used to pressurise Black's queen's wing.

The English is not an immediately confrontational opening and so Black has various ways to deploy his forces. A common approach is to play ....e7-e5 at some point when the game often resembles a Reversed Sicilian. As White is now a tempo ahead on such lines, Black will generally choose a quiet formation. Another frequently seen approach is for Black to adopt a system which involves the move ...c7-c5. Both positions are then highly flexible and complex middlegames often result. We will consider both of these Black approaches in this chapter.

The English with ...e5

1 c4 e5

When White starts with 1 c4 he is generally aiming to avoid the more forcing 1 e4 and 1 d4 openings. The English is often a prelude to a quieter opening involving Nb1-c3 and typically g2-g3 and Bf1-g2. The rest of White's development typically depends on Black's choice of set-up.

Black has a wide choice of replies but it is prudent to have a plan for developing his forces, even if your opponent has no direct threats. The popular 1...e5 can be used for an early development of the king's bishop to c5 or b4 but it's primarily to claim an important part of the centre.

What is White's Strategy?

The move c4 controls the important d5-square without using one of his own central pawns to do so. The e- and d-pawns are held in reserve as useful assets for the future. If Black at some point plays ...d7-d5 then the exchange of White's c-pawn for Black's d-pawn leaves White the bonus of a central majority.

The characteristic c4 of the English Opening prepares Nb1-c3 and frees the queen for an eventual outing. The typical g2-g3 and Bf1-g2 leaves the bishop bearing down on e4, d5 and the rest of the long diagonal.

Once Black decides on ...e7-e5, he usually concentrates his forces towards the kingside; therefore White may pick a solid development around his king (to thwart Black's intentions) and push his b-pawn to increase space and generate play on the queenside.

What is Black's Strategy?

The most common development involves ...Nb8-c6, ...d7-d6, ...g7-g6, ...Bf8-g7, 0-0 and at some point ...f7-f5. Note that if ...Ng8-f6 is played early on then the knight has to relocate in order to facilitate this advance.

Then Black may wish to advance further his kingside pawns, or negate White's efforts on other fronts with ideas such as ...a7-a5, ...Rf8-e8 or an eventual ...c7-c6 and ...d6-d5 but this plan should only be considered once his development is advanced.

Sharper ideas involving ...c7-c6 and ...d7-d5, or the immediate ...Nf6 and ...d5, or a precocious ...f5 are possible but risky; White has the advantage of an extra tempo in the opening and no immediate targets if the game becomes tactical.

Black sometimes chooses another positional form of development ...Ng8-f6 and ...Bf8-b4 followed by ...0-0 which has proven to be solid in practise.

Tactical/Strategic/Dynamic?

The early phase is slow and strategic, but the tension builds and arising middlegames can be complex. White's opening can be described as patient and flexible and Black does well to mimic this strategy.

Theoretical?

Plans, manoeuvres an ideas abound but very little forcing theory. So it's very non-theoretical.

How Popular is it?

At a higher level 1 c4 is popular but it's sometimes used as a roundabout route to get into a desired queen's pawn opening. The most dynamic and popular reply 1...e5, is an ideal way of obtaining an unbalanced struggle, and players of all standards are attracted to this and to an opening that requires little homework.

Most club players generally choose more direct openings, but some prefer the chance to be more original.

Illustrative Games

Game 129
☐ **Kasparov** ■ **Ivanchuk**
Moscow 1988

---

1 c4 Nf6 2 Nc3 e5 3 Nf3 Nc6 4 g3 Bb4 5 Bg2 0-0 6 0-0 e4 7 Ng5 Bxc3 8 bxc3 Re8 9 f3 exf3 10 Nxf3 d5 11 d4

White has some structural weaknesses in his position, but he is relying on the energy of his bishop pair and central pawns to compensate.

11...Ne4 12 Qc2 dxc4 13 Rb1 f5 (Diagram 1) 14 g4

A powerful flanking blow, undermining Black's centre.

14...Qe7 15 gxf5 Nd6 16 Ng5 Qxe2 17 Bd5+ Kh8 18 Qxe2 Rxe2 19 Bf4 Nd8

The opening has been a big success for White. Black's pieces have been driven back in confusion and White's are running riot.

20 Bxd6 cxd6 21 Rbe1 Rxe1 22 Rxe1 Bd7 23 Re7 Bc6 24 f6 1-0

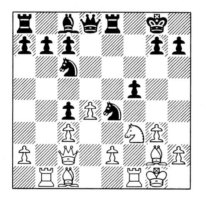

Diagram 1
White wants to undermine the e4-knight

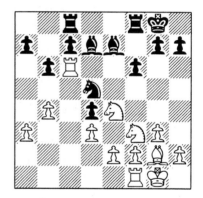

Diagram 2
A powerful exchange sacrifice

Game 130
☐ **Karpov** ■ **Hjartarson**
Seattle 1989

---

1 c4 e5 2 Nc3 Nf6 3 g3 d5 4 cxd5 Nxd5 5 Bg2 Nb6 6 Nf3 Nc6 7 0-0 Be7 8 a3 Be6 9 b4 0-0 10 Rb1 f6 11 d3 Qd7 12 Ne4

White is playing a kind of 'reversed Sicilian Dragon'. He is hoping to generate pressure on the queenside thanks to his bishop on g2, the open c-file and his advancing queenside pawns.

12...Nd5 13 Qc2 b6 14 Bb2 Rac8 15 Rbc1 Nd4 16 Bxd4 exd4 17 Qc6 Qxc6 18 Rxc6 Bd7 (Diagram 2) 19 Nxd4

This is a powerful exchange sacrifice, clearing away the black centre and liberating White's minor pieces.

19...Bxc6 20 Nxc6 Rce8 21 Rc1 f5 22 Nd2 Nf6 23 Nxa7 Bd6 24 e3 c5 25 Nc4 Bb8 26 Nc6 b5 27 N4a5 cxb4 28 axb4 Nd7 29 d4

White's strategy has succeeded – a piece and two solid central pawns should be worth more than a rook.

29...g5 30 Nxb8 Rxb8 31 Rc7 Nf6 32 Nc6 Rb6 33 Ne7+ Kh8 34 Nxf5 Ra6 35 Rc1 Ra2 36 h3 Rb2 37 e4 Rxb4 38 g4 h5 39 e5 hxg4 40 exf6 gxh3 41 Bxh3 Rxf6 42 Rc8+ Kh7 43 Rc7+ Kg6 44 Rg7+ Kh5 45 f3 1-0

TIP: When playing a 'Reversed Sicilian' as Black, it is usually better to keep the position closed when the missing tempo is less of a problem.

Game 131
☐ **Psakhis** ■ **Kasparov**
Murcia 1990

1 c4 g6 2 Nc3 Bg7 3 g3 Nc6 4 Bg2 d6 5 Nf3 e5 6 d3 f5 7 0-0 Nf6 8 Rb1 h6 9 b4 0-0

Black has adopted a 'reversed Closed Sicilian' set-up. Although it is often dangerous to play 'White' openings with Black (due to the lost tempo) it is usually okay with an opening such as this where there is minimal early contact.

10 b5 Ne7 11 a4 Be6 12 Ba3 Rc8 13 Nd2 b6 14 e3 g5 15 d4 exd4 16 exd4 (Diagram 3) 16...f4

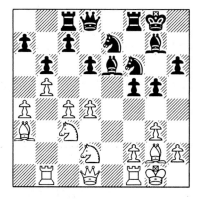

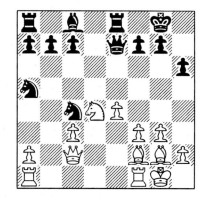

| **Diagram 3** | **Diagram 4** |
| Black is ready to roll on the kingside | White has good bishops but weak pawns |

Black powers forward on the kingside.

17 Re1 Bg4 18 Nf3 Qd7 19 c5 Rce8 20 Rc1 Nf5 21 Qd3 Kh8 22 cxd6 cxd6 23 Rxe8 Qxe8 24 Rf1 Qh5

The black forces are gathering ominously in the vicinity of the white king.

25 Ne4 Nxe4 26 Qxe4 Bh3 27 Ne5 Bxg2 28 Kxg2 g4 29 Bxd6 Rf6 30 Bb8 Qh3+ 0-1

Game 132
□ **Kasparov** ■ **Karpov**
Seville 1987

---

1 c4 e5 2 Nc3 Nf6 3 Nf3 Nc6 4 g3 Bb4 5 Bg2 0-0 6 0-0 Re8 7 d3 Bxc3 8 bxc3 e4 9 Nd4 h6 10 dxe4 Nxe4 11 Qc2 d5 12 cxd5 Qxd5 13 e3 Na5 14 f3 Nd6 15 e4 Qc5 16 Be3 Ndc4 17 Bf2 Qe7 (Diagram 4)

This is a complex position. White has the bishop pair and a strong centre but Black has easy development and good control on the queenside where White has weak pawns.

18 Rad1 Bd7 19 f4 Rad8 20 e5 Bg4 21 Nf5 Qe6 22 Rxd8 Rxd8 23 Nd4 Qc8 24 f5

White is trying to force the pace but Black is well placed to meet this advance.

24...c5 25 Qe4 cxd4 26 Qxg4 Nxe5 27 Qe2 Nec6

White was hoping to create active play with his pawn sacrifice but it comes to very little.

28 cxd4 Nxd4 29 Bxd4 Rxd4 30 f6 Qe6 31 Qb2 Qe3+ 32 Kh1 b6 33 fxg7 Nc4

Although the black king is slightly vulnerable, the rest of his position is beautifully centralised and can beat off White's threats in this sector.

34 Qc2 Kxg7 35 Bd5 Nd6 36 Qb2 Qe5 37 Bb3 a5 38 Qf2 f5 39 Qb2 b5 40 a3 Kg6 41 Qf2 0-1

The English with ...c5

1 c4 c5

Black's symmetrical answer doesn't mean that he lacks original ideas! Black too wishes to claim some of the centre in an indirect fashion and to reserve his d- and e-pawns for later. He cannot however simply copy White for long and does best to vary in the early stages and create his own plans for the middlegame. These can revolve around a number of different ideas such as ...d7-d5, ...d7-d6 combined with ...e7-e5, or even ...e7-e6 and ...d7-d5.

What is White's Strategy?

White will usually play for an eventual d2-d4, which typically liquidates the black c-pawn leaving White's to maintain the bind on d5. One way is after 1 c4 c5 to play the direct 2 Nf3 Nf6 3 d4 with an open centre reminiscent of a queen's pawn opening. Another version of this idea is to follow the symmetrical sequence 1 c4 c5 2 Nc3 Nc6 3 g3 g6 4 Bg2 Bg7 5 Nf3 Nf6 6 0-0 0-0 with 7 d4.

White can opt to maintain the tension in the centre and instead develop quietly with b2-b3 and Bc1-b2, but another dynamic plan is to play for an early b2-b4 (another way of dissolving the c-pawn) i.e. 1 c4 c5 2 Nc3 Nc6 3 g3 g6 4 Bg2 Bg7 5 a3 and after most replies White can try Ra1-b1 with ideas of b2-b4.

What is Black's Strategy?

Sometimes Black is content to copy White's play for the early moves and wait for White to think of something creative. By playing like this Black is indicating that he believes that White cannot do anything too drastic. The most common approach however is to decide how and when to vary from White's development method.

The more dynamic ways of switching can involve an early ...b7-b6: 1 c4 c5 2 Nf3 Nf6 3 g3 b6 4 Bg2 Bg7 5 0-0 and now either 5...e6 or 5...g6; or 1 c4 c5 2 Nf3 Nf6 3 d4 cxd4 4 Nxd4 b6; or even 2 Nc3 Nf6 3 Nf3 b6. These often lead to so-called 'Hedgehog' systems where White has more central space but Black is solid and has long term dynamic possibilities. Another series of ideas are based on a rapid reaction with ...d7-d5: 1 c4 c5 2 Nf3 Nf6 3 g3 d5; or 1 c4 c5 2 Nc3 Nf6 3 g3 d5; or 1 c4 c5 2 Nc3 Nf6 3 Nf3 d5.

A common method to create some dynamism is to follow suit and decide to simply develop the king's knight to another square; e.g. 1 c4 c5 2 Nc3 Nc6 3 g3 g6 4 Bg2 Bg7 5 Nf3 and now 5...e6 and 6...Nge7 or 5...e5 and 6...Nge7.

Tactical/Strategic/Dynamic?

These lines are very strategic with many options for either player. Again events seems sluggish at first but often results in a dynamic struggle if Black can find a way to break the symmetry at an appropriate moment.

There is little tactical play early on, but there is much latent tension in the position.

Theoretical?

There is so much choice that it's hard to force either player into any overtly theoretical lines. However both players have to be aware that the closed nature of the opening can rapidly change if either player goes for quick central action. In this case the pace of the game can accelerate, leading to a more lively and possibly theoretical struggle.

How Popular is it?

A much more popular choice amongst stronger players who are often attracted to the great wealth of possibilities inherent in such a flexible variation. There is great scope to outplay a generally less-experienced opponent.

Club players often shy away from subtle manoeuvring and thus prefer to play 1 d4 or 1 e4 as White and to answer 1 c4 with a King's Indian set-up or 1...e5.

TIP: The positions arising after 1 c4 c5 are well worth studying, even if you do not intend to play them, as they are strategically very rich and the play can be highly instructive.

Illustrative Games

Game 133
□ **Petrosian** ■ **Radulov**
Amsterdam 1973

1 c4 c5 2 Nf3 Nc6 3 Nc3 e5 4 g3 g6 5 a3 Bg7 6 Rb1 Nge7 7 Bg2 a5

This is a risky strategy from Black. He is trying to clamp down on White's play everywhere at once but in doing so is creating nasty light square weaknesses in his own camp.

8 d3 0-0 9 Bg5 f6 10 Bd2 d6 11 0-0 Be6 12 Ne1 f5 13 Nc2 d5 (Diagram 5) 14 b3

Petrosian is in no hurry – Black's light square problems will not go away.

14...d4 15 Nb5 f4 16 b4 b6 17 bxc5 bxc5 18 a4 Qd7 19 Na1 Bh3 20 Nb3

Black now has serious problems with his c-pawn and tries to solve these with tactical play.

20...Bxg2 21 Kxg2 e4 22 Nxc5 f3+ 23 exf3 exf3+ 24 Qxf3 Rxf3 25 Nxd7 Rxd3 26 Bg5

Black is now lost as Nc5 will inevitably win too much material.

26...Nf5 27 g4 h6 28 Nc5 Rc3 29 Nxc3 dxc3 30 gxf5 hxg5 31 f6

Bf8 32 Ne4 c2 33 Rb2 Nd4 34 Rc1 Re8 35 Nxg5 1-0

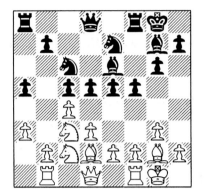

Diagram 5
White takes his time

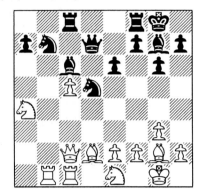

Diagram 6
White's c-pawn is solidly blockaded

Game 134
□ **Petrosian** ■ **Fischer**
Belgrade 1970

---

1 c4 g6 2 Nc3 c5 3 g3 Bg7 4 Bg2 Nc6 5 Nf3 e6 6 0-0 Nge7 7 d3 0-0 8 Bd2 d5 9 a3 b6 10 Rb1 Bb7

Black's development, with his knight on e7, is slightly more comfortable than White's and this guarantees him a comfortable game. White's natural plan is to advance on the queenside but Black is well placed to meet this.

11 b4 cxb4 12 axb4 dxc4 13 dxc4 Rc8 14 c5 bxc5 15 bxc5 Na5 16 Na4 Bc6 17 Qc2 Nb7 18 Rfc1 Qd7 19 Ne1 Nd5 (Diagram 6) 20 Nb2

White's c-pawn is firmly blockaded and is a source of weakness rather than strength.

20...Bb5 21 Ned3 Bd4 22 Qb3 Nxc5 23 Nxc5 Rxc5 24 Rxc5 Bxc5 25 Nd3 Bxd3 26 Qxd3 Rd8 27 Bf3 Qc7 28 Bg5 Be7 29 Bxe7 Qxe7

Black now slowly but surely nurses his extra pawn to victory.

30 Qd4 e5 31 Qc4 Nb6 32 Qc2 Rc8 33 Qd3 Rc4 34 Bg2 Qc7 35 Qa3 Rc3 36 Qa5 Rc5 37 Qa3 a5 38 h4 Nc4 39 Qd3 Nd6 40 Kh2 Kg7 41 Rd1 Ne8 42 Qd7 Qxd7 43 Rxd7 Nf6 44 Ra7 Ng4+ 45 Kg1 Rc1+ 46 Bf1 Ra1 47 e4 a4 48 Kg2 Ra2 49 Rxf7+ Kxf7 50 Bc4+ Ke7 51 Bxa2 a3 52 Kf3 Nf6 53 Ke3 Kd6 54 f4 Nd7 55 Bb1 Nc5 56 f5 Na6 57 g4 Nb4 58 fxg6 hxg6 59 h5 gxh5 60 gxh5 Ke6 61 Kd2 Kf6 62 Kc3 a2 63 Bxa2 Nxa2+ 64 Kb2 Nb4 65 Kc3 Nc6 66 Kc4 Nd4 0-1

Game 135
□ **Piket** ■ **Kasparov**
Internet Match 2000

1 Nf3 Nf6 2 c4 c5 3 Nc3 d5 4 cxd5 Nxd5 5 g3 Nc6 6 Bg2 Nc7 7 d3 e5 8 0-0 Be7

In this variation Black takes a slight risk by falling behind in development in the interests of setting up a strong centre.

9 Nd2 Bd7 10 Nc4 0-0 11 Bxc6 Bxc6 12 Nxe5 Be8 (Diagram 7)

This is a familiar theme in this variation. Black gives up a pawn in return for the two bishops and, in the long term, has potential weaknesses around the white king to aim at.

13 Qb3 Bf6 14 Ng4 Bd4 15 e3 Bxc3 16 Qxc3 b6 17 f3 Bb5 18 Nf2 Qd7 19 e4 Ne6 20 Be3 a5 21 Rad1 Rad8 22 Rd2 Qc6 23 Rc1 Qb7 24 a3 Nd4 25 Kg2

White still has the extra pawn but Black has strong pressure.

25...Rc8 26 Rb1 Rfd8 27 Bxd4 Rxd4 28 b4 axb4 29 axb4 Qd7 30 bxc5 bxc5 31 Rbb2 h6 32 Ra2 Kh7 33 Ra5 Rd8 34 Qxc5 Bxd3 35 Rxd3 Rxd3 36 Nxd3 Qxd3 37 Ra2 Qb3 38 Qc2

The position has fizzled out and should now be a draw. However, Black was short of time and did not find the correct way to defend.

38...Qxc2+ 39 Rxc2 h5 40 f4 g6 41 e5 Rd3 42 Kh3 Re3 43 Kh4 Kg7 44 Kg5 Re1 45 Rc7 Re2 46 Re7 Ra2 47 f5 gxf5 48 e6 h4 49 Rxf7+ Kg8 50 Kf6 1-0

WARNING: When playing lines with ...d7-d5, Black must be careful not to fall too far behind in development.

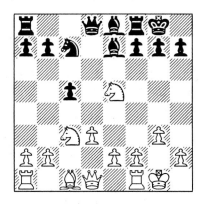

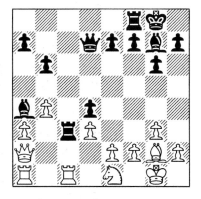

Diagram 7
Black's bishops are compensation

Diagram 8
Black has a useful outpost

Game 136
□ Ribli ■ Miles
Amsterdam 1978

1 Nf3 Nf6 2 c4 c5 3 Nc3 d5 4 cxd5 Nxd5 5 g3 g6 6 Bg2 Bg7 7 0-0 0-0 8 Nxd5 Qxd5 9 d3 Nc6 10 a3 b6 11 Rb1 Bb7 12 b4 Qa2 13 Be3 Nd4

Black's strange queen invasion has proved awkward for White who is now obliged to improve Black's pawn structure by capturing on d4.

14 Bxd4 cxd4 15 Ra1 Qd5 16 Qa4 Bc6 17 Qc2 Rac8 18 Rfc1 Bd7 19 Qb2 Ba4 20 Ne1 Qd7 21 Qa2 Rc3 (Diagram 8)

Black makes full use of the strong pawn on d4.

22 Rxc3 dxc3 23 Rc1 e6 24 e3 Rc8 25 d4 e5 26 d5 f5 27 Bf1 e4 28 Nc2 Rd8 29 Nd4 Bxd4 30 exd4 c2 31 Bc4 Kf8 32 Bb3 Bxb3 33 Qxb3 Qxd5 34 Qxd5 Rxd5 35 Rxc2 Ke7 36 Rc4 Rd7

Black has a big advantage in this endgame thanks to the weak white d-pawn and his pawn wedge on the kingside.

37 h4 Ke6 38 b5 Kd5 39 Ra4 h6 40 Kf1 g5 41 hxg5 hxg5 42 Ke2 f4 43 gxf4 gxf4 44 Kd2 Rc7 45 Kd1 e3 46 fxe3 f3 47 Ke1 Ke4 48 Rb4 Rc1+ 49 Kf2 Rc2+ 50 Ke1 Kxe3 51 Rb3+ Kf4 52 d5 Re2+ 0-1

GLENVIEW PUBLIC LIBRARY
1930 GLENVIEW ROAD
GLENVIEW, ILLINOIS 60025
847-729-7500

3 1170 00584 0933